Modern Indices for International Economic Diplomacy

Vincent Charles · Ali Emrouznejad
Editors

Modern Indices for International Economic Diplomacy

palgrave
macmillan

Editors
Vincent Charles
CENTRUM Católica Graduate
Business School
Lima, Peru
Pontifical Catholic University of Peru
Lima, Peru

Ali Emrouznejad
Surrey Business School
University of Surrey
Guildford, UK

ISBN 978-3-030-84534-6   ISBN 978-3-030-84535-3 (eBook)
https://doi.org/10.1007/978-3-030-84535-3

© The Editor(s) (if applicable) and The Author(s), under exclusive license to Springer Nature Switzerland AG 2022
This work is subject to copyright. All rights are solely and exclusively licensed by the Publisher, whether the whole or part of the material is concerned, specifically the rights of translation, reprinting, reuse of illustrations, recitation, broadcasting, reproduction on microfilms or in any other physical way, and transmission or information storage and retrieval, electronic adaptation, computer software, or by similar or dissimilar methodology now known or hereafter developed.
The use of general descriptive names, registered names, trademarks, service marks, etc. in this publication does not imply, even in the absence of a specific statement, that such names are exempt from the relevant protective laws and regulations and therefore free for general use.
The publisher, the authors and the editors are safe to assume that the advice and information in this book are believed to be true and accurate at the date of publication. Neither the publisher nor the authors or the editors give a warranty, expressed or implied, with respect to the material contained herein or for any errors or omissions that may have been made. The publisher remains neutral with regard to jurisdictional claims in published maps and institutional affiliations.

This Palgrave Macmillan imprint is published by the registered company Springer Nature Switzerland AG
The registered company address is: Gewerbestrasse 11, 6330 Cham, Switzerland

Preface

Both globalisation and technological revolution have increased the speed of change and have further transformed the organisation of international economic relationships around the world, affecting the economic, social, cultural, psychological, and political aspects of societies and citizens, in general. The concept of economic diplomacy has evolved and nowadays encompasses not only state actors (economic and commercial diplomats), but also non-state actors (corporate, business, national, and transnational diplomats).

Faced with growing complexities of markets and states, enterprises and governments alike must devise strategies to cope with the post-modern environment. It is in this context that a multitude of standards that govern business behaviour have emerged; this has further led to the appearance of a range of modern composite indices for development and well-being, against which the performance of institutions and nations is to be judged. Furthermore, in the amidst of today's changes, it is of paramount importance that all six forms of diplomacies mentioned above (economic, commercial, business, corporate, national, and transnational) are represented in the most competent manner possible to ensure sustainable economic development. Thus, it is necessary that different policymakers in the enlarged sphere of post-modern diplomacy are well-informed and employ the relevant indices for development and well-being to guide policies, evaluate progress, and engage constructively in policy dialogue.

Aggregate indices play a vital role in every macro-level decision-making process—take, for example, the cases of GDP, GDP per capita, inflation, government debt, external balance, and unemployment rate, among others. However, along with the said classic indices, there are also many recent indices for development and well-being, which may give support in such a decision process. Hence, this book aims to renew interest in some of the most widely used modern indices for development and well-being, namely the OECD Better Life Index, the Gini Index, the Gender Equality/Inequality Index, the International Energy Security Risk Index, the Big Mac Index, the Country Risk Index, the Corruption Perceptions Index, and the Global Terrorism Index. The book positions itself as unique on the market, aiming to bring a fresh look onto the modern indices for international economic diplomacy and the various ways that these could be used to unleash more societal value and drive national productivity.

Composite indices are used by national and international organisations, and governments and businesses alike, to monitor different performance aspects of the economy of a country and the people therein; and they have historically been valuable as communication tools and as inputs into decision and policymaking. In Chapter 1, "The Role of Composite Indices in International Economic Diplomacy", Vincent Charles, Tatiana Gherman, and Ali Emrouznejad delve into the relevant literature to explore the link between international diplomacy, institutions, and composite indices, with the overall aim of renewing interest in composite indices and highlighting the need to periodically revisit them, in an attempt to develop improved ones that can better serve the objectives for which they were created in the first place, helping to guide and move the field and practice forward. From a very practical perspective, there is a need for indices that can accommodate new challenges, for which a greater level of collaboration between a wider range of stakeholders, from researchers to data scientists, regulators and policymakers, business executives and members of civil societies, is also required.

Addressing the world's challenges collectively through constructive diplomacy will enable governments to deliver better lives for their citizens. In this respect, it is of outmost importance to construct reliable well-being measures that can be employed as tools to support international economic diplomacy. In Chapter 2, "The OECD Better Life Index: A Guide for Well-being Based Economic Diplomacy", Gregory Koronakos, Yiannis Smirlis, Dimitris Sotiros, and Dimitris K. Despotis present the Better Life Index developed by the Organization for Economic Cooperation and Development (OECD) as part of the OECD Better Life initiative to facilitate a better understanding of what drives the well-being of people and aid governments to place welfare at the centre of policymaking. The authors discuss the applications of the index in the literature and present a hierarchical (bottom-up) evaluation methodology that is based on Multiple Objective Programming, which they apply to the data of 38 countries. The Better Life Index provides measures for several well-being aspects; it can reveal the real needs of people and serve as a tool for economic diplomacy to pursue international goals for economy and sustainability.

The problem of inequality has become more salient in recent years. Data shows that the degree of inequality has increased in most countries, generating concerns both from the perspective of the sustainability of economic growth, as well as from the perspective of social cohesion. Preventing and reducing inequality depends largely on the actions and reforms taken by the countries' governments. The Gini index is a prominent measure of income or wealth inequality, with relevancy at an international level. In Chapter 3, "The Gini Index: A Modern Measure of Inequality", Vincent Charles, Tatiana Gherman, and Juan Carlos Paliza introduce the original Gini index, as well as the various existent alternative Gini formulations, while also exploring various traditional and modern applications of the index in different settings at national and international levels. The authors further discuss the implications of the Gini index for international diplomacy and policymaking and conclude with future research directions.

Gender equality is a central issue on the global agenda. To track progress towards the goal of gender equality, the United Nations Development Programme developed the Gender Inequality Index (GII). In Chapter 4, "The Gender Inequality Index Through the Prism of Social Innovation", Vanina Farber and Patrick Reichert highlight the special role of social innovation in tackling the issue of gender inequality. For each sub-component of the GII, examples are given that illustrate to power of social innovation to reduce gender inequalities through three mechanisms: resources, attitudes, and power. The authors review some criticism that has been levied towards the GII and identify other measures and indices that have been developed to capture gender inequality. They further illustrate how the GII informs concrete actions that empower women and reduce gender-based discrimination and inequality. Additionally, they offer a discussion of how social innovation can help government, non-profit, and business actors move towards the 2030 SDG goal of gender equality.

In recent decades, there have been a series of positive changes that contribute to generating more egalitarian societies. Within this process, gender equality has become an internationally recognised and promoted concept, since it is part of the foundations that contribute to the development of countries and the world. Despite this, there are still troubling gender inequalities in the world that need to be addressed. In Chapter 5, "Gender Equality Index for Country Regions (GEICR)", Beatrice Avolio and Luis del Carpio propose a Gender Equality Index for Country Regions, which aims to provide a comprehensive approach to the quantitative measurement of gender equality and social development in a sub-national setting and to show how resources are distributed between women and men, with an application to the 25 regions of Peru. The GEICR should be seen as a part of the development process of necessary tools to identify inequalities. The GEICR can be used by policymakers and other relevant stakeholders for policy and strategy design and development at the national and international levels, making it an important tool for the International Economic Diplomacy.

Energy has long been recognised as a core requirement for economic growth and development, prosperity, well-being, and strategic priority, probably only after air, water, and food. Nevertheless, increases in demand and trade competitions between countries for energy are considered main sources of energy security risks. Motivated by the increasing interest in the topic, in Chapter 6, "International Energy Security Risk Index and Energy Diplomacy", Mohga Bassim and Vincent Charles look at the energy security risks, risk evaluation metrics, indexes, proposed mitigation strategies, and policies and discuss two of the indexes used to evaluate the energy security risks. Among others, the authors highlight that the complexity of energy security calls for a collective international effort to reach balanced policies that would help all countries, including developing countries, with growing needs for energy at affordable costs. International efforts for mitigating energy security threats through robust energy trade agreements and diplomatic efforts are essential for maintaining the basics goals of energy availability, affordability, sustainability, and economic growth.

The Big Mac Index was developed by "The Economist" in 1986 and has remained till date one of the most profoundly influential economic indices to gauge the relative valuation of currencies vis-à-vis price of "hamburgers", lending comparability across economies in the wake of unmatched advantage emerging from product standardisation. In Chapter 7, "On Re-imagining the Role of Big Mac Index in Promoting International Economic Diplomacy: Some Perspectives", Ullas Rao, Paul J. Hopkinson, and N. R. Parasuraman investigate the divergent issues at play in respect of the Big Mac by screening through the prism of both developed economies and emerging markets. Employing the index stands as the first barometer of performance to gauge the relative under or overvaluation in comparison to exchange rates determined by the demand and supply principles of the foreign exchange market. Valuation of exchange rates has assumed considerable significance in recent times owing to the re-emergence of the "external threats" posed on country's international trade. So, to that extent, the role of the index in contributing to the wider implications on economic diplomacy cannot be undermined.

The country risk analysis is vital for any investor in the international market. Governments of different countries find merit in constructing such an index because, among others, international lending relies on the relative positioning of the country on such index. Many international aids are, therefore, related to the evaluation of the status of risk of investment in a country. In Chapter 8, "Country Risk Analysis: Theory, Methodology, and Applications", Nitin Arora and Sunil Kumar present a compact prologue to the concept of country risk. The authors present the prominent indices of country risk and discuss some widely used methods to generate weights and construct the composite index of country risk and its sub-indices. The authors conclude with a call for alternative country indices to be constructed, with rank distributions built based on each measure of country risk.

The Corruption Perceptions Index has been impacting the national and international economics, businesses, corporate diplomacy, and the related decision-making around policies for reducing the level of corruption. In Chapter 9, "Understanding the Corruption Perceptions Index", Emigdio Alfaro introduces the index and its construction methods, contributing to the understanding of the index in terms of impact and context, as well as its role in guiding decision-making for governmental organisations and for managers and directors of organisations. The chapter further lays out diverse important concepts around corruption, its types, and its consequences, exploring the results of prior studies on the topic. Finally, conclusions and recommendations for future research are presented. The author indicates that future research must look at simplified ways for measuring corruption, considering the indicators for other human problems: education, health, environment, economics, etc.

Global terrorism poses a serious threat for economies around the world, which must be treated at the national and the international level jointly. It also reflects a serious problem for diplomacy inside and outside the countries and must be treated in a holistic manner considering global indexes for comparing the respective situation in each country by multinational institutions. In Chapter 10, "Understanding the Global Terrorism Index", Emigdio Alfaro introduces the Global Terrorism Index developed by the Institute for Peace & Economy, discusses the construction of the index, and then critically evaluates the application of the index, detailing views and applications at the national and international levels. The chapter concludes with recommendations for future research. Among others, it is proposed that future research must also include the effect on terrorism of the indicators associated with the COVID-19 pandemic, global health indicators including mental health indicators, type of political regime, and sustainable land management indicators jointly with risk management indicators.

The many academics and researchers who contributed chapters and the experts within the field who reviewed the chapters made this book possible—we thank you! The chapters contributed to this book should be of considerable interest and provide our readers with informative reading.

Lima, Peru Vincent Charles
Guildford, UK Ali Emrouznejad
March 2022

Contents

1 **The Role of Composite Indices in International Economic Diplomacy**   1
Vincent Charles, Tatiana Gherman, and Ali Emrouznejad

2 **The OECD Better Life Index: A Guide for Well-Being Based Economic Diplomacy**   19
Gregory Koronakos, Yiannis Smirlis, Dimitris Sotiros, and Dimitris K. Despotis

3 **The Gini Index: A Modern Measure of Inequality**   55
Vincent Charles, Tatiana Gherman, and Juan Carlos Paliza

4 **The Gender Inequality Index Through the Prism of Social Innovation**   85
Vanina Farber and Patrick Reichert

5 **Gender Equality Index for Country Regions (GEICR)**   121
Beatrice Avolio and Luis del Carpio

6 **International Energy Security Risk Index and Energy Diplomacy**   157
Mohga Bassim and Vincent Charles

7	On Re-Imagining the Role of Big Mac Index in Promoting International Economic Diplomacy: Some Perspectives Ullas Rao, Paul J. Hopkinson, and N. R. Parasuraman	193
8	Country Risk Analysis: Theory, Methodology, and Applications Nitin Arora and Sunil Kumar	213
9	Understanding the Corruption Perceptions Index Emigdio Alfaro	233
10	Understanding the Global Terrorism Index Emigdio Alfaro	271

Index   295

Editors and Contributors

About the Editors

Vincent Charles, Ph.D., PDRF, FRSS, FPPBA, MIScT is a Full Professor and the Director of the Centre for Value Chain Innovation at CENTRUM Católica Graduate Business School, PUCP, Lima, Peru. He holds multiple visiting professorship positions across the Globe. He is an experienced researcher in the fields of artificial intelligence, (big) data science, and OR/MS. He has more than two decades of teaching, research, and consultancy experience in various countries, having been a full professor and director of research for more than a decade in triple-crown business schools. He holds Executive Certificates from the MIT, HBS, and IE Business School. He has published over 150 research outputs and is a recipient of many international academic honours and awards. An AWS Certified Cloud Practitioner, AWS Accredited Educator, Certified Six Sigma Black Belt, and Advance HE Certified External Examiner, UK. He is the Editor-in-Chief of the *International Journal of Business and Emerging Markets*, and an Associate Editor for the *Journal of the Operational Research Society*, *RAIRO—Operations Research*, *Expert Systems with Applications*, *Machine Learning with Applications*, *Intelligent Systems with Applications*, and *Decision Analytics Journal*.

Ali Emrouznejad is a Professor and Chair in Business Analytics at Surrey Business School, University of Surrey, UK. His areas of research interest include performance measurement and management, efficiency and productivity analysis, as well as big data and data mining. Prof. Emrouznejad is an editor of *Annals of Operations Research*, associate/guest editor or member of editorial board in a number of other journals including *European Journal of Operational Research*, *Journal of Operational Research Society*, *Socio-Economic Planning Sciences*, *IMA Journal of Management Mathematics*, *OR Spectrum*, and *RAIRO—Operations Research*. He has published over 200 articles in top-ranked journals; he is the author of the book on *Applied Operational Research with SAS*, and editor of the books on *Performance Measurement with Fuzzy Data Envelopment Analysis* (Springer), *Managing Service Productivity* (Springer), *Big Data Optimization* (Springer), *Big Data for Greater Goods* (Springer), and *Handbook of Research on Strategic Performance Management and Measurement* (IGI Global). He is also a co-founder of Performance Improvement Management Software (PIM-DEA), see http://www.Emrouznejad.com.

Contributors

Emigdio Alfaro Universidad César Vallejo, Lima, Peru

Nitin Arora Department of Economics, Panjab University, Chandigarh, India

Beatrice Avolio CENTRUM Católica Graduate Business School, Lima, Peru;
Pontificia Universidad Católica del Perú, Lima, Peru

Mohga Bassim Department of Economics and International Studies, Faculty of Business, Humanities, and Social Sciences, The University of Buckingham, Buckingham, UK

Luis del Carpio CENTRUM Católica Graduate Business School, Lima, Peru;
Pontificia Universidad Católica del Perú, Lima, Peru

Vincent Charles CENTRUM Católica Graduate Business School, Lima, Peru;
Pontifical Catholic University of Peru, Lima, Peru

Dimitris K. Despotis Department of Informatics, University of Piraeus, Piraeus, Greece

Ali Emrouznejad Surrey Business School, The University of Surrey, Guildford, UK

Vanina Farber Elea Center for Social Innovation, International Institute for Management Development, Lausanne, Switzerland

Tatiana Gherman Faculty of Business and Law, University of Northampton, Northampton, UK

Paul J. Hopkinson Edinburgh Business School, Heriot-Watt University, Dubai, United Arab Emirates

Gregory Koronakos Department of Informatics, University of Piraeus, Piraeus, Greece

Sunil Kumar Faculty of Economics, South Asian University, New Delhi, India

Juan Carlos Paliza Alliance Manchester Business School, University of Manchester, Manchester, UK

N. R. Parasuraman Shri Dharmasthala Manjunatheshwara Institute for Management Development, Mysore, India

Ullas Rao Edinburgh Business School, Heriot-Watt University, Dubai, United Arab Emirates

Patrick Reichert Elea Center for Social Innovation, International Institute for Management Development, Lausanne, Switzerland

Yiannis Smirlis School of Economics, Business and International Studies, University of Piraeus, Piraeus, Greece

Dimitris Sotiros Department of Operations Research and Business Intelligence, Wroclaw University of Science and Technology, Wrocław, Poland

List of Figures

Chapter 2

Fig. 1	The hierarchical structure of the OECD Better Life Index	23
Fig. 2	Boxplots of the weights of the 11 topics derived by the public opinion	40
Fig. 3	BLI scores as derived by models (9) and (12) with Ω	47
Fig. 4	Top 10 countries	48
Fig. 5	Heat map of the BLI performance of the 38 countries provided by the min-sum model (10) with Ω	49

Chapter 3

Fig. 1	Gini indices by country 2021 (*Source* https://worldpopulationreview.com/country-rankings/gini-coefficient-by-country)	56
Fig. 2	Lorenz curves	67

Chapter 4

Fig. 1	Gender inequality index	89
Fig. 2	Gender Inequality Index 1995–2017 (*Note* Figure constructed by authors based on source data from the UNDP Human Development Reports)	96
Fig. 3	Mother mortality rate by region 1990–2015 (*Note* Figure constructed by authors based on source data from the UNDP Human Development Reports)	99

Fig. 4	Adolescent fertility rate by region 1990–2017 (*Note* Figure constructed by authors based on source data from the UNDP Human Development Reports)	102
Fig. 5	Parliamentary representation by region 2005–2017 (*Note* Figure constructed by authors based on source data from the UNDP Human Development Reports)	106
Fig. 6	Parliamentary representation in Balkan States (*Note* Figure constructed by authors based on source data from the UNDP Human Development Reports)	107
Fig. 7	Education gender gap (*Note* Figure constructed by authors based on source data from the UNDP Human Development Reports)	110
Fig. 8	Labour force participation gender gap (*Note* Figure constructed by authors based on source data from the UNDP Human Development Reports)	114

Chapter 5

| Fig. 1 | Indicator's operationalization process | 129 |

Chapter 6

Fig. 1	Crude oil average prices (US$/bbl)—2014–2016 (*Source* World Bank. [2021]. Commodity Price Data. *The Pink Sheet*)	168
Fig. 2	UK final energy consumption (mtoe) (*Source* UK National Statistics, Department for Business, Energy and Industrial Strategy. [2019]. Energy Consumption in the UK [ECUK] 1970 to 2018, Consumption Tables, Chart C1)	170
Fig. 3	Energy use (KG of oil equivalent per capita) (*Source* Based on World Bank. [2020]. *World Bank database*. https://data.worldbank.org/indicator/EG.use.pcap.kg.OE?locations)	171
Fig. 4	Schematic diagram for identifying energy profiles in IEA countries (*Source* Jewell, J. [2011]. *The IEA Model of Short-Term Energy Security [MOSES]*)	178
Fig. 5	Changes in forecasts of US energy security index after 2010 (*Source* Global Energy Institute. [2020a, b]. International Index of Assessing Risk in a Global Energy Market, U.S. Chamber of Commerce, USA)	183

Chapter 7

Exhibit 1	Developed Economies' GDP Per Capita: PPP vs. Market-based exchange rate (*Source* World Bank Open Data)	206
Exhibit 2	BRICS Economies' GDP Per Capita: PPP vs. Market-based exchange rate (*Source* World Bank Open Data)	207

Chapter 8

Fig. 1	A CFA-based model to measure country risk (*Source* Authors' Elaborations)	226

LIST OF TABLES

Chapter 1

Table 1	Pros and cons of composite indices	4

Chapter 2

Table 1	Descriptive statistics of the data of indicators—Level 1	35
Table 2	Average score for each topic as derived by each model	36
Table 3	Standard deviation of scores for each topic as derived by each model	36
Table 4	Normalized weights retrieved from OECD about the topics of level 2	38
Table 5	Lower and upper bounds of the weights of the eleven topics—Level 2	41
Table 6	BLI scores—Level 3	42
Table 7	No of BLI efficient countries, average score and standard deviation derived by each model	44

Chapter 3

Table 1	Measures of inequality	60
Table 2	Composition of income per capita by the methodology of measurement	66
Table 3	Alternative Gini formulations	69

Chapter 4

Table 1	An overview of gender inequality indices and their indicators	93
Table 2	GII by region	95
Table 3	Top and worst performing countries	97
Table 4	Mother mortality rate by region	99
Table 5	Top and worst performing countries (Mother mortality rate)	100
Table 6	Adolescent fertility rate by region	103
Table 7	Top and worst performing countries (Adolescent fertility rate)	104
Table 8	Parliamentary representation by region (reports percentage of women in parliament)	105
Table 9	Top and worst performing countries (parliamentary representation)	108
Table 10	Education gap by region	111
Table 11	Labour force participation gap by region	112

Chapter 5

Table 1	Gender indexes	127
Table 2	Factors, indicators, variables, unit and objectives of the education pillar	135
Table 3	Factors, indicators, variables, unit and objectives of the health pillar	136
Table 4	Factors, indicators, variables, unit and objectives of the autonomy pillar	137
Table 5	Factors, indicators, variables, unit and objectives of the opportunities pillar	138
Table 6	Statistical analysis by dimension—Peruvian GEICR	144
Table 7	General results of the Peruvian GEICR—2019	146

Chapter 6

Table 1	IEA Energy Security Model (MOSES)—Measured dimensions	175
Table 2	Risk and resilience (Res.) indicators used in MOSES	176
Table 3	Variables used in the US energy security index system	180
Table 4	The international energy security index metrics	184

Chapter 8

Table 1	Methods of country risk assessment	218
Table 2	Risk categories and their sub-categories in the country risk analysis of IHS Markit	222
Table 3	HIS country risk bands	223
Table 4	Comparable risk categories for an individual country	225

CHAPTER 1

The Role of Composite Indices in International Economic Diplomacy

Vincent Charles, Tatiana Gherman, and Ali Emrouznejad

1 International Economic Diplomacy

Diplomacy can be defined as "the conduct of international relations by negotiation and dialog or by any other means to promote peaceful relations among states. Besides this widely accepted single definition, diplomacy is also a set of practices, institutions, and discourses which is crucial for the basic understanding of the historical evolution of the

V. Charles (✉)
CENTRUM Católica Graduate Business School, Lima, Peru
e-mail: vcharles@pucp.pe

Pontifical Catholic University of Peru, Lima, Peru

T. Gherman
Faculty of Business and Law, University of Northampton, Northampton, UK
e-mail: tatiana.gherman@northampton.ac.uk

A. Emrouznejad
Surrey Business School, University of Surrey, Guildford, UK
e-mail: a.emrouznejad@surrey.ac.uk

© The Author(s), under exclusive license to Springer Nature Switzerland AG 2022
V. Charles and A. Emrouznejad (eds.), *Modern Indices for International Economic Diplomacy*, https://doi.org/10.1007/978-3-030-84535-3_1

international system and its evolving functional and normative needs" (Cornago, 2008, p. 574).

In the post-modern environment, the concept of "diplomacy" has undergone substantial mutations. To begin with, the phenomenon of "globalisation" has transformed international economic relationships around the world; then, a growing number of actors (state and non-state) have begun to emerge and impact such relationships, increasing interconnectivities and interdependencies. In turn, all of these have affected the economic, social, and political spheres of societies and citizens (Saner & Yiu, 2001).

Diplomacy, in its various forms, plays a vital role in international relationships. First, diplomacy provides the means for measuring international relations; and generally, such measurements involve comparisons across countries at the same point in time. Second, diplomacy is a veritable means for conflict resolution and peace-building in crisis situations among nations. Diplomacy facilitates information, communication, and knowledge exchange among nations.

In every-day language, diplomacy is most widely thought of from the perspective of the political aspect. However, this chapter (and entire book, for that matter), is not intended for covering the political aspect of diplomacy, which is nonetheless, an important dimension. Rather, the interest is to explore the more socio-economic dimension of diplomacy: how diplomacy can support country competitiveness, social progress, and people's well-being, as well as the stability and resilience in nations around the world through reliance on various composite indices.

2 Composite Indices

In recent years, there has been increased interest in studying (composite) indices for the betterment of the public. A recent special issue of the journal Socio-Economic Planning Sciences, edited by Charles, Emrouznejad, and Johnson (2020), stands as proof of this assertion. The special issue focused on the conceptualisation and development of new indices for the betterment of the public and novel algorithms and approaches that integrated or refined those indices, as well as novel ways of using the existing indices to improve the public policies that serve the greater good. The articles contained therein aimed to position themselves beyond purely suggesting new/modern/revised indices with the economics view and conceivably validating them using real-life vital data sets; rather, the scope of the articles was to help policymakers gain an advanced understanding of the ways that would unleash greater long-term social success, as well as propose strategies that would create the conditions for the betterment of the public.

Composite indices are used by a range of governments, national, and international organisations, as well as businesses to monitor different performance aspects of the economy of a country and the people therein. In a nutshell, composite indices are synthetic indices of individual indices which compare and rank entities (*e.g.*, countries, organisations, and so on) in different performance areas, such as competitiveness, innovation, gender equality, human development, governance, and environmental sustainability, just to name a few (n/a, 2003). Composite indices can surmount national particularities and bring the consideration to a common denominator (Tangian, 2004).

Munda and Nardo (2003, p. 2) noted that:

> *Composite indicators stem from the need to rank countries and benchmarking their performance whenever a country does not perform strictly better than another. Composite indicators are very common in fields such as economic and business statistics (e.g., the OECD Composite Leading Indicators) and are used in a variety of policy domains such as industrial competitiveness, sustainable development, quality of life assessment, globalization and innovation* (see Cox and others 1992; Huggins, 2003; Wilson & Jones, 2002; Guerard, 2001; Färe et al., 1994; Lovell et al., 1995; Griliches, 1990; Saisana & Tarantola, 2002 among others) ... *A general objective of most of these indicators is the ranking of countries according to some aggregated dimensions* . (see Cherchye, 2001; Kleinknecht, 2002)

Of course, it is always a challenge to reduce complex socio-economic phenomena to a single index; so, it is important to remember that composite indices are limited in that way, reflecting only a simplified version of reality. As emphasised by the OECD (2003, p. 3), "composite indicators are valued for their ability to integrate large amounts of information into easily understood formats for a general audience... Despite their many deficiencies, composite indicators will continue to be developed due to their usefulness...". So, we must also acknowledge that being developed in this way is useful in a very practical sense, in that they can better focus and direct policy debates. Needless to say, then, that historically composite indices have been valuable as communication tools and as inputs into decision and policymaking.

2.1 Pros and Cons of Composite Indices

The number of composite indices that are constructed and used nationally and internationally is growing very fast; it is, therefore, necessary to understand their benefits and limitations. In their technical report on tools for composite indicators building, Nardo et al. (2005, p. 6) elegantly summarised the pros and cons of composite indices, which are conveyed here in Table 1.

Table 1 Pros and cons of composite indices

Pros of composite indices	Cons of composite indices
Summarise complex or multi-dimensional issues, in view of supporting decision-makers	May send misleading policy messages, if they are poorly constructed or misinterpreted
Are easier to interpret than trying to find a trend in many separate indicators	May invite drawing simplistic policy conclusions, if not used in combination with the indicators
Facilitate the task of ranking countries on complex issues in a benchmarking exercise	May lend themselves to instrumental use (e.g., be built to support the desired policy), if the various stages (e.g., selection of indicators, choice of model, weights) are not transparent and based on sound statistical or conceptual principles
Assess progress of countries over time on complex issues	The selection of indicators and weights could be the target of political challenge
Reduce the size of a set of indicators or include more information within the existing size limit	May disguise serious failings in some dimensions of the phenomenon, and thus increase the difficulty in identifying the proper remedial action
Place issues of countries performance and progress at the centre of the policy arena	May lead wrong policies, if dimensions of performance that are difficult to measure are ignored
Facilitate communication with ordinary citizens and promote accountability	

Source Taken from Nardo et al. (2005, p. 6)

2.2 Characteristics of Good Composite Indices

There are a number of general characteristics that indicators should have in order to be both useful and efficient. Although not constituting a comprehensive list, the following are examples of guidelines or best practices (of a theoretical, technical, or procedural nature) most commonly invoked; in this sense, indicators should be:

2.3 Clearly Defined

Indicators should have clear and intelligible definitions. In this sense, the intended users of the indicators should be able to understand them even if the definitions contain technical terms. At the same time, another aspect that needs to be considered is that narrowing or broadening too much the definition of an indicator can also create problems; hence, finding the right balance is an art.

2.4 Theoretically Sound

This aspect is many times underlooked; however, it is important that the composite index has a strong theoretical foundation. This means that the various variables, pillars, and/or subpillars, and factors composing the index should be informed by relevant theoretical and policy underpinning. Moreover, such consideration will also be useful in further decisions related to the weighting mechanism to be used; for example, variables with greater relevance or importance to the phenomenon being analysed should be given a greater weight. Of course, weights may be assigned both qualitatively (*e.g.*, through expert opinion) and quantitatively (*e.g.*, through techniques such as principal component analysis or factor analysis).

2.5 Relevant

The variables, pillars, and/or subpillars, and factors composing the index should not only be analytically sound but should further be relevant to the phenomenon being measured. There should also be a clear articulation of the stakeholders to whom indicators will be useful. Differences in interests and perspectives will make an indicator more relevant to some users and less to others. As such, indicators need to be aligned with the strategic goals and objectives of the organisations that intend to use them.

2.6 Comparable

Variables come in a variety of statistical units with different ranges or scales; hence, variables should undergo standardisation or normalisation to bring them to a common basis that in turn will render them comparable. Furthermore, the indicators should ideally be able to be compared with a consistent database, both between organisations and with historical values. Additionally, a vital element around comparability involves the consideration of the context and the conditions therein, which if highly different across contexts, might render the comparison invalid.

2.7 Verifiable

Statistical validation is another criterion to be considered. First, indicators must be collected and calculated in a way that allows the data and results to be verified (thus, ensuring transparency and accessibility); in other words, relevant parties should be in a position to verify the accuracy of the information included, the consistency of the methods used, and the robustness of the composite index developed. Second, methodological practicalities need to be acknowledged and clearly stated: for example, how are missing values being dealt with, whether there are any issues regarding the double-counting of phenomena, how the qualitative data are being integrated into the index, and so on. Third, sensitivity tests should be conducted to assess the impact of including or excluding variables, changing weights, and using different standardisation or normalisation techniques, among others.

2.8 Flexible

Indicators should be adaptable to changes that may occur both nationally and internationally. In this sense, indicators should be able to accommodate new variables or methods of computation, encouraging innovation.

2.9 Placed in Time

Indicators should be based on data that are available within a reasonable period of time, depending on how and when the information is used. Some data are collected daily or weekly, while other data are only available once a year and across years.

2.10 Visually Sound

Lastly, it is important to remember that visualisation matters, mostly because it can be deceptive. As it is well known, the same information can be presented in very different ways, leading to different interpretations; some of the most common misleading visualisation techniques involve cherry picking, omitting the baseline, manipulating the axes, using wrong graphs, overloading or underloading with data, and so on. Considering that composite indices have the power to influence the policy message, the presentation of the results of composite indices should be carefully considered so as to acknowledge their limitations, and possibly show the results and impact of the sensitivity tests results.

2.11 Governments and International Organisations

One of the roles of both national and international organisations (such as the United Nations, The Organisation for Economic Co-operation and Development—OECD, World Economic Forum—WEF, International Institute for Management—IMD, Social Progress Imperative, etc.) is to assist governments in their efforts to design and implement better policies for better development on a national and global scale. Thus, the role that the composite indices developed by these organisations have for diplomacy as a policy advisor to foster progresses of its various forms is more than evident. "A significant and rapidly growing number of international business and policy decisions directly rely on such indicators. A growing amount of analysis that influences broader perceptions, and often directly or indirectly shapes future decisions, does likewise" (Arndt & Oman, 2006, p. 13).

As risks (be them economic or financial crises, terrorism acts, or pandemics, just to name a few) keep on characterising and affecting all aspects of life globally, at the individual and societal level, governments need to be constantly adapting and collaborating through international diplomacy to pursue common goals for people's well-being (such as increasing economic growth, decreasing inequalities, and enforcing environmental regulations). True well-being means achieving a balance between various development goals, such as economic, social, and environmental. In this sense, it is worth pointing out the 17 global Sustainable Development Goals (SDGs) adopted by the United Nations in 2015, aimed at achieving a better and more sustainable future by 2030. The 17 SDGs are:

1. No Poverty;
2. Zero Hunger;
3. Good Health and Well-being;
4. Quality Education;
5. Gender Equality;
6. Clean Water and Sanitation;
7. Affordable and Clean Energy;
8. Decent Work and Economic Growth;
9. Industry, Innovation, and Infrastructure;
10. Reducing Inequality;
11. Sustainable Cities and Communities;
12. Responsible Consumption and Production;
13. Climate Action;
14. Life Below Water;
15. Life On Land;
16. Peace, Justice, and Strong Institutions;
17. Partnerships for the Goals.

Each goal typically has 8–12 targets, and each target has between 1 and 4 indices used to measure progress towards reaching the targets. In total, the initiative started with 169 targets and 232 indices. In time, because of measurement difficulties (Winfried, 2021), revisions have been made; for example, in 2020, 36 changes to the global index framework were proposed, with some indices being replaced or revised, while others deleted (United Nations, 2020).

All in all, the document that contains these goals, titled "Transforming Our World: The 2030 Agenda for Sustainable Development", represents a commitment of heads of state and government to eradicate poverty and achieve sustainable development by 2030 worldwide. Importantly, this document also differentiates between gross domestic product (GDP) and social progress when it formulated its objective as: "By 2030, build on existing initiatives to develop measurements of progress on sustainable development that complement gross domestic product, and support statistical capacity-building in developing countries" (Charles & D'Alessio, 2019). And this is a critical observation because "'The Beyond

GDP' initiative has brought together a large number of countries who found themselves cooperating in developing indicators that are as clear as the GDP, but more inclusive of environmental and social aspects of progress" (Charles, Gherman, & Tsolas, 2020, p. 160).

2.12 Methodological and Computational Aspects

As previously mentioned, composite indices represent a useful tool for policymaking and public communications. However, the process of creating a composite index is not simple, and the methodological and computational aspects present a number of technical issues that, if not addressed properly, can lead to composite indices being misread or manipulated. Of course, views differ quite widely. For example, back in 2004, Sharpe (2004) noted that:

> *The aggregators believe there are two major reasons that there is value in combining indicators in some manner to produce a bottom line. They believe that such a summary statistic can indeed capture reality and is meaningful, and that stressing the bottom line is extremely useful in garnering media interest and hence the attention of policy makers. The second school, the non-aggregators, believe one should stop once an appropriate set of indicators has been created and not go the further step of producing a composite index. Their key objection to aggregation is what they see as the arbitrary nature of the weighting process by which the variables are combined.*

So, it is equally difficult to know where to start and when to stop. Despite the existence of so many indices, there is no single methodology for the computation of any of them. There is no general agreement on the existence of a set of standardised or holistic indices to measure progress in its various forms. Some indices may lack a certain level of transparency, while others may suffer from bias, and others may not be applicable to developed and developing countries in the same way. Needless to say, this is not just a problem of the past or the present, but also of the future; the perfect index will undoubtedly never exist. Nevertheless, indices are needed to monitor conditions and assess prospects for future developments in countries around the world in terms of political stability, social progress, poverty reduction, gender equality, human rights and human development, and so on. So, efforts can be made to periodically renew interest in composite indices and reiterate the need to revise them, developing improved ones that can better serve the objectives for which they were created in the first place. Below, we discuss two directions that such studies have generally taken.

The first group of studies seek to make changes at the conceptual level. For example, Coronado et al. (2017) computed a regional competitiveness index by taking agricultural resources as determinant factors, which represents a novel conceptualisation of the regional competitiveness index. In this sense, the authors identified regional factors related to the use of water, soil, production, revenues, and rural population, which conform a total of six productivity indices, that the authors then employed to calculate the regional agricultural competitiveness index.

The second group of studies acknowledges that changes are needed not just at the conceptual level, but also at the methodological level. For example, take the case of the computation of regional competitiveness. Charles and Diaz (2016), Charles and Sei (2019), and Charles and Zegarra (2014) observed that generally, the existing methodologies to compute a regional competitiveness index use the information of several variables to measure the performance across a specific number of dimensions, or pillars, that are considered to be the fundamental components of competitiveness. Now, taking these pillars as the inputs for computations, the computations follow a non-optimisation approach most of the times, where the indices are derived in an absolute sense, and the pillars are given equal importance in terms of weights. But, as the authors noted, "this approach raises two concerns, which have been treated in the literature of composite indicators (Cherchye et al., 2007), namely that: (1) the indices are absolute, so then the results are sensitive to the units of measurement of the pillars, and (2) some value judgements are implicit in the choice of weights (in this case, pillars may not play an equal role in the competitiveness of every region)" (Charles & Diaz, 2016). The studies mentioned above attempted to address such shortcomings by proposing envelopment-based models.

Similarly, using the theoretical framework of the World Bank, Charles (2015) developed a novel methodology based on data envelopment analysis to compute doing business index that could more accurately capture the efficiency of the business climate of 189 countries. The objective was to rank the economies according to the outcomes achieved in the various factors. But in contrast with the methodology employed by the World Bank (which is an equal weight methodology, where each variable has the same weight in each of the 10 factors and each factor has the same weight in the global index), a data envelopment analysis approach does not impose ad-hoc weights. In the author's words, "the reasoning behind is the following: with multiple outcomes to evaluate, different weights could produce different orderings in the ranking; furthermore, imposing the same weights for every economy could fail to reflect their individual preferences or constraints" (Charles, 2015, p. 15). The proposed methodology overcomes all of these barriers. Moreover, the model is both unit invariant and translation invariant.

More recently, Charles, Gherman and Tsolas (2020) showed a novel way to compute a regional social progress index, under a two-phase approach. Building upon the framework provided by the Social Progress Imperative (2016), in the first phase, the authors aggregated the item-level information into subfactor-level indices and the subfactor-level indices into a factor-level index using an objective general index (Sei, 2016); in the second phase, they use the factor-level indices to obtain the regional social progress index through a pure data envelopment analysis approach.

The nicety of these recent methodological developments is that they can be used for the computation of various other indices. For example, the proposed model by Charles and Diaz (2016) does not only serve to compute the index of regional competitiveness, but it can also be used to construct other index systems, such as the Social Progress Index, Doing Business Index, Happiness Index, Innovation Index, and so on.

At this point, it is also important to acknowledge that there is a third strand of research, an emergent and promising one, that advocates for changes that go beyond conceptual and methodological aspects, emphasising a need for more collaborative, inter- and intra-disciplinary efforts. This is because, in the context of the ever-changing conditions in the world economy, we require a much broader set of indicators to examine and monitor performance and progress towards achieving the intended aims and determine where resources and support are needed. This also means higher level of cooperation, with all stakeholders involved.

We join all these calls; more specifically, we join the calls for the development of improved conceptual frameworks and methodologies to measure the various dimensions of progress and people's well-being, as well as we join the calls for a more efficient social and civil dialogue between various interested groups (Charles et al., 2019). These new and revised indices can further be utilised by international diplomacy to promote international consensus and reach new milestones in terms of economic, social, and environmental agreements. International economic diplomacy requires indices that allow the design and implementation of relevant policies at both national and international levels. Hence, indices can be used by policymakers and other interested parties to monitor different performance aspects of the economy of a country and the people therein.

2.13 Final Thoughts

Composite indices are useful for monitoring different performance aspects of the economy of a country and the people therein; and they have historically been valuable as communication tools and as inputs into decision and policymaking. However, the process of creating a composite index is not simple, and the methodological and computational aspects present a number of technical issues that, if not addressed properly, can lead to composite indices being misread or manipulated. Over time, indices have been met with various criticism, among which, the fact that they may be biased or may lack theoretical support, transparency, or operational rules. Despite the existence of so many indices, there is no single methodology for the computation of any of them. So, it comes as no surprise that there is no general agreement on the existence of a set of standardised or holistic indices to measure progress in its various forms. Yet, composite indices are increasingly being used by governments, national and international organisations, and businesses alike, for cross-country comparisons. As Saisana et al. (2005) pointed out:

> *[...] it is hard to imagine that debate on the use of composite indicators will ever be settled [...] official statisticians may tend to resent composite indicators, whereby a lot of work in data collection and editing is "wasted" or "hidden" behind a single number of dubious significance. On the other hand, the temptation of stakeholders and practitioners to summarise complex and sometime elusive processes (e.g. sustainability, single market policy, etc.) into a single figure to benchmark country performance for policy consumption seems likewise irresistible.*

So, it is fair to say that indices will always be among us. Considering the importance of composite indices for monitoring and benchmarking the mutual and relative progress of countries in a variety of policy areas, improvements in the way indices are constructed and used are a very important research issue from a theoretical, methodological, and practical point of view (Munda & Nardo, 2003).

Our aim in this manuscript has been to renew interest in composite indices and highlight the need to periodically revisit them, in an attempt to develop improved ones that can better serve the objectives for which they were created in the first place, helping to guide and move the field and practice forward. From a very practical perspective, there is a need for indices that can accommodate the new challenges in a world impacted not only by the characteristics of today's business environment [i.e., volatility, uncertainty, complexity, and ambiguity—or VUCA], but also by the characteristics of the big data age (among which we mention context, complexity, and connectedness—see Charles and Gherman [2013]), of course, within an ethical framework (Charles et al., 2015).

As Charles et al. (2021) noted, "the relatively recent phenomenon posed by the exponential growth of big data has brought with it new challenges, one of the most intriguing of which deals with knowledge discovery and large-scale data-mining (Emrouznejad & Marra, 2016). The presence of big data has been 'pushing' organisations [N.B. of all sorts, we may add] to review their practices and identify opportunities that would allow them to base a substantial portion of their operational decisions on data, otherwise known as data-driven decision-making (Charles, Aparicio, & Zhu, 2020)".

Studies aimed at bringing together the topic of composite indices and large/big data have started emerging and, without a doubt, represent one of the future directions of research. For example, Resce and Maynard (2018) aggregated millions of tweets and proposed a composite Better Life Index (BLI) based on the weighted average of the national performances in each dimension of the BLI, using the relative importance that the topics have on Twitter as weights. The idea is novel not only methodologically, but also conceptually, since this exercise develops a composite index that considers social priorities in the aggregation. Indeed, different computational approaches and different data collection methods will yield different insights. So, another implication is that there is a need for more cross- and inter-disciplinary empirically grounded research, more specifically, for new research approaches to study people and practice in truly insightful and impactful ways (for an example, please see Charles and Gherman (2018; Gherman [2018]), which can then translate into the creation of better, more comprehensive composite indices.

The development of such indices will further require a greater level of collaboration between a wider range of stakeholders, from researchers to data scientists, regulators and policymakers, business executives and members of civil societies, just to name a few. This is because while traditionally, diplomacy has been the prerogative of ambassadors and official envoys, today, the management of international economic relations is no longer confined to the state, but rather extended to civil and commercial affairs (Saner & Yiu, 2001). In a nutshell, therefore, there is a need to create an extended network of experts who can engage in constructive policy dialogue. Part of such dialogue would encompass not only efforts to construct better composite indices, but also to develop quality guidelines for the construction of such indices, with clear policy implications.

Acknowledgements The authors are thankful to the reviewers for their valuable comments on the previous version of this work.

REFERENCES

Arndt, C., & Oman, C. (2006). *Uses and abuses of governance indicators*. OECD Development Centre Studies.

Charles, V. (2015). Doing business across the continents: A quick heads-up. *Strategia, 37*, 8–18.

Charles, V., & D'Alessio, F. A. (2019). An envelopment-based approach to measuring regional social progress. *Socio-Economic Planning Sciences, 70*, 100713.

Charles, V., & Diaz, G. (2016). A non-radial DEA index for Peruvian regional competitiveness. *Social Indicators Research, 134*(2), 747–770.

Charles, V., & Gherman, T. (2013). Achieving competitive advantage through big data. Strategic implications. *Middle-East Journal of Scientific Research, 16*(8), 1069–1074.

Charles, V., & Gherman, T. (2018). Big data and ethnography: Together for the greater good. In A. Emrouznejad & V. Charles (Eds.), *Big data for the greater good* (pp. 19–34). Springer.

Charles, V., & Sei, T. (2019). A two-stage OGI approach to compute the regional competitiveness index. *Competitiveness Review: An International Business Journal, 29*(2), 78–95.

Charles, V., & Zegarra, L. F. (2014). Measuring regional competitiveness through data envelopment analysis: A peruvian case. *Expert Systems with Applications, 41*, 5371–5381.

Charles, V., Aparicio, J., & Zhu, J. (Eds.). (2020). *Data science and productivity analytics*. Springer.

Charles, V., Emrouznejad, A., & Gherman, T. (2021). Strategy formulation and service operations in the big data age: The essentialness of technology, people, and ethics. In A. Emrouznejad & V. Charles (Eds.), *Big data for service operations management* (pp. 1–30). Springer's International Series in Studies in Big Data, Springer-Verlag, UK. (Forthcoming).

Charles, V., Emrouznejad, A., & Johnson, M. P. (2020). Indices for the betterment of the public. *Socio-Economic Planning Sciences, 70*, 100767.

Charles, V., Gherman, T., & Paliza, J. C. (2019). Stakeholder involvement for public sector productivity enhancement: Strategic considerations. *ICPE Public Enterprise Half-Yearly Journal, 24*(1), 77–86.

Charles, V., Gherman, T., & Tsolas, I. E. (2020). A Novel two-phase approach to computing a regional social progress index. In J. Aparicio, C. A. K. Lovell, J. T. Pastor, & J. Zhu (Eds.), *Advances in efficiency and productivity II* (pp. 159–172). Springer's International Series in Operations Research & Management Science.

Charles, V., Tavana, M., & Gherman, T. (2015). The right to be forgotten—is privacy sold out in the big data age? *International Journal of Society Systems Science, 7*(4), 283–298.

Cherchye, L. (2001). Using data envelopment analysis to assess macroeconomic policy performance. *Applied Economics, 33*, 407–416.

Cherchye, L., Moesen, W., Rogge, N., & Van Puyenbroeck, T. (2007). An introduction to the 'benefit of the doubt' composite indicators. *Social Indicators Research, 82*, 111–145.

Cornago, N. (2008). Diplomacy. In L. Kurtz (Ed.), *Encyclopedia of violence, peace, & conflict* (2nd ed., pp. 574–580). Academic Press.

Coronado, F., Charles, V., & Dwyer, R. J. (2017). Measuring regional competitiveness through agricultural indices of productivity: The Peruvian case. *World Journal of Entrepreneurship, Management and Sustainable Development, 13*(2), 78–95.

Cox, D., Fitzpatrick, R., Fletcher, A., Gore, S., Spiegelhalter, D., & Jones, D. (1992). Quality-of-life assessment: Can we keep it simple? *Journal of the Royal Statistical Society, 155*(3), 353–393.

Emrouznejad, A., & Marra, M. (2016). Big data: Who, what and where? Social, cognitive and journals map of big data publications with focus on optimization. In A. Emrouznejad (Ed.), *Big data optimization: Recent developments and challenges* (pp. 1–16). Springer.

Färe, R., Grosskopf, S., Norris, M., & Zhang, Z. (1994). Productivity growth, technical progress and efficiency change in industrialised countries. *American Economic Review, 84*(1), 66–83.

Gherman, T. (2018, Spring/Summer). Machine learning and ethnography: A marriage made in heaven. *Informs OR/MS Tomorrow*, 12–13.

Griliches, Z. (1990). Patent statistics as economic indicators. *Journal of Economic Literature, 28*, 1661–1707.

Guerard, J. B. (2001). A note on the forecasting effectiveness of the US leading economic indicators. *Indian Economic Review, 36*(1), 251–268.

Huggins, R. (2003). Creating a UK competitive index: Regional and local benchmarking. *Regional Studies, 37*, 89–96.

Jolly, R. (1999). New composite indices for development co-operation. *Development, 42*, 36–42.

Kleinknecht, A., Van Montfort, K., & Brouwer, E. (2002). The non-trivial choice between innovation indicators. *Economic Innovation and New Technologies, 11*(2), 109–121.

Lovell, C. A. K., Pastor, J. T., & Turner, J. A. (1995). Measuring macroeconomic performance in the OECD: A comparison of European and non-European countries. *European Journal of Operational Research, 87*, 507–518.

Munda, G., & Nardo, M. (2003, May 12). *On the methodological foundations of composite indicators used for ranking countries.* In OECD/JRC Workshop on composite indicators of country performance, Ispra (VA), Italy.

n/a. (2003, May 12). *Summary: First workshop on composite indicators of country performance.* Ispra (VA). Joint Research Centre of the European Commission https://www.oecd.org/sti/ind/2511317.pdf

Nardo, M., Saisana,M., Saltelli, A., & Tarantola, S. (2005). Tools for composite indicators building. *Technical Report EUR 21682 EN*. Institute for the Protection and Security of the Citizen Econometrics and Statistical Support to Antifraud Unit, I-21020 Ispra (VA), Italy.

OECD. (2003). *Composite indicators of country performance: A critical assessment.* DSTI/DOC (2003)16. OECD.

Resce, G., & Maynard, D. (2018). What matters most to people around the world? Retrieving better life index priorities on Twitter. *Technological Forecasting and Social Change, 137*, 61–75.

Saisana, M., & Tarantola, S. (2002). State-of-the-art report on current methodologies and practives for composite indicator development. *EUR 20408 EN Report*. European Commission, JRC, Ispra, Italy.

Saisana, M., Tarantola, S., & Saltelli, A. (2005). Uncertainty and sensitivity techniques as tools for the analysis and validation of composite indicators. *Journal of the Royal Statistical Society A, 168*(2), 1–17.

Saner, R., & Yiu, L. (2001). *International economic diplomacy: Mutations in Post-modern times.* Discussion Papers in Diplomacy, Netherlands Institute of

International Relations 'Clingendael'. https://www.clingendael.org/sites/default/files/pdfs/20030100_cli_paper_dip_issue84.pdf

Sei, T. (2016). An objective general index for multivariate ordered data. *Journal of Multivariate Analysis, 147*, 247–264.

Sharpe, A. (2004). *Literature review of frameworks for macro-indicators*. Centre for the Study of Living Standards.

Social Progress Imperative. (2016). *2016 social progress index*. http://www.socialprogressimperative.org/

Tangian, A. S. (2004). Constructing the composite indicator "quality of work" from the third European survey on working conditions. *Diskussionspapier Nr. 132*. https://www.boeckler.de/pdf/p_wsi_diskp_132.pdf

United Nations. (2020). *IAEG-SDGs 2020 comprehensive review proposals submitted to the 51st session of the United Nations statistical commission for its consideration*. United Nations, Department of Economic and Social Affairs, Statistics Division. Retrieved October 10, 2021, from https://unstats.un.org/sdgs/iaeg-sdgs/2020-comprev/UNSC-proposal/

Wilson, J. W., & Jones, C. P. (2002). An analysis of the S&P 500 index and Cowles's extensions: Price indexes and stock returns, 1870–1999. *Journal of Business, 75*, 505–533.

Winfried, H. (2021). The UN sustainable development goals and the governance of global public goods. In M. Iovane, F. Palombino, D. Amoroso, & G. Zarra (Eds.), *The protection of general interests in contemporary international law: A theoretical and empirical inquiry*. Oxford University Press.

CHAPTER 2

The OECD Better Life Index: A Guide for Well-Being Based Economic Diplomacy

Gregory Koronakos, Yiannis Smirlis, Dimitris Sotiros, and Dimitris K. Despotis

1 Introduction

The recent global threats, such as climate change, financial crisis and pandemics, evidently manifest their direct impact on the well-being of people. At the same time, the international competition among the countries has sharpened to attract foreign investments, to gain access to foreign markets and to protect their domestic markets. However, these conflicting

---

G. Koronakos (✉) · D. K. Despotis
Department of Informatics, University of Piraeus, Piraeus, Greece
e-mail: gkoron@unipi.gr

Y. Smirlis
School of Economics, Business and International Studies, University of Piraeus, Piraeus, Greece

D. Sotiros
Department of Operations Research and Business Intelligence, Wrocław University of Science and Technology, Wrocław, Poland

© The Author(s), under exclusive license to Springer Nature Switzerland AG 2022
V. Charles and A. Emrouznejad (eds.), *Modern Indices for International Economic Diplomacy*, https://doi.org/10.1007/978-3-030-84535-3_2

interests in conjunction with the economic interdependencies of markets and the fragmented political relationships have negative effect on the living conditions and the quality of life. Obviously, such a volatile environment renders imperative for the governments to interact and effectively cooperate to promote the international relations and reach economic and climate agreements. Addressing the world's challenges collectively through constructive diplomacy will enable governments to deliver better lives for their citizens. In this respect, it is of utmost importance to construct reliable well-being measures that can be employed as tools to support international economic diplomacy.

Well-being is multidimensional as it depends on a wide range of socio-economic aspects, such as material conditions, quality of life and sustainability. However, the multifaceted factors of well-being are of different importance and they may not follow the same trend. For instance, the economic growth is not always followed by other societal aspects, nor it is equally shared to all parts of societies. In addition, the quality of life is more important than income. Hence, to derive a better picture of how society performs in all areas, it is crucial to depart from the ordinary income-based measures (e.g., gross domestic product-GDP), which are inadequate to capture the societal progress, and shift the awareness to more comprehensive measures that incorporate multifaceted human-centric criteria.

On this basis, the Organization for Economic Co-operation and Development (OECD) launched the OECD Better Life initiative (Durand, 2015; OECD, 2011) with the aim to develop better well-being metrics, to facilitate the better understanding of what drives well-being of people and guide the policy-making. The initiative provides regular monitoring and benchmarking through the "*How's Life?*" reports (OECD, 2011, 2013a, 2015, 2017, 2020) and the interactive web platform (oecdbetterlifeindex.org) that promotes the OECD Better Life Index (BLI). The OECD BLI covers several socio-economic aspects by incorporating eleven key topics (factors) that the OECD has identified as essential to well-being in terms of material living conditions and quality of life. The BLI has a hierarchical structure with three levels. In a bottom-up representation, the first (bottom) level comprises of the indicators that form the eleven topics of the second level, which subsequently form the BLI at the third level. The web application is designed to disseminate the BLI as well as to prompt people to share their views about the topics that matter most to them. The public participation is critical considering the varying needs and the unequal distribution of the well-being outcomes among different regions and groups of the population. Also, the public opinion allows to focus on true-life conditions, hence it should be considered when creating well-being measures and policies. The OECD, except measures about the well-being at country (international) level, provides measures for regional well-being via the OECD regional well-being web platform (oecdregionalwellbeing.org). Hence, the concept of BLI can be readily applied at national level, i.e., for regional assessments.

Obtaining a single measure of well-being by synthesizing the multifaceted components of BLI is challenging. However, the OECD has not adopted, so far, an aggregation approach for the case of BLI. It is left to the citizens though to create the BLI based on their views. This is explicitly declared in the BLI's website: "*Your Better Life Index is designed to let you, the user, investigate how each of the 11 topics can contribute to wellbeing*". The OECD Handbook for the construction of composite indices (OECD, 2008) provides directives and methodological tools. Nevertheless, there is still a great debate about the aggregation techniques that should be adopted (Greco et al., 2019a). In the frame of BLI, it is arbitrary to consider that the eleven topics are of equal importance, i.e., that people believe that each topic has the same impact on their life. Assuming equal weights for the construction of composite indices has justifiably faced criticism since it implies equal worth and contribution of the included topics, see Nardo et al. (2005). An alternative to the equal or fixed weighting procedure is the *Benefit of the Doubt* (BoD) approach, which is based on Data Envelopment Analysis (DEA) (Cooper et al., 2011). The BoD approach (Cherchye et al., 2007; Melyn & Moesen, 1991), is a popular approach for constructing composite indices where the weights derive endogenously from the optimization process. The BoD approach estimates different weights for each unit under assessment in its most favorable way to reach the highest possible performance. Rogge (2018) explored various weighted average functions in a BoD framework for the construction of composite indices. Smirlis (2020) introduced a trichotomic segmentation approach as initial preference information to estimate the values of composite indices. The aggregation procedure employs the BoD approach with common weights for all the assessed countries. However, in the BoD approach compensability among the different components of the indices is assumed.

An increasing literature body is focused on the construction of noncompensatory composite indicators. Bouyssou (1986) introduced general aggregation methods that allow for a mix of compensatory and non-compensatory components. The non-compensatory aggregation methods do not allow an unfavorable value in one topic to be compensated by a favorable value in another topic (Roy, 1996). Despite their desirable properties, the non-compensatory methods are not as popular as the enhanced compensatory methods, which are preferred due to their simplicity in implementation. For instance, a solution to overcome the hypothesis of compensation that retains the simplicity of the implementation is to adopt the geometric aggregation method (Van Puyenbroeck & Rogge, 2017). Fusco (2015) dealt with non-compensability by introducing a directional penalty in the BoD model according to the variability of each topic. Zanella et al. (2015) proposed a directional BoD model for the assessment of composite indicators and imposed weight restrictions on the virtual weights, which reflect the relative importance of the topics in percentage terms. Similarly, Rogge et al. (2017) imposed weight restrictions in a directional distance BoD model.

In this chapter, we present the BLI and we discuss its applications reported in the literature. As BLI is not provided directly as an index by the OECD we present a hierarchical (bottom-up) evaluation methodology developed by Koronakos et al. (2019) that is based on Multiple Objective Programming. Also, the real views of people about well-being, as recorded by the OECD BLI web platform, are incorporated into the assessment models in the form of weight restrictions. The rest of the chapter unfolds as follows. In Sect. 2 we present the hierarchical structure of the BLI and its role in international economic diplomacy. In Sect. 3, we discuss the different methods proposed in the literature and in Sect. 4 we apply the approach introduced by Koronakos et al. (2019) for the BLI assessment of 38 countries (35 OECD and 3 non-OECD economies) for the year 2017. Conclusions are drawn in Sect. 5.

2 The OECD Better Life Index

The OECD framework covers dimensions of well-being that are universal and relevant for all people across the world. These dimensions are represented by eleven topics that compose the OECD Better Life Index. Each one of the eleven topics (level 2) of BLI is composed of one to four indicators (level 1). The indicators, as noticed in OECD (2011, 2013b), have been chosen in accordance with theory, practice and consultation

Fig. 1 The hierarchical structure of the OECD Better Life Index

with experts from various OECD directorates, about the issue of appropriate measuring of the well-being. The hierarchical three-level structure of Better Life Index is exhibited in Fig. 1. The indicators lie at the first (bottom) level, the topics are at the second level, and at the third level lies the resulting Better Life Index.

Among the eleven topics, the first three reflect material living conditions and the remaining eight are characterized as determinants of quality of life. A complete description of each topic and indicator included in the BLI can be found in the *"How's Life?"* report of OECD (2011) and the web platform.[1] The OECD provides for each indicator a clear picture about the specific aspects of well-being that it covers, its unit of measurement and the source of the data. The data mostly originate from official sources such as the OECD or National Accounts, United Nations Statistics and National Statistics Offices. The OECD BLI web platform presents the profiles and the performance in each indicator of the OECD countries and three key partners, namely Brazil, Russia and South Africa. Shortly, other countries will be included in OECD BLI such as China, India and Indonesia.

The BLI derives from the aggregation of the components that lie on three different levels. The indicators of level 1 are aggregated with equal weights to derive the values of each topic of level 2. This method, besides being employed by OECD for the BLI, it also prevails in the literature. On the other hand, the OECD has not proposed any specific weighting scheme for the aggregation of the eleven topics of level 2, whereas the

---

[1] The OECD Better Life Index web platform https://www.oecdbetterlifeindex.

reported approaches in the literature are mainly devoted to this task. Up to now, OECD has focused on the dissemination of BLI and the recording of what matters most to the people about well-being. The BLI is not provided directly as an index by the OECD, also in the online platform is stated that *"the OECD has not assigned rankings to countries"*. However, the aggregation scheme of the eleven topics for its construction is left to the people.

2.1 The Role of the OECD Better Life Index in International Economic Diplomacy

Economic Diplomacy, although driven by economic interests, indirectly is affected by the level of development of a country and by the well-being of its people. This link is mentioned in several research articles describing the exercise of Economic Diplomacy for different countries. Mudida (2012) focuses on aspects of the economic diplomacy of African countries, names it "diplomacy of development" and relates it with the quality of life of African citizens. Shichao (2012) ascertain that Singapore, although being a small country, achieved rapid growth, great improvements in its people's level of well-being and consequently developed Economic Diplomacy that in turn has put to reaching political and security goals.

The role of OECD is to assist governments to design and implement better policies for better well-being on a global scale. In the context of OECD 60th anniversary, the OECD Secretary-General Angel Gurría noticed *"Over the past 60 years, the OECD has been a catalyst for change in many aspects of public policy. We encourage debate, provide evidence and promote a shared understanding of critical global issues"*. The OECD launched the Better Life initiative and the program on Measuring Well-Being and Progress to find answers to questions such as *"Are our lives getting better?"*, *"How can policies improve our lives?"*, *"Are we measuring the right things?"*, etc. Thus, it is evident the role of OECD to diplomacy as a policy advisor for well-being based on BLI analysis.

The political and the economic environment influence the well-being. For instance, the implemented environmental policies and the economic conditions (income, unemployment, etc.) affect the quality of life. The OECD's How's Life? 2020 report illustrates that two-thirds of people in OECD countries are exposed to dangerous levels of air pollution. On average the footprint of the OECD residents is increased, only 10.5% of energy consumption is produced by renewable sources and in almost half of OECD countries thousands of species face extinction. In addition, the report shows that on average the household wealth and the performance of school students in international science tests have fallen. According to the report inequalities persist, with unequal income distribution, insecurity, despair and disconnection affecting large part of the population. In particular, more than 1 in 3 OECD households are financially insecure (household debt exceeds the household disposable income), 7% of people in OECD countries express very low satisfaction and the deaths due to depression exceeded the deaths from homicide and road accidents. The BLI incorporates the aforementioned aspects into the analysis and provides measures and insights for the well-being.

BLI also serves as an international public opinion repository about well-being. The online BLI platform records the priorities and views of citizens from different socio-economic environments worldwide. This interactive communication tool reveals what matters most to the people. For instance, exposure to dangerous levels of fine particulate matter may affect a small part of the population in one region while affecting a larger part in another. Thus, the answers given online can be used to elicit valuable information about the weighting scheme that should be used for the construction of BLI. In this way, the real priorities of people will be incorporated in the BLI and their views will further play a key role in the recommendations and advice to the policy makers.

As the emerging natural and economic risks threaten all aspects of life globally, the governments should adapt and collectively cooperate through international diplomacy to pursue common goals for well-being. Recognizing that the development must balance social, economic and environmental sustainability, the United Nations adopted the Sustainable Development Goals (a collection of 17 global goals) in 2015 for a better and more sustainable future to be achieved by the year 2030. The future of well-being will be ensured by preserving global financial stability and fair competition, stimulating the economic growth, reducing the inequalities and implementing international environmental regulations. The BLI provides measures for the several well-being aspects and demonstrates how policy can be a collaborative process. It enables worldwide comparisons and illustrates the individual issues of each region on which focus must be placed. In this vein, BLI can be employed to determine where resources are needed as well as to examine if policies are underperforming or achieving their strategic goals. Thus, it can straightforwardly serve as a tool to aid international diplomacy, e.g., United Nations, to reach economic and climate agreements (see Berridge, 2015).

3 Methods

Mizobuchi (2014) applied the BoD approach to construct the BLI for 34 countries (32 OECD members, Brazil and Russia) for the data of year 2011. The BoD was applied for the aggregation of the eleven topics (level 2), whose scores were estimated by the original averaging formula proposed by the OECD BLIOECD Better Life Index (BLI) initiative.[2] The obtained BLI scores were used to further investigate the link between the countries' well-being and the economic development, as reflected by per capita GDP. However, the approach of Mizobuchi (2014) generates country-specific weights that maximize the performance (composite indicator) of each country, failing in this way to provide a common basis for comparisons among the countries. Mizobuchi (2017) introduced another topic to BLI, apart from the 11 initial topics to account for the sustainability of well-being. Such an addition has been also proposed by OECD as a future complement in the BLI. In contrast to Mizobuchi (2014, 2017) applied the corrected convex non-parametric least squares (C^2NLS) method for constructing the BLI. Barrington-Leigh and Escande (2018) conducted a comparative study of indicators that measure progress and countries' well-being, reviewing the BLI and highlighting its advantages. In the same context, Lorenz et al. (2017) developed BoD based models to estimate the weighting schemes that allow each country to attain the highest possible rank according to its BLI performance. In addition, Peiro-Palomino and Picazo-Tadeo (2018) calculated the BLI based only on ten topics. They used instead the "*Life Satisfaction*" topic for comparison purposes with the calculated BLI. They employed the goal-programming model proposed by Despotis (2002) for the assessment and they also performed hierarchical cluster analysis to group the assessed countries in terms of well-being. However, in these models, compensability among the different components of the indices is assumed, i.e., trade-off relations exist among the topics and a country's low performance in a topic may be "compensated" by a high performance

---

[2] The method proposed by OECD for the aggregation of the indicators of level 1 can be found in https://www.oecdbetterlifeindex.org/about/better-life-initiative/#question15.

in another topic. Koronakos et al. (2019) modeled the assessment of BLI as a multiple objective programming (MOP) problem. They developed a hierarchical (bottom-up) procedure to aggregate the components of each level of BLI in separate phases. They also incorporated the public opinion, acquired from the OECD BLI web platform, into the assessment models in the form of weight restrictions. In this way, the effect of compensation imposed by the modeling approach is reduced. Greco et al. (2019b) also employed the ratings provided by people on the OECD BLI web platform for the eleven factors of BLI, but for the estimation of the aggregate societal loss of well-being. For this purpose, for each country they first transformed the performance of the factors into a discrete scale. Then they calculated each individuals' loss in well-being as the distance between the transformed performance in each factor and the collected individuals' views (weights).

3.1 Normalization

As the multilateral indicators are expressed in different units (dollars, years, etc.), the composition of BLI requires a data transformation step, prior to the aggregation of the raw data. The transformation is accomplished by applying the following formula to the original values of the indicators[3]:

$$\frac{ACV - MINOV}{MAXOV - MINOV} \quad (1)$$

When an indicator depicts a negative aspect of well-being (e.g., air pollution) the formula is modified as:

$$1 - \frac{ACV - MINOV}{MAXOV - MINOV} \quad (2)$$

In formulas (1) and (2) ACV denotes the actual country's value, whereas MINOV and MAXOV denote the minimum and maximum observed value among all countries, respectively. The normalization procedure converts the values of the indicators (level 1) in the [0,1] range, where

---

[3] The normalization formulas used by OECD for the data of the indicators of level 1 can be found in https://www.oecdbetterlifeindex.org/about/better-life-initiative/#question16.

"0" represents the worst possible performance and "1" the best possible one.

Notice that the normalization procedure described above involves, only for the year under assessment, the minimum and maximum observed values of the indicators from the participating countries. However, Koronakos et al. (2019) noticed that these values may have been changed dramatically among the years. As a result, the dispersion of the indicators' (level 1) values among the years is not considered during the necessary normalization process. They proposed instead to smooth the deviations of indicators' values and to establish cross-year compatibility by incorporating in the normalization process their minimum and maximum observed values[4] across the years (i.e., of the available data of 2013–2017). In this way, the absolute values of the indicators are converted to relative ones. For this purpose, they modified the formulas (1) and (2) accordingly. For the indicators that exhibit positive contribution to the BLI (e.g., Life expectancy, Water Quality, etc.), they employed the following adjusted formula:

$$\frac{ACV - MINOV^{(2013-2017)}}{MAXOV^{(2013-2017)} - MINOV^{(2013-2017)}} \qquad (3)$$

Similarly, for the indicators that exhibit negative contribution to the BLI (e.g., Housing Expenditure, Air pollution, etc.), the normalization formula becomes:

$$1 - \frac{ACV - MINOV^{(2013-2017)}}{MAXOV^{(2013-2017)} - MINOV^{(2013-2017)}} \qquad (4)$$

where ACV denotes the actual country's value, whereas $MINOV^{(2013-2017)}$ and $MAXOV^{(2013-2017)}$ denote the minimum and maximum observed value among all countries, respectively from 2013 to 2017.

3.2 Aggregation

The common practice adopted in the literature for the construction of three-level hierarchical composite indices such as BLI, is the use of the

---

[4] The complete data of the indicators for the years 2013–2017 can be found in the online database of OECD https://stats.oecd.org/Index.aspx?DataSetCode=BLI.

simple arithmetic average for the aggregation of the indicators (level 1). However, Koronakos et al. (2019) focused on the whole hierarchical structure of the index and aggregated the indicators of level 1 as weighted arithmetic averages, where the weights are obtained endogenously from optimization process. They developed a bottom-up procedure to aggregate, in two separate phases, the components of the index. In the first phase of the procedure, they derived through optimization the aggregation scheme of the indicators (level 1) to obtain the values of the topics that lie on the next level (level 2). Then, in the second phase of the procedure, they utilized the values of the 11 topics (level 2) obtained from the first phase, to derive through optimization of the aggregation weighting scheme that constructs the BLI (level 3).

The BoD is a prevailing approach in the literature of composite indices and has been already utilized for the aggregation of the topics (level 2) of BLI (Mizobuchi, 2014). The conventional form of BoD model (5) below, can be characterized as an index maximizing linear programming model that is solved for one country at a time (Despotis, 2005). The composite index h_j for the specific country j ($j = 1,...,n$) derives as the weighted sum $h_j = uY_j$, where $Y_j = (Y_{j1}, Y_{j2}, ..., Y_{jm})^T$ denotes the vector of the m components' values and $u = (u_1, u_2, ..., u_m)$ denotes the vector of the variables used as weights.

$$\max h_{j0} = uY_{j0}$$
$$s.t.$$
$$uY_j \leq 1, \quad j = 1, ..., n$$
$$u \geq \varepsilon \tag{5}$$

Model (5) provides a relative measure for a composite index and it is solved for each country individually. Thus, the optimal values u^* of the multipliers vary from country to country. The different country-specific weighting schemes derived by model (5) allow each country to achieve the highest possible score. In this respect, the BoD model (5) lacks a common basis for cross-country comparisons and ranking. Koronakos et al. (2019) argued that a common basis for fair evaluation can be established by finding a common set of multipliers u that will be used to obtain the composite index for each country. They formulated the following multiple objective programming model where the performance of each country ($h_j = uY_j$) is treated as a distinct objective-criterion:

$$\max \{ h_1 = uY_1, \ldots, h_n = uY_n\}$$
s.t.
$$uY_j \leq 1, \ j = 1, \ldots, n$$
$$u \geq \varepsilon \quad (6)$$

The MOP (6) can be converted and solved as a single objective program through scalarization. For this purpose, Koronakos et al. (2019) employed the *method of the global criterion* (c.f. Mietinnen, 1999) that is a no-preference method, i.e., no priority is assigned to the objectives. In this method, the distance between some reference point and the feasible objective region is minimized. They selected the vector $e = (1,\ldots,1)$ as the reference point to derive ratings for each country as near as possible to the highest level of the index, i.e. $h_j = 1, j = 1,\ldots,n$. The distance between the reference point and the feasible objective region can be measured by employing different metrics, thus they formulated the L_p problem as follows:

$$\min \left(\sum_{j=1}^{n} |1 - uY_j|^p \right)^{1/p}$$
s.t.
$$uY_j \leq 1, \ j = 1, \ldots, n$$
$$u \geq \varepsilon \quad (7)$$

The MOP (6) is scalarized via the method of the global criterion by employing the L_1 metric, i.e., $p = 1$ in (7), as follows:

$$\min \sum_{j=1}^{n} (1 - uY_j)$$
s.t.
$$uY_j \leq 1, \ j = 1, \ldots, n$$
$$u \geq \varepsilon \quad (8)$$

The single objective model (8), also known as the *min-sum* method, simultaneously minimizes the sum of the deviations (L_1 metric) for all countries between the performance that they can achieve using the common multipliers and the selected reference point. In other words, the aim of model (8) is to maximize the performances of all countries simultaneously under a common weighting scheme. Model (8) can be straightforwardly transformed to model (9) by introducing the deviation variables ($d_j = 1 - uY_j$) at the constraints and replacing the corresponding terms in the objective function.

$$\min \sum_{j=1}^{n} d_j$$

s.t.

$$uY_j + d_j = 1, \ j = 1, \ldots, n$$
$$u \geq \varepsilon, \ d_j \geq 0 \quad (9)$$

Model (9), as it is equivalent to model (8), is solved only once and provides higher discrimination regarding the performance of the evaluated countries as well as it allows for ranking. This approach can be characterized as fair and democratic since all countries collectively and equally participate in the generation of the optimal set of weights that is commonly used to derive their performance. Notice that the optimal solution of models (8) and (9) is Pareto optimal to the MOP (6).

Koronakos et al. (2019) noted that if the analysis is oriented to the disadvantaged countries to give them the opportunity to be heard, then the L_∞ metric can be utilized, i.e., $p = \infty$ in (7). Also, the L_∞ metric can be used to examine how the countries perform from the viewpoint of the weakest one. In this way, variations on their performances can be detected. Utilizing the L_∞ metric, the model (7) takes the following form:

$$\min \max_{j=1,\ldots n} \left[|1 - uY_j| \right]$$

s.t.

$$uY_j \leq 1, \ j = 1, \ldots, n$$
$$u \geq \varepsilon \quad (10)$$

Model (10) is also known as the *Tchebycheff* or *min-max* method that is among the most common scalarization methods in multiple criteria optimization. Model (10) can be equivalently transformed to the linear program (11):

$$\min \delta$$
$$s.t.$$
$$uY_j + \delta \geq 1, \quad j = 1, \ldots, n$$
$$uY_j \leq 1, \quad j = 1, \ldots, n$$
$$u \geq \varepsilon, \ \delta \geq 0 \tag{11}$$

Notice that the optimal solution of model (11) is in general weakly Pareto optimal to the MOP (6) (c.f. Yu, 1973). Steuer and Choo (1983) introduced a variant of the *Tchebycheff* method called *augmented Tchebycheff* method, which secures the Pareto optimality of the solutions. This is accomplished by adding to the objective function of model (11) the aggregate of the deviations from the reference point (L_1-*term*), which is called correction or augmentation term. The formulation of the *augmented Tchebycheff* method that guarantees to derive a Pareto optimal solution to model (6) is model (12):

$$\min \delta + \rho \sum_{j=1}^{n} (1 - uY_j)$$
$$s.t.$$
$$uY_j + \delta \geq 1, \quad j = 1, \ldots, n$$
$$uY_j \leq 1, \quad j = 1, \ldots, n$$
$$u \geq \varepsilon, \ \delta \geq 0 \tag{12}$$

In model (12) the parameter ρ is a sufficiently small positive scalar. Model (12) minimizes the distance between the reference point and the feasible objective region by employing the augmented Tchebycheff metric. In model (12), the optimal solution is primarily determined by the largest deviation δ from the reference point, i.e., by the objective (country) with the lowest performance. Thus, the obtained weighting scheme (set of common weights) provides performance measures for all countries from the viewpoint of the weakest one.

3.3 Public Opinion

Mizobuchi (2017) mentioned "*it is particularly difficult to reach consensus on the relative importance of different socio-economic conditions*". Indeed, different weighting schemes provide different scores and country rankings that raise the argument. In the ten Step Guide published by the Competence Centre on Composite Indicators and Scoreboards of the European Commission, it is noted that public opinion polls are often launched to elicit the relative weights, from a societal aspect, for the aggregation of composite indicators. In this context, the OECD BLI web platform prompts people to declare their views on the relative importance of the eleven topics of level 2 to build their own Better Life Index. The preferences expressed by people are stored in a publicly accessible database that enables the cross-country comparisons and aid the OECD to better understand what is most important for the well-being. Thus, as Barrington-Leigh and Escande (2018) noticed, the online platform serves also "*as a research tool because it records user interaction*". Koronakos et al. (2019) argued that although people's authentic responses are subjective judgments, they reveal the true needs and beliefs. Hence, public opinion is the best driver for assessing the countries concerning the well-being, despite the different necessities and cultures that might exist across countries or even within same regions. Including the global responses from all parts of societies, enables to consider equally all the different views in a democratic form of assessment. The public opinion over the significant issues of what makes for a quality life, can and should be employed by policy makers to shape a better picture of well-being across countries, with the ultimate goal to designate and deliver accurate and successful policies.

Similar to Zanella et al. (2015) and Rogge et al. (2017) who introduced weight restrictions in their formulations to deal with the compensability, Koronakos et al. (2019) incorporated the public opinion into the evaluation models (5), (9) and (12) in the form of weight restrictions (see Allen et al., 1997). In this manner, as they noted, they incorporated a non-compensatory preference relation in their assessment. They translated the reported people's views for the eleven topics (level 2) that compose the BLI to absolute limits that the corresponding weights (u) can receive (see Roll et al., 1991). The lower and upper bounds of the weight given to each topic derive from the minimum and maximum values of the responses for each topic. The whole set of the weight restrictions is denoted with Ω.

$$u \in \Omega \qquad (13)$$

Notice that by imposing rational restrictions on the weights' limits, if not eliminates, the compensation among the 11 topics of BLI assumed in the models (5), (9) and (12). Moreover, the incorporation of the weight restrictions Ω into the evaluation models does not allow the variables (weights) to get zero values at optimality. Thus, the constraints $u \geq \varepsilon$ are omitted as redundant. Alternative types of weight restrictions can be also employed, such as assurance region constraints in which upper and lower bounds are imposed on the ratio of pairs of weights (Thompson et al., 1986).

4 Assessment of OECD BLI

In this section we apply the two-phase bottom-up approach introduced by Koronakos et al. (2019) for the BLI assessment of 38 countries (35 OECD and 3 non-OECD economies) for the year 2017.

4.1 Normalization of the Raw Data of Indicators (Level 1)

Table 1 summarizes the statistics of the indicators at level 1, as they were rescaled by means of the formulas (3) and (4). The raw data of the indicators can be found in the online database[4] of OECD.

4.2 Calculation of the Topics (Level 1 to Level 2)

The indicators (level 1) are aggregated as weighted arithmetic averages, where the aggregation weighting schemes for the calculation of the values of the next level are derived through optimization. At the first phase of the procedure, models (5), (9) and (12) were applied separately to the normalized values of the indicators (level 1) to derive the aggregation weighting scheme that yields the values of the topics (level 2). As argued in Koronakos et al. (2019), in this way, the rationale and the properties of each modeling approach are conveyed to the whole structure of the composite index. Nine out of eleven topics comprise of more than one indicator, thus each model exclusively was applied to the indicators of each topic so as to obtain its value. Notice that only two topics, namely

Table 1 Descriptive statistics of the data of indicators—Level 1

	Min	Max	Mean	Median	Variance	St.Dev	Skew	Q1	Q3
Dwellings without basic facilities	0	1	0.907	0.984	0.032	0.179	−3.835	0.884	0.997
Housing expenditure	0.063	0.750	0.382	0.375	0.023	0.151	0.138	0.250	0.438
Rooms per person	0	0.947	0.496	0.553	0.062	0.249	−0.152	0.263	0.632
House hold net adjusted disposable income	0.061	1	0.464	0.458	0.052	0.227	0.282	0.283	0.612
House hold net financial wealth	0	1	0.271	0.214	0.050	0.223	1.158	0.094	0.397
Labor market insecurity	0.176	0.974	0.847	0.895	0.027	0.163	−2.686	0.846	0.939
Employment rate	0	1	0.575	0.605	0.036	0.191	−0.765	0.512	0.715
Long-term unemployment rate	0.129	0.999	0.836	0.899	0.037	0.191	−2.555	0.799	0.936
Personal earnings	0.107	1	0.559	0.573	0.062	0.249	−0.005	0.323	0.767
Community	0.258	0.968	0.711	0.726	0.022	0.148	−1.010	0.645	0.806
Educational attainment	0.094	1	0.722	0.789	0.062	0.250	−1.330	0.695	0.887
Student skills	0.044	0.912	0.646	0.704	0.044	0.211	−1.537	0.613	0.767
Years in education	0.099	1	0.461	0.451	0.038	0.196	0.478	0.327	0.563
Air pollution	0.500	1	0.792	0.780	0.014	0.118	−0.232	0.710	0.875
Water quality	0.182	1	0.696	0.727	0.039	0.198	−0.579	0.541	0.868
Stakeholder engagement for developing regulations	0	1	0.463	0.481	0.066	0.258	−0.019	0.259	0.667
Voter turnout	0.043	0.957	0.501	0.489	0.064	0.254	0.013	0.332	0.668
Life expectancy	0.022	1	0.839	0.899	0.030	0.173	−3.151	0.789	0.939
Self-reported health	0.050	0.967	0.624	0.667	0.054	0.233	−0.744	0.533	0.767
Life Satisfaction	0.032	0.903	0.590	0.629	0.063	0.250	−0.458	0.387	0.831
Feeling safe walking alone at night	0	1	0.608	0.641	0.061	0.247	−0.726	0.465	0.818
Homicide rate	0	0.964	0.900	0.971	0.040	0.200	−3.326	0.948	0.985
Employees working very long hours	0.269	1	0.814	0.868	0.029	0.170	−1.617	0.734	0.921
Time devoted to leisure and personal care	0.186	1	0.670	0.684	0.027	0.163	−0.924	0.593	0.742

the "Life Satisfaction" and the "Community", consist of one indicator. Therefore, the normalized values of these indicators directly become the values of the corresponding one-dimensional topics. We provide descriptive measures for the values of the topics (level 2) as derived by each model in Tables 2 and 3.

Table 2 Average score for each topic as derived by each model

Model	HO	IW	JE	SC	ES	EQ	CG	HS	SW	PS	WL
BoD model (5)	0.936	0.465	0.902	0.711	0.824	0.818	0.686	0.887	0.590	0.903	0.833
Min-sum model (9)	0.907	0.464	0.878	0.711	0.774	0.792	0.604	0.864	0.590	0.900	0.817
Min-max model (12)	0.700	0.387	0.851	0.711	0.698	0.756	0.592	0.760	0.590	0.640	0.817

HO: Housing, IW: Income, JE: Jobs, SC: Community, ES: Education, EQ: Environment, CG: Civic engagement, HS: Health, SW: Life Satisfaction, PS: Safety, WL: Work-Life Balance

Table 3 Standard deviation of scores for each topic as derived by each model

Model	HO	IW	JE	SC	ES	EQ	CG	HS	SW	PS	WL
BoD model (5)	0.091	0.226	0.161	0.148	0.204	0.110	0.214	0.121	0.250	0.198	0.163
Min-sum model (9)	0.179	0.227	0.173	0.148	0.247	0.118	0.236	0.175	0.250	0.200	0.169
Min-max model (12)	0.129	0.214	0.185	0.148	0.202	0.129	0.218	0.175	0.250	0.252	0.169

HO: Housing, IW: Income, JE: Jobs, SC: Community, ES: Education, EQ: Environment, CG: Civic engagement, HS: Health, SW: Life Satisfaction, PS: Safety, WL: Work-Life Balance

Table 2 presents the average score of all countries in each topic as obtained from each model. Analogously, Table 3 exhibits the standard deviation of all counties' scores per topic in each model separately. Notably, in Community (SC) and Life Satisfaction (SW) all models provide the same average score and standard deviation. This is attributed to the fact that these topics consist of a single indicator. Thus, independently of the model employed, the countries' scores on these topics coincide with the levels of the corresponding normalized indicators. Furthermore, as the BoD (5) grants the flexibility to each country to maximize its performance, it provides higher scores compared to the other models. Consequently, the average scores derived by BoD (5) are the highest ones with the lowest standard deviations in all indicators apart from Income (IW) and Education (ES), as presented in Table 3. Regarding the min-sum model (9) and the min-max model (12), the former yields higher average scores than the latter in all topics. This is attributed to the "*democratic*" and "*fair*" character of the min-sum model (9) where all countries together and equally decide the optimal solution. On the other hand, in min-max model (12) the country with the poorest performance plays a decisive role and primarily decides the optimal solution.

4.3 Incorporation of Public Opinion

To date, more than 132,566 users from 218 countries have shared their views on the OECD web platform. The responses are updated daily, and grouped by country, age and gender. The 57% of the respondents are male while the 43% of them are female. Also, the respondents are divided into seven age groups, namely <15, 15–24, 25–34, 35–44, 45–54, 55–64 and >65. Most of the respondents belong to the groups 15–24 (33%) and 25–34 (28%). The complete list of the responses of people worldwide is publicly available at the web platform (oecdbetterlifeindex.org/bli/rest/indexes/stats/country). In this study, we have chosen to include the 117,434 responses that derive from the citizens of the 35 members of the OECD and the 3 partner countries for which OECD provides data and metrics. Table 4 presents the normalized weights for the 11 topics (level 2), which are retrieved from the responses of the 38 countries that participate in the assessment. The last row of Table 4 contains the representative (total) weights of the worldwide responses as provided by OECD.

Table 4 Normalized weights retrieved from OECD about the topics of level 2

	Country	HO	IW	JE	SC	ES	EQ	CG	HS	SW	PS	WL
1	Australia	0.090	0.087	0.084	0.074	0.098	0.083	0.063	0.103	0.099	0.092	0.127
2	Austria	0.091	0.083	0.086	0.080	0.098	0.095	0.068	0.107	0.103	0.097	0.091
3	Belgium	0.094	0.087	0.087	0.079	0.100	0.092	0.065	0.107	0.103	0.092	0.094
4	Canada	0.090	0.088	0.089	0.080	0.099	0.091	0.064	0.107	0.104	0.096	0.093
5	Chile	0.090	0.089	0.092	0.076	0.106	0.092	0.073	0.104	0.096	0.090	0.093
6	Czech Republic	0.085	0.092	0.092	0.076	0.098	0.094	0.068	0.104	0.103	0.098	0.090
7	Denmark	0.083	0.081	0.087	0.081	0.103	0.094	0.073	0.102	0.112	0.091	0.094
8	Estonia	0.096	0.090	0.090	0.078	0.099	0.097	0.067	0.103	0.100	0.099	0.083
9	Finland	0.087	0.083	0.085	0.079	0.099	0.098	0.069	0.105	0.107	0.097	0.091
10	France	0.094	0.087	0.091	0.088	0.099	0.092	0.062	0.108	0.099	0.088	0.093
11	Germany	0.090	0.084	0.086	0.083	0.099	0.092	0.068	0.105	0.109	0.090	0.094
12	Greece	0.086	0.090	0.092	0.077	0.102	0.092	0.066	0.110	0.100	0.094	0.090
13	Hungary	0.092	0.090	0.085	0.084	0.096	0.093	0.062	0.101	0.105	0.099	0.095
14	Iceland	0.097	0.089	0.090	0.081	0.101	0.085	0.064	0.108	0.094	0.104	0.087
15	Ireland	0.088	0.089	0.089	0.083	0.099	0.087	0.068	0.101	0.111	0.085	0.100
16	Israel	0.094	0.103	0.088	0.077	0.103	0.082	0.064	0.107	0.101	0.088	0.093
17	Italy	0.086	0.082	0.093	0.083	0.098	0.095	0.072	0.104	0.103	0.088	0.095
18	Japan	0.090	0.088	0.087	0.081	0.098	0.087	0.063	0.103	0.102	0.111	0.090
19	Korea	0.093	0.089	0.088	0.080	0.096	0.086	0.069	0.097	0.107	0.101	0.094
20	Latvia	0.087	0.094	0.087	0.080	0.094	0.097	0.069	0.093	0.103	0.097	0.097
21	Luxembourg	0.089	0.098	0.094	0.078	0.092	0.093	0.062	0.106	0.101	0.093	0.092
22	Mexico	0.091	0.091	0.092	0.076	0.104	0.088	0.074	0.100	0.097	0.093	0.092
23	Netherlands	0.093	0.085	0.084	0.079	0.099	0.092	0.067	0.105	0.111	0.092	0.095
24	New Zealand	0.088	0.085	0.086	0.081	0.099	0.096	0.067	0.102	0.108	0.091	0.097
25	Norway	0.093	0.088	0.090	0.079	0.095	0.092	0.065	0.107	0.105	0.093	0.095
26	Poland	0.090	0.094	0.091	0.078	0.101	0.086	0.061	0.098	0.109	0.098	0.095

	Country	HO	IW	JE	SC	ES	EQ	CG	HS	SW	PS	WL
27	Portugal	0.088	0.084	0.093	0.078	0.096	0.090	0.069	0.104	0.104	0.099	0.096
28	Slovak Republic	0.085	0.088	0.092	0.081	0.096	0.093	0.068	0.104	0.104	0.097	0.091
29	Slovenia	0.089	0.084	0.087	0.083	0.099	0.102	0.065	0.101	0.099	0.100	0.092
30	Spain	0.086	0.084	0.091	0.078	0.102	0.087	0.075	0.109	0.097	0.094	0.097
31	Sweden	0.088	0.084	0.089	0.079	0.097	0.096	0.070	0.105	0.107	0.090	0.095
32	Switzerland	0.090	0.089	0.089	0.083	0.097	0.092	0.064	0.103	0.106	0.092	0.093
33	Turkey	0.091	0.093	0.088	0.083	0.099	0.090	0.073	0.100	0.095	0.094	0.094
34	United Kingdom	0.091	0.089	0.090	0.079	0.098	0.091	0.062	0.105	0.111	0.086	0.097
35	United States	0.086	0.087	0.087	0.081	0.099	0.092	0.063	0.104	0.112	0.091	0.098
36	Brazil	0.090	0.087	0.089	0.074	0.107	0.087	0.065	0.104	0.102	0.103	0.092
37	Russia	0.096	0.095	0.090	0.080	0.094	0.088	0.074	0.100	0.095	0.096	0.092
38	South Africa	0.095	0.093	0.091	0.074	0.096	0.088	0.061	0.100	0.106	0.097	0.100
	Total	0.090	0.088	0.089	0.080	0.099	0.090	0.066	0.104	0.104	0.092	0.097

Figure 2 depicts the variability of the weights presented in Table 4, where the symbol "o" denotes outlier and the symbol "*" denotes extreme outlier. As shown for example, responses originated from Australia (numbered 1 in Table 4) give the highest priority to Work–Life Balance (WL), which is characterized as extreme outlier. As can be seen, the topic Civic Engagement (CG) has been assigned the lowest weight values.

The public opinion can be incorporated into the evaluation models by translating it into direct weight restrictions. In Table 5 we present the lower and upper bounds that the weight of each topic can receive. These bounds derive from the minimum and maximum values of each column (topic) of Table 5. The whole set of the weight restrictions is denoted with Ω (13).

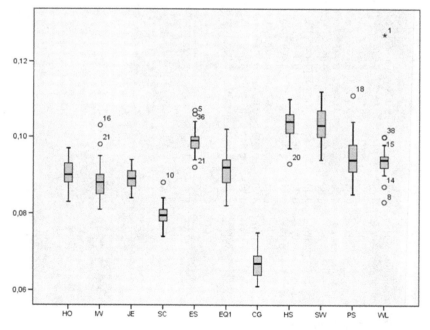

Fig. 2 Boxplots of the weights of the 11 topics derived by the public opinion

Table 5 Lower and upper bounds of the weights of the eleven topics—Level 2

	HO	IW	JE	SC	ES	EQ	CG	HS	SW	PS	WL
Lower Bound	0.083	0.081	0.084	0.074	0.092	0.082	0.061	0.093	0.094	0.085	0.083
Upper Bound	0.097	0.103	0.094	0.088	0.107	0.102	0.075	0.110	0.112	0.111	0.127

HO: Housing, IW: Income, JE: Jobs, SC: Community, ES: Education, EQ: Environment, CG: Civic engagement, HS: Health, SW: Life Satisfaction, PS: Safety, WL: Work-Life Balance

4.4 Calculation of the BLI (Level 2 to Level 3)

At the second phase of the bottom-up procedure we employ, similar to the first phase, the models (5), (9) and (12) derive the BLI for each country under each different concept and draw comparisons. However, at this phase we incorporate into the models (5), (9) and (12) the weight restrictions Ω described in Table 5.

In Table 6, we present the results obtained by applying each of the aforementioned models to the corresponding data of the topics that derived in the first phase of the bottom-up procedure. The BLI scores of BoD model (5) with the weight restrictions Ω as well as the ranking are presented in column 4 of Table 6. Similarly, the column 5 presents the BLI scores and the ranking derived by the min-sum model (9) with the weight restrictions Ω. The column 6 of Table 6 exhibits the BLI scores and the ranking that obtained by applying the min-max model (12) with the weight restrictions Ω. For comparison purposes, we also present in column 3 of Table 6 the results obtained by applying the BoD model (5) without the weight restrictions Ω. In addition, the second column of Table 6, exhibits the ranking of the countries obtained directly from the OECD platform given the same importance to the 11 topics. Notice that the online platform does not provide the BLI scores of the countries, but only their rank depending on the weighting scheme given by the user.

The conventional BoD model (5) without the weight restrictions Ω ranks many countries in the first position, thus the comparisons with the ranking provided from the OECD web platform cannot be safely drawn. On the contrary, as we observe from Table 6, the rankings derived by models (5), (9) and (12) with the weight restrictions Ω are close to the ranking provided from the OECD web platform. In these four rankings Norway is ranked first while South Africa is ranked last. Comparing the

Table 6 BLI scores—Level 3

Country	OECD ranking with equal importance	BoD model (5) Ranking	BoD model (5) with Ω Ranking	Min-sum model (9) with Ω Ranking	Min-max model (12) with Ω Ranking
Australia	(3)	1 (1)	0.992 (4)	0.984 (5)	0.925 (7)
Austria	(17)	0.998 (26)	0.940 (14)	0.912 (16)	0.850 (14)
Belgium	(12)	1 (1)	0.935 (15)	0.917 (15)	0.865 (12)
Canada	(5)	1 (1)	0.991 (5)	0.990 (2)	0.942 (3)
Chile	(31)	0.898 (37)	0.747 (31)	0.729 (31)	0.638 (31)
Czech Republic	(21)	1 (1)	0.889 (19)	0.880 (19)	0.755 (22)
Denmark	(2)	1 (1)	0.997 (3)	0.986 (4)	0.935 (5)
Estonia	(22)	1 (1)	0.844 (24)	0.837 (22)	0.747 (23)
Finland	(9)	1 (1)	0.985 (8)	0.990 (2)	0.923 (8)
France	(18)	1 (1)	0.904 (18)	0.883 (18)	0.786 (19)
Germany	(13)	1 (1)	0.956 (12)	0.949 (11)	0.879 (11)
Greece	(35)	0.986 (30)	0.716 (34)	0.705 (34)	0.565 (35)
Hungary	(32)	0.968 (34)	0.745 (33)	0.738 (30)	0.622 (34)
Iceland	(7)	1 (1)	0.974 (11)	0.960 (8)	0.913 (9)
Ireland	(15)	1 (1)	0.935 (15)	0.910 (17)	0.844 (15)
Israel	(24)	0.989 (29)	0.853 (22)	0.832 (23)	0.759 (21)
Italy	(25)	0.985 (31)	0.843 (25)	0.807 (27)	0.690 (26)
Japan	(23)	1 (1)	0.837 (26)	0.816 (26)	0.694 (25)
Korea	(29)	1 (1)	0.800 (28)	0.764 (28)	0.671 (28)
Latvia	(30)	0.984 (32)	0.762 (30)	0.764 (28)	0.661 (29)
Luxembourg	(14)	1 (1)	0.986 (7)	0.952 (9)	0.863 (13)
Mexico	(37)	1 (1)	0.628 (37)	0.613 (37)	0.558 (37)

Country	OECD ranking with equal importance	BoD model (5) Ranking	BoD model (5) with Ω Ranking	Min-sum model (9) with Ω Ranking	Min-max model (12) with Ω Ranking
Netherlands	(10)	1 (1)	0.975 (9)	0.935 (12)	0.910 (10)
New Zealand	(11)	1 (1)	0.947 (13)	0.931 (13)	0.841 (16)
Norway	(1)	1 (1)	1 (1)	1 (1)	0.973 (1)
Poland	(27)	0.996 (27)	0.828 (27)	0.826 (24)	0.709 (24)
Portugal	(28)	0.973 (33)	0.775 (29)	0.720 (33)	0.643 (30)
Slovak Republic	(26)	0.993 (28)	0.846 (23)	0.841 (21)	0.690 (26)
Slovenia	(20)	1 (1)	0.877 (20)	0.863 (20)	0.808 (18)
Spain	(19)	1 (1)	0.865 (21)	0.825 (25)	0.776 (20)
Sweden	(4)	1 (1)	0.990 (6)	0.981 (6)	0.943 (2)
Switzerland	(6)	1 (1)	0.998 (2)	0.976 (7)	0.936 (4)
Turkey	(36)	0.950 (35)	0.677 (35)	0.623 (36)	0.565 (35)
United Kingdom	(16)	1 (1)	0.915 (17)	0.918 (14)	0.831 (17)
United States	(8)	1 (1)	0.975 (9)	0.952 (9)	0.935 (5)
Brazil	(34)	0.909 (36)	0.668 (36)	0.660 (35)	0.626 (32)
Russia	(33)	1 (1)	0.747 (31)	0.725 (32)	0.626 (32)
South Africa	(38)	0.752 (38)	0.515 (38)	0.358 (38)	0.364 (38)

rankings obtained from model (12) with the Ω and the OECD web platform, we observe slight differences, e.g., Australia 7/3, Austria 14/17 and Israel 21/24. The major differences between the ranking of model (5) with the Ω and the ranking of the OECD web platform, are detected for Luxembourg 7/14, Belgium 15/12 and Iceland 11/7. The major differences between the ranking of model (9) with the Ω and the ranking of the OECD web platform, are detected for Finland 2/9, Spain 25/19, Luxembourg 9/14, Portugal 33/28 and Slovak Republic 21/26.

As expected, the conventional BoD model (5) yields the highest possible score for each country (the average score is 0.984) and lacks discriminating power since 25 countries out of the 38 are deemed as BLI efficient. On the contrary, the inclusion of public opinion with the form of weight restrictions Ω in the BoD model (5), imposes limits to the trade-offs among the 11 topics of BLI and reduces drastically the compensation among them. Indeed, the BoD model (5) with the weight restrictions Ω identifies only one country as BLI efficient, namely Norway, and the obtained average score is considerably lower than the one derived from the BoD model (5). There is a reduction of 12.1% (from 0.984 to 0.865) between the average scores obtained from the BoD model (5) and the BoD model (5) with the weight restrictions Ω. The incorporation of the weight restrictions Ω improves the discriminating power of the BoD model (5). Similarly, from the results of models (9) and (12) we deduce that the weight restrictions Ω play a key role in the assessment. In Table 7 we provide the average score, the standard deviation of the scores and the number of the BLI efficient countries derived by each model.

Table 7 No of BLI efficient countries, average score and standard deviation derived by each model

	BoD model (5)	BoD model (5) with Ω	Min-sum model (9) with Ω	Min-max model (12) with Ω
No of BLI efficient countries	25	1	1	0
Average score	0.984	0.865	0.843	0.770
Standard deviation of scores	0.045	0.121	0.137	0.143

The optimal solution of the min-sum model (9) is decided collectively by all countries, i.e., all countries are assessed under a common weighting scheme. Thus, the min-sum model (9) generates lower scores than the BoD approach and has higher discriminating power. Indeed, the min-sum model (9) with Ω deems as BLI efficient only one country (namely Norway) and on average yields lower scores compared to the BoD model (5) with Ω. In general, the BLI scores derived from the min-sum model (9) with Ω are lower than the scores of BoD model (5) with Ω, the average reduction of the BLI scores is 2.82%, with a significant reduction of 30.5% to the performance of South Africa (0.358 vs 0.515). However, for three countries the BLI scores of the former are higher, namely for Finland (0.99 (2) vs 0.985 (8)), Latvia (0.764 (28) vs 0.762 (30)) and United Kingdom (0.918 (14) vs 0.915 (17)). This clearly occurs because in the bottom-up procedure each model is separately applied to all levels of the BLI. As a result, in the second phase of the bottom-up procedure each model is applied to different data (values of topics). Notice that the values of the topics (level 2) are derived in the first phase of the bottom-up procedure, by applying separately each model to the values of the indicators (level 1). Thus, the resulting values of the topics (level 2) obtained from the different approaches are generally different.

The BLI scores derived from the min-max model (12) with Ω, are in average considerably lower than the ones obtained from the other approaches, for instance we observe an average reduction of 11.03% and 8.86% in comparison with the BoD model (5) with Ω and the min-sum model (9) with Ω, respectively. The scores obtained from the min-max model (12) with Ω are remarkably decreased for all countries as compared with the corresponding ones derived by the BoD model (5) with Ω. For instance, there is a significant reduction on the performance of Greece by 21% (0.565 vs 0.716) and Slovak Republic by 18% (0.69 vs 0.846). Also, the scores obtained from the min-max model (12) with Ω are decreased for all countries but one, namely South Africa (0.364 vs 0.358), as compared with the corresponding ones obtained from the min-sum model (9) with Ω. Again, we spot significant reduction on the performance of some countries, for instance the performance of Greece is decreased by 20% (0.565 vs 0.705) and the one of Italy by 18% (0.69 vs 0.807).

The discrepancies on the BLI scores derived by models (9) and (12), with the weight restrictions Ω, are clearly justified by the different optimality criterion of each model. Although each model yields a common optimal solution for all the countries, these solutions are generally different. The optimal solution of model (9) with Ω is absolutely determined by all countries, since all the constraints, except the ones imposed by the weight restrictions, should structurally be binding at optimality. On the other hand, the optimal solution of the min-max model (12) with Ω is determined by the country whose performance has the largest deviation from the selected reference point (ideal rating), i.e., the binding constraint corresponds to South Africa. Clearly, South Africa plays a key role in model (12), although we did not assign any priority to this country. This holds because it is a structural property of model (12) to give the opportunity to the weakest country to be heard and let the optimal solution to be primarily decided by the country with the poorest performance. Thus, the obtained weighting scheme provides performance measures for all countries from the viewpoint of the weakest one. This justifies also the reduction in the performance in all other countries than South Africa. Obviously, this effect is mitigated to some extent by bringing into play the views of people about well-being, i.e., the weight restrictions Ω. This happens because the voice of the rest countries can be still heard in model (12) via the weight restrictions Ω. Indeed, the BLI scores and ranking derived by model (12) with Ω indicate that Norway is still ranked first even though the weighting scheme is primarily decided by the weakest country (South Africa) that is ranked at the last position. The South Africa clearly does not act like a benchmark for Norway, since model (12) with Ω does not deem any country as BLI efficient. This is attributed to the impact of the weight restrictions Ω. Notice that when the weight restrictions are omitted from model (12), at optimality, only Australia and Norway are deemed as BLI efficient, which are also the *benchmarks* of South Africa in this case.

A general observation is that the BLI scores obtained from all models as well as the rankings differentiate. However, for the most countries we do not observe great differences on the rankings generated by models (9) and (12), with the weight restrictions Ω. Considerable differentiations are observed for Finland (2/8), Luxembourg (9/13) and Switzerland (7/4). Thus, it is concluded that the incorporation of the public opinion, in the form of the weight restrictions Ω, restrain significantly the flexibility of the models and play a crucial role to the assessment of BLI. Notice that these models without the weight restrictions yield very different scores and rankings. Figure 3 provides a schematic representation of the BLI scores derived by the models (9) and (12) with the weight restrictions Ω.

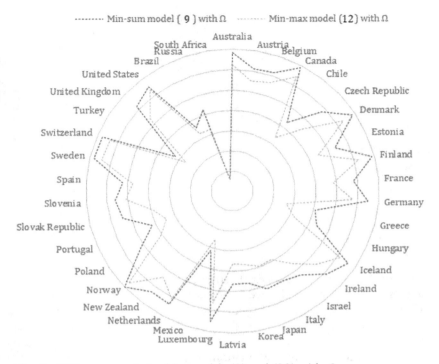

Fig. 3 BLI scores as derived by models (9) and (12) with Ω

The results reveal that there is a clear divide between the Nordic countries as well as Switzerland, Australia and Canada which achieve high BLI scores and the rest of countries that generally achieve relatively low BLI scores. The results verify the objective reality of the balanced economic growth with the well-being in the aforementioned countries. In Fig. 4 we present the countries ranked in Top 10 by models (5), (9) and (12) with the weight restrictions Ω. It is noteworthy that the top five rankings provided by the above mentioned models include only eight countries. Notice that the Southern and Eastern European countries are absent from the Top 10 as well as the countries from Asia, South America and Africa.

Based on the analysis of the results and the characteristics of the min-sum model (9) with Ω and the min-max model (12) with Ω, we propose the former for the evaluation of BLI as it is more democratic

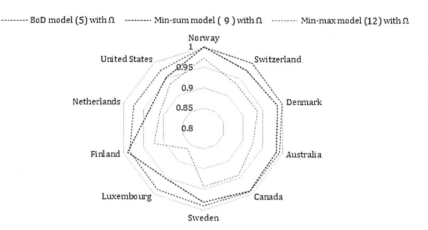

Fig. 4 Top 10 countries

than the latter one. It also establishes a common basis for fair evaluation assessment, where the weighting scheme is determined jointly by all the countries and none of them is favored. In addition, the min-sum model (9) with Ω proves to have higher discriminating power than the BoD model (5). As more revealing than mere numbers is the full picture of the 38 countries under evaluation, Fig. 5 exhibits a visualization of their performance as derived by the min-sum model (9) with Ω. In the heat map of Fig. 5 the darker colors indicate high performance while the brighter colors indicate low performance.

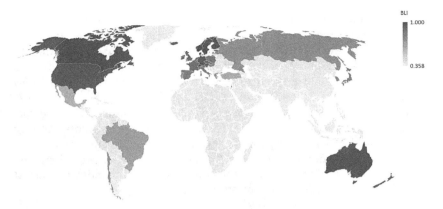

Fig. 5 Heat map of the BLI performance of the 38 countries provided by the min-sum model (10) with Ω

5 Conclusion

In this chapter we presented the OECD Better Life Index that covers several socio-economic aspects and facilitates the better understanding of what drives well-being of people. We discussed the three-level hierarchical structure of the index and we presented the hierarchical bottom-up procedure, proposed by Koronakos et al. (2019), for the aggregation of the components of BLI that lie on different levels. In the context of this approach, the values of each topic (level 2) are obtained from optimization process, instead of commonly aggregating with equal weights the indicators (level 1) that they comprise. Also, we discussed the normalization issues for the indicators (level 1) stemming from possible extreme variations of their values between the years. We showed that the incorporation of data from previous years into the normalization process, absorbs the possible discrepancies. In addition, we demonstrated that the real view of people, captured from the global responses in the web platform of OECD BLI, can be translated to weight restrictions and incorporated into the assessment models. In this way, a non-compensatory preference relation for the weights of the topics was specified. Also, we showed that the incorporation of public opinion can effectively drive the optimization process and depict the collective preferences to the BLI scores.

We illustrated that the assessment of BLI can be modeled as a MOP problem, where the performance of each country is treated as a distinct objective-criterion. The scalarizing methods that can be applied for the MOP have different properties and thus can be employed for different scenarios. We applied the discussed modeling approaches to the data of 38 countries (35 OECD and 3 Non-OECD economies) for the year 2017. Each approach was applied to all levels of BLI to examine how the performance of each country is affected under the different concepts. Among the employed models, we propose the use of the min-sum model (9), because it establishes a *"fair"* and *"democratic"* assessment, where the aggregation weighting scheme of the components of the index is decided collectively and equally by all countries.

Given the global concern for the countries to improve the quality of life for their citizens, the concept of BLI can be applied both to international and national level, e.g., among regions, municipalities, etc. The proposed approach for the BLI identifies, based on the real priorities of people, the different parts of the global society that need improvement. In this respect, BLI illustrates the true-life conditions and needs. Thus, it can be employed to examine the performance of the implemented policies and to determine where resources are needed. These results can be further utilized by the international diplomacy to promote the international consensus and reach economic and environmental agreements.

Acknowledgements This research is co-financed by Greece and the European Union (European Social Fund-ESF) through the Operational Programme "Human Resources Development, Education and Lifelong Learning" in the context of the project "Reinforcement of Postdoctoral Researchers - 2nd Cycle" (MIS-5033021), implemented by the State Scholarships Foundation (IKΥ).

References

Allen, R., Athanassopoulos, A., Dyson, R. G., & Thanassoulis, E. (1997). Weights restrictions and value judgments in data envelopment analysis: Evolution, development and future directions. *Annals of Operations Research, 73*, 13–34.

Barrington-Leigh, C., & Escande, A. (2018). Measuring progress and well-being: A comparative review of indicators. *Social Indicators Research., 135*(3), 893–925.

Berridge, G. R. (2015). Economic and commercial diplomacy. In *Diplomacy*. Palgrave Macmillan. https://doi.org/10.1057/9781137445520_15

Bouyssou, D. (1986). Some remarks on the notion of compensation in MCDM. *European Journal of Operational Research, 26*, 150–160.

Cherchye, L., Moesen, W., Rogge, N., & Van Puyenbroeck, T. (2007). An introduction to 'benefit of the doubt' composite indicators. *Social Indicators Research, 82*(1), 111–145.

Cooper, W. W., Seiford, L. M., & Zhu, J. (2011). *Handbook on data envelopment analysis*. Springer.

Despotis, D. K. (2002). Improving the discriminating power of DEA: Focus on globally efficient units. *Journal of the Operational Research Society, 53*(3), 314–323.

Despotis, D. K. (2005). A reassessment of the human development index via data envelopment analysis. *Journal of the Operational Research Society, 56*(8), 969–980.

Durand, M. (2015). The OECD better life initiative: How's life? and the measurement of well-being. *Review of Income and Wealth, 61*(1), 4–17.

Fusco, E. (2015). Enhancing non-compensatory composite indicators: A directional proposal. *European Journal of Operational Research, 242*(2), 620–630.

Greco, S., Ishizaka, A., Tasiou, M., & Torrisi, G. (2019a). On the methodological framework of composite indices: A review of the issues of weighting, aggregation, and robustness. *Social Indicators Research, 61–94*, 141.

Greco, S., Ishizaka, A., Resce, G., & Torrisi, G. (2019b). Measuring well-being by a multidimensional spatial model in OECD Better Life Index framework. *Socio-Economic Planning Sciences*. https://doi.org/10.1016/j.seps.2019.01.006

Koronakos, G., Smirlis, Y., Sotiros, D., & Despotis, D. K. (2019). Assessment of OECD Better Life Index by incorporating public opinion. *Socio-Economic Planning Sciences*. https://doi.org/10.1016/j.seps.2019.03.005

Lorenz, J., Brauer, C., & Lorenz, D. (2017). Rank-optimal weighting or "'How to be best in the OECD Better Life Index?'" *Social Indicators Research, 134*(1), 75–92.

Melyn, W., & Moesen, W. W. (1991). *Towards a synthetic indicator of macroeconomic performance: unequal weighting when limited information is available* (Public Economics Research Papers, CES, KU Leuven, 17), 1–24.

Miettinen, K. (1999). Nonlinear multiobjective optimization. *International Series in Operations Research & Management Science, 12*. https://doi.org/10.1007/978-1-4615-5563-6

Mizobuchi, H. (2014). Measuring world better life frontier: A composite indicator for OECD better life index. *Social Indicators Research, 118*, 987–1007.

Mizobuchi, H. (2017). Incorporating sustainability concerns in the Better Life Index: Application of corrected convex non-parametric least squares method. *Social Indicators Research, 131*(3), 947–971.

Mudida, R. (2012). Emerging trends and concerns in the economic diplomacy of African states. *International Journal of Diplomacy and Economy, 1*(1), 95–109.

Nardo, M., Saisana, M., Saltelli, A., Tarantola, S., Hoffman, A., & Giovannini, E. (2005). *Handbook on constructing composite indicators* (OECD statistics working papers (2005/03)).

OECD. (2008). *Handbook on constructing composite indicators: Methodology and user guide*. OECD Publishing.

OECD. (2011). *How's life? Measuring well-being*. OECD Publishing.

OECD. (2013a). *How's life? Measuring well-being*. OECD Publishing.

OECD. (2013b). *OECD guidelines on measuring subjective well-being*. OECD Publishing.

OECD. (2015). *How's life? Measuring well-being*. OECD Publishing.

OECD. (2017). *How's life? Measuring well-being*. OECD Publishing.

OECD. (2020). *How's life? Measuring well-being*. OECD Publishing.

Peiro-Palomino, J., & Picazo-Tadeo, A. J. (2018). OECD: One or many? Ranking countries with a composite well-being indicator. *Social Indicators Research, 139*, 847–869.

Rogge, N. (2018). Composite indicators as generalized benefit-of-the-doubt weighted averages. *European Journal of Operational Research, 267*(1), 381–392.

Rogge, N., De Jaeger, S., & Lavigne, C. (2017). Waste performance of NUTS 2-regions in the EU: A conditional directional distance benefit-of-the-doubt model. *Ecological Economics, 139*, 19–32.

Roll, Y., Cook, W. D., & Golany, B. (1991). Controlling factor weights in data envelopment analysis. *IIE Transactions, 23*(1), 2–9.

Roy, B. (1996). *Multicriteria methodology for decision aiding*. Springer.

Shichao, Y. (2012). *Singapore's economic diplomacy* (Bluebook 21st ed.). 37 CHINA INT'l Stud. 112.

Smirlis, Y. (2020). A trichotomic segmentation approach for estimating composite indicators. *Social Indicators Research*. https://doi.org/10.1007/s11205-020-02310-1

Steuer, R. E., & Choo, E. (1983). An interactive weighted Tchebycheff procedure for multiple objective programming. *Mathematical Programming, 26*, 326–344.

Thompson, R. G., Singleton, F. D., Jr., Thrall, R. M., & Smith, B. A. (1986). Comparative site evaluations for locating a high-energy physics lab in Texas. *Interfaces, 16*, 35–49.

Van Puyenbroeck, T., & Rogge, N. (2017). Geometric mean quantity index numbers with Benefit-of-the-Doubt weights. *European Journal of Operational Research, 256*(3), 1004–1014.

Yu, P. L. (1973). A class of solutions for group decision problems. *Management Science, 19*, 936–946.

Zanella, A., Camanho, A. S., & Dias, T. G. (2015). Undesirable outputs and weighting schemes in composite indicators based on data envelopment analysis. *European Journal of Operational Research, 245*(2), 517–530.

CHAPTER 3

The Gini Index: A Modern Measure of Inequality

Vincent Charles, Tatiana Gherman, and Juan Carlos Paliza

1 Introduction

Inequality among people has always been a problem but has become more salient in recent years. Indeed, data and research show that the degree of inequality has increased in most countries around the world, which in turn, has generated concerns both from the perspective of the

---

V. Charles
CENTRUM Católica Graduate Business School, Lima, Peru
e-mail: vcharles@pucp.pe

Pontifical Catholic University of Peru, Lima, Peru

T. Gherman (✉)
Faculty of Business and Law,
University of Northampton, Northampton, UK
e-mail: tatiana.gherman@northampton.ac.uk

J. C. Paliza
Alliance Manchester Business School, University of Manchester, Manchester, UK

sustainability of economic growth, as well as from the perspective of social cohesion and well-being.

In economics, the Gini index or coefficient (also known as the Gini ratio) is a measure of statistical dispersion intended to denote the income inequality or the wealth inequality within a nation or a social group. Figure 1 shows the world map of the Gini indices by country, as of 2021, with higher values indicating greater inequality.

It is noted that income distribution can vary greatly from wealth distribution in a given country; by all accounts, in practice, income and wealth are two distinct concepts. For example, the income originating from the black-market economic activity, a subject of current economic research, is not included.

The Gini index has been most widely used in the field of economics. However, fields as diverse as sociology, health science, ecology, engineering, and agriculture have also benefited from the same (Sadras & Bongiovanni, 2004). The existing literature demonstrates the breadth of applications of the Gini index. As with any other index, the Gini index has

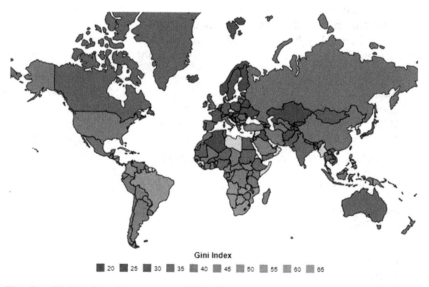

Fig. 1 Gini indices by country 2021 (*Source* https://worldpopulationreview.com/country-rankings/gini-coefficient-by-country)

been used by a range of actors, from governments to national and international organisations and businesses alike, to monitor income inequality within a given country or across countries.

For policymakers, the Gini index plays a vital role, as it can assist in determining where resources and support are most needed. For example, the Pan American Health Organization (PAHO) uses a Sustainable Health Index (SHI), which contains the Gini index as one of its components, in order to allocate its budget among its member states. It is worth mentioning that this budget policy formula is composed of a floor component (core staff and general operating expenses), a needs-based component (SHI), a resource mobilisation component (ability to raise resources by a country), and a variable component (to address emergent situations that may not be reflected in the needs-based calculation, for example, natural disasters, epidemics, and so on) (PAHO, 2019).

In view of the above, the Gini index is more relevant today than ever before, being a powerful inequality measure and the most popular of all to help understand the economic diversity of an area, especially when used along with additional data on income, education, and poverty, among others. In this work, our aim is to present the original Gini index, as well as some of the various existent alternative Gini formulations, while also exploring various traditional and modern applications of the index in different settings, at national and international levels. We further discuss the implications of the traditional Gini index for international diplomacy and policymaking and conclude with some future directions on the topic.

2 History of the GINI Index

The Gini index is a commonly used objective measure of inequality (Wu & Chang, 2019), which was first introduced by the Italian statistician Corrado Gini (1912, cited in Luebker, 2010). It can theoretically take any value between zero (perfect equality, *i.e.*, everybody has the same income) and one (perfect inequality, *i.e.*, all income goes to a single person) (Luebker, 2010, p. 1). In other words, the Gini index measures the degree of wealth concentration among citizens on a 0–1 scale, wherein a Gini index of 1 indicates the most unequal situation, in which all income is owned by a single person and all others have nothing (Wu & Chang, 2019, p. 1479).

2.1 Uses and Purposes of the Gini Index

It is widely acknowledged that both growth and equity play a role in poverty reduction. Since economic and financial crises have undermined development prospects over time, many policymakers have revived their focus on greater equity as a means out of poverty (Luebker, 2010, p. 6). As a result, the Gini index becomes even more vital and relevant.

Ceriani and Verme (2015) defined the Gini index as the sum of individual contributions where individual contributions are interpreted as the degree of diversity of each individual from all other members of society (p. 637). As the authors further elegantly highlighted, "one cannot talk of individual inequality but one can talk of individual diversity and it can be reasonably argued that the sum of individual income diversities in a given population is one possible measure of societal income inequality" (p. 638).

The Gini index (just like the Bonferroni index and the De Vergotinni index) can be interpreted as a measure of social deprivation, as well as a measure of social satisfaction. The absolute Gini index is a measure of mean social deprivation or mean social satisfaction when an individual (a) considers the whole distribution when he compares his/her income with each and all of the incomes of others and (b) he/she does not identify with any group (Imedio-Olmedo et al., 2012, pp. 479, 484). Imedio-Olmedo et al. (2012) argued that "the social deprivation and social satisfaction measures are the expected value of the functions that assign deprivation or satisfaction to each income level. However, when aggregating these two concepts along the income distribution, a policymaker may want to discriminate between different parts of the distribution by attaching different weights. This can be done by computing the mean social deprivation or the mean social satisfaction as weighted means using different weighting profiles" (p. 485). Because of the relationship between deprivation, satisfaction, and inequality, inequality indices in general can be thought of as aggregate measures of the feelings of people who perceive themselves to be disadvantaged or advantaged in terms of income (Temkin, 1986, 1993).

2.1.1 Advantages of the Gini Index

Among the advantages of the Gini index are:

(a) The Gini index is a prominent measure of income or wealth inequality, with relevancy at an international level. The Gini index is used by almost all governmental and international bodies to summarise income inequality in a country or the world (Liu & Gastwirth, 2020, p. 61). It will not be an overstatement to say that the Gini index is the most widely accepted across the Globe.

(b) Although originally developed to be a standardised measure of statistical dispersion intended to understand income distribution, the Gini index has evolved to quantify inequity in all kinds of wealth distributions, gender parity, access to education and health services, and environmental regulations, among others (Mukhopadhyay & Sengupta, 2021).

(c) Also, it is worth noting that the appeal of the Gini index comes from its simplicity, as it condenses a country's total income distribution on a scale of 0 to 1; the higher the number, the higher the degree of inequality (Adeleye, 2018, cited in Osabohien et al., 2020, p. 581). It is, therefore, quite easy to interpret, helping in easily drawing conclusions.

(d) Its popularity also comes from the fact that as the amount and quality of inequality data have increased, the Gini index, in particular, has become a "cross-over statistic", known and understood by non-specialists (Moran, 2003, p. 353).

(e) There are a variety of summary measures of inequality (please see Table 1, compiled by Kokko et al., 1999), each with its own set of assumptions and mathematical properties. Only two of these, however, the Gini index and Henri Theil's (1967 cited in Moran, 2003, p. 373) entropy measure, satisfy the five most sought-after features or properties. In order to satisfy these properties, an inequality indicator must be: (1) symmetrical, (2) income scale invariant, (3) invariant to absolute population levels, (4) defined by upper and lower bounds, and (5) able to satisfy the Pigou-Dalton Principle of Transfers, which states that any redistribution from richer to poorer reduces inequality and vice versa. To satisfy the transfer principle, inequality measures must reflect any income transfer, regardless of where it occurs in the distribution. None of

Table 1 Measures of inequality

Measure	Equation
Sample variance, s_y^2	$\frac{1}{n-1}\sum_{i=1}^{n}(y_i - \overline{y})^2$
Index of dispersion, I	$\frac{s_y^2}{\overline{y}}$
Coefficient of variation, CV	$\frac{s_y}{\overline{y}}$
Morisita coefficient, I_δ	$\frac{n}{(n\overline{y})^2 - n\overline{y}}\sum_{i=1}^{n}y_i^2 - n\overline{y}$
Standardised Morisita coefficient, I_p	See Krebs (1989) or Tsuji and Tsuji (1998) for adjustment procedure
Herfindahl index, H (or Simpson's index, S)	$\sum_{i=1}^{n}p_i^2$
Bradbury's bounded skew index, B (originally: H)	ns_p^2
Keller's weighted skew index, W	$\frac{n_0+n_+B_+}{n_0+n_+}$, where $B_+ = \begin{cases} n_+s_p^2+ & if\ n_+ > 1 \\ 1 & if\ n_+ = 1 \end{cases}$
Keller's corrected skew index, $\widetilde{W}$	$\frac{W - E[W|H_0]}{1 - E[W|H_0]}$
Kokko's iterative skew, K_{med} (originally: λ)	Iterative solution of $y_i \sim \frac{K(1-K)^{i-1}}{1-(1-K)^n}$ such that resampled s_y^2 agrees with observed value
Hovi's mean error skew, M	$\frac{n}{2} \times \frac{1}{n-1}\sum_{i=1}^{n}|p_i - \overline{p}|$
Pamilo's linear skew, L (originally: S_3)	$\frac{1}{n-1}\left[n - \left(\sum_{i=1}^{n}p_i^2\right)^{-1}\right]$
Pietra ratio ("Robin Hood index"), P	$\max_{j=1,\ldots,n}\left|\sum_{i=1}^{j}p_i - \frac{j}{n}\right|$

Measure	Equation
Alatalo's cumulative skew, C_t	$\sum_{i=1}^{\frac{nt}{100}} y_i$, where t is a threshold $(0 < t < 100)$
Poissonian deviance, δ	$\frac{s_y^2 - \bar{y}}{n\bar{y}^2 - \bar{y}}$
Index of monopolisation, Q (Green's coefficient, F)	$\frac{s_y^2 - \bar{y}}{n\bar{y}^2 - \bar{y}}$
Lloyd's mean crowding index, m^*	$\bar{y} + \frac{s_y^2}{\bar{y}} - 1$
Gini coefficient, G	$\frac{1}{2n^2\bar{y}} \sum_{i=1}^{n} \sum_{j=1}^{n} \lvert y_i - y_j \rvert$
Theil index, I_v	$\ln(n) + \sum_{i=1}^{n} p_i \ln(n p_i)$
Moment skewness, g_1	$\frac{n}{s_y^3(n-1)(n-2)} \sum_{i=1}^{n} (y - \bar{y})^3$
L-moment skewness, g_L	$\frac{2w_2 - \bar{y}}{6w_3 - 6w_2 + \bar{y}}$,
	where $w_2 = \frac{1}{n(n-1)} \sum_{i=2}^{n} (i-1) y_i$
	and $w_3 = \frac{1}{n(n-1)(n-2)} \sum_{i=3}^{n} (i-1)(i-2) y_i$
	with y_i ordered: $y_1 \leq y_2 \leq \ldots \leq y_n$

Source Kokko et al. (1999, pp. 362–363)

the other summary metrics have all of these properties (Moran, 2003, pp. 355, 373).

(f) The Gini index satisfies the following four essential conditions which are frequently imposed on any good poverty index: (1) Continuity (Gini values for closed distributions are similar); (2) Anonymity (the invariance of the Gini index to a permutation of the income values); (3) Invariance when the income measure scale is changed; and as aforementioned; (4) the Dalton-Pigou transfer principle. However, it is noteworthy that these four essential requirements are insufficient for choosing an acceptable poverty indicator (Stefanescu, 2011, pp. 256–257).

2.1.2 Disadvantages of the Gini Index

Among the disadvantages of the Gini index are:

(a) The Gini index does not directly reflect people's views on income distribution (Wu & Chang, 2019, p. 1479). Specifically, Gimpelson and Treisman (2018, cited in Wu & Chang, 2019, p. 1479) found that the Gini index is not related to people's support for redistribution. Instead, as the perceived levels of inequality rise, so do the demands for redistribution (Wu & Chang, 2019, p. 1479).

(b) Mathematically, the Gini index is most sensitive to income transfers towards the middle of the distribution, whereas Theil's index, for example, becomes progressively receptive to transfers near the lower end of the income scale (Allison, 1978, cited in Moran, 2003, p. 373).

(c) The Gini ratios' absolute magnitudes are not consistent across surveys or in view of changes in measurement specifications within surveys (Moran, 2003, p. 364).

(d) The Gini index has often been chastised for yielding results that are equal when calculated from two different distributions (p. 61). However, Liu and Gastwirth (2020) showed that expecting a single measure to completely describe the entire income distribution is unrealistic. As a result, researchers may benefit from combining the Gini index with another measure that emphasises the section of the underlying distribution that is most important to the research problem. For instance, Foster and Wolfson (2010, cited in Liu &

Gastwirth, 2020, p. 68) combined the Gini index with the relative median deviation, *i.e.*, $(\mu_U - \mu_L)/\mu$, where μ_U is the mean of those above the median and μ_L is the mean of those below the median, to measure the polarisation of an income distribution.

(e) Needless to say, on its own, the Gini index presents a narrow view of overall inequality prevailing in a society and does not measure the quality of life.

2.2 Construction of the Gini Index to Measure Inequality

2.2.1 Data and Variables Used in the Index System

Some authors utilise Gini indices that have been derived directly from a household survey to measure income distribution disparity, using household per capita income as a welfare indicator (Székely & Mendoza, 2015, p. 399).

It should be noted that the sensitivity of all inequality measures to the measurement choices on which they are based is one of the most important yet ignored elements of all inequality measures.

The choice of income-receiving unit (*e.g.*, households, person equivalents) is statistically as well as conceptually significant, yet it is a topic that is frequently disregarded in inequality studies. Adopting a larger unit should, on the surface, reduce the degree of assessed disparity because the incomes of the various members are essentially averaged (Moran, 2003, pp. 358–359).

Different aggregations of the same distribution will return conflicting Gini ratio estimations, similar to discrepancies in receiving units. Even if the poorest population quintile has the same number of households as the highest quintile (*e.g.*, both 20%), it may (and often does) contain fewer people of working age, and thus the quintile's low overall income can be attributed in part to having comparatively fewer income-receiving people (Moran, 2003, p. 360).

The next methodological concern is agreeing on a definition of "income" after the receiving unit has been decided and the level of aggregation has been established. The more progressive and effective the national tax system is, the more crucial it is to quantify income in pre- or post-tax statistics for inequality measurements. Estimates of inequality based on gross income should, by definition, provide larger Gini indices than those based on income net of taxes, especially in developed countries with progressive tax systems. Significant discrepancies in inequality measurements could also be due to how non-monetary expenditures are accounted for (such as in-kind government transfers and benefits) (Moran, 2003, p. 360).

Although Gini indices are commonly employed to measure income disparity, some relate to market earnings (*i.e.*, income before taxes and transfers) and others refer to disposable incomes (*i.e.*, income after taxes and transfers). Calculating Gini indices for wages or earnings, while omitting income from other sources, can be useful at times. Furthermore, Gini indices can be calculated using consumption or expenditure data (rather than income), or taxable income can be calculated using tax records. They can also be computed for other types of distributions, such as wealth or land ownership (Luebker, 2010, p. 1).

Gini indices are reported exclusively by most major cross-national data aggregates, and they are regularly released by both national statistical agencies like the UK Government Office of National Statistics and the US Census Bureau, as well as international development organisations like the United Nations and the World Bank (Moran, 2003, p. 353).

The European Union's statistical office, EUROSTAT, calculates a standard Gini index, which measures how far a country's wealth distribution deviates from a fully equal wealth distribution, with 0 representing complete equality and 100 indicating complete inequality when expressed in percentages (EUROSTAT, 2021; Tammaru et al., 2020, p. 6).

As a particular case, there are some differences and similarities between the Gini index published by the Organisation for Economic Co-operation and Development (OECD) and the one published by the National Institute of Statistics and Informatics (INEI, for its acronym in Spanish) in Peru, a developing country in Latin America. In this sense, although the Gini index published by INEI showed a decreasing trend from 2007 to 2017 (Castillo, 2020, p. 4), the level of inequality in Peru was higher than the levels of inequality in countries from the European Union, members of OECD (Yamada et al., 2016, p. 4).

INEI measured inequality both for real household income and expenditure per capita using data from the National Household Survey of Peru (ENAHO, for its acronym in Spanish; Castillo, 2020, p. 3). Also, INEI (2018, cited in Castillo, 2020, p. 5) published the Gini estimates for real household income per capita at the regional level, using for its classification a geographical criterion. In Peru, there are three main geographical regions: the Coast, the Highlands, and the Jungle. According to INEI (2018, cited in Castillo, 2020, p. 5), the Coast appears to be the most equal, while there is no clear dominance between the Highlands and the Jungle.

The measurement of per capita income used by INEI to calculate the Gini index was obtained after adding the following income components at the household level (A + B + C + D), dividing this addition by the number of the household members, and deflating the result in order to express it in terms of prices from the Lima Metropolitan area in 2014 (Yamada et al., 2016, pp. 6–7):

(A) Income from Employment comprises salaries received from the main and secondary employment activities, including extra payments and commissions, whether the individual is an employee or involved in self-employment jobs. Also, it includes goods and services produced for own consumption (mainly, from agriculture), extraordinary payments (gratuities, bonuses, and termination pay), and payments made with free or subsidised goods.
(B) Property Income includes interests from financial assets, royalties and income from properties, and payments received for the use of properties.
(C) Private Monetary Transfers include transfers from resident and non-resident private agents (specifically, remittances), but none of them includes employment pensions.
(D) Private Non-Monetary Transfers comprise transfers from private institutions including non-governmental organisations (NGOs).

Nevertheless, OECD defined income and its components based on the principle of disposable income. Therefore, OECD considered the following sources of income, which were not considered by INEI (Yamada et al., 2016, p. 7):

(E) Public Monetary Transfers or Transfers received from Social Security refer to transfers delivered by the government in order to subsidise the population in poverty or the target population according to the type of programme.
(F) Public Employment Pensions received by retired workers.
(G) Workers' Contributions paid through pension schemes to which the individual is affiliated when accessing the employment market.
(H) Direct Taxes paid proportionally to the individual income.

Table 2 Composition of income per capita by the methodology of measurement

	Sources of income	INEI	OECD
1.	+Income from employment	x	x
2.	+Property income	x	x
3.	+Private monetary transfers	x	x
4.	+Private non-monetary transfers	x	
5.	+Public monetary transfers		x
6.	+Public employment pensions received		x
7.	−Workers' contributions paid		x
8.	−Direct taxes paid		x

Source Yamada et al. (2016, p. 8)

These differences and similarities regarding the sources of income considered by INEI and OECD are shown in Table 2 (Yamada et al., 2016, p. 8).

Furthermore, OECD used the following formula to calculate the disposable income adjusted per capita (Yamada et al., 2016, p. 8):

$$\frac{Y_i}{S_i^\epsilon},$$

where Y_i is the total disposable income in household i, S_i is the number of household members, and ϵ is defined as the equivalent elasticity.

2.2.2 Methods to Compute the Gini Index

The Gini index is conceptualised geometrically in terms of the quintile–quintile plot, often known as the Lorenz curve. The Gini index is defined as the ratio of the area between the Lorenz curve and the diagonal (area A) to the total area under the diagonal (area A + B), as shown in Fig. 2. The Gini indices can range from 0 (complete equality, area A = 0 and the Lorenz curve follows the 45° diagonal, so that 20% of the population receives 20% of total income and so on) to 1 (total inequality, all of the area A + B). Greater differences between a given distribution and

Fig. 2 Lorenz curves

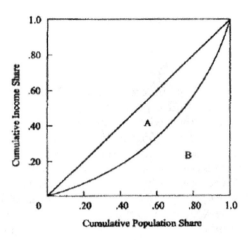

the criterion of complete equality are represented by higher Gini ratios (Moran, 2003, pp. 354–355).

The Gini index (G) is determined mathematically as the average of the absolute value of the relative mean difference in incomes between all possible pairs of individuals, as shown in the equation below (Osberg, 2017, p. 575):

$$G = \frac{1}{2\bar{y}.n.(n-1)} \cdot \sum_{i \neq j}^{n} \sum_{j}^{n} |y_i - y_j|$$

where $y_i, y_j = $ income of individuals i and j, $n = $ total population size, and $\bar{y} = $ average income of all individuals.

Alternatively, if we let y_i designate a random distribution such as income, let $\pi = F(y_i)$ indicate the distribution for y_i, and let $\eta = F_1(y_i)$ represent the corresponding first-moment distribution function, then the relation between η and π, defined for $0 \leq y_i < \infty$, is the Lorenz curve, and the relation can be denoted by $\eta = L(\pi)$. Thus, the Gini index can be defined accordingly (Liao, 2006, pp. 203–204):

$$G = 1 - 2\int_0^1 L(\pi)d\pi$$

Outside of the economics field, the Gini index is significantly less well-known, and even within economics, different indices of inequality are frequently used to substitute the Gini index. The critiques regarding the Gini index's computability are one explanation for this (Furman et al., 2019, p. 1). In their note, Furman et al. (2019) proposed an alternate expression and interpretation of the Gini index based on the concept of a size-biased distribution (p. 1). The authors demonstrated that the Gini index, as opposed to the distribution of the actual wealth (random variable X), measures the size-bias hidden in the random sample distribution (random variable Y*). The closer the Gini index value is to zero, the more accurate the sampling technique (in terms of size-bias) is (p. 2).

Since its inception, the Gini index has been reformulated in a variety of ways that can be stated as sums of individual observations throughout the population and that reflect various individual functions. These formulations are listed in Table 3, considering a population of N individuals, $i = 1, 2, \ldots, n$, $n \in \mathbb{N}$, $n \geq 3$, and an income distribution $Y = (y_1, y_2, \ldots, y_i, \ldots, y_n)$, where $Y \in \mathbb{R}^n_{++}$, $y_1 \leq y_2 \leq \ldots \leq y_n$, μ_Y and y_M are, respectively, the arithmetic mean and the median of distribution Y, and M is the rank of the individual with the median income (Ceriani & Verme, 2015, pp. 639–640):

Ceriani and Verme (2015) proved that, among these eight possible formulations of the Gini index, only the index of individual diversity g_i^{III} satisfies the desirable properties that a measure of individual diversity should have, which are the following: Continuity, Additivity, Linear homogeneity, Translation invariance, Symmetry, and Anonymity (pp. 642–643). The definition of individual contribution to inequality proposed in the paper allows for a distinct type of additive Gini index decomposition by population subgroups. Individual contributions to the Gini index are seen as a measure of individual variety. We can simply sum up the individual values by group to get the Gini value when we aggregate these individual degrees of diversity across groups such as males and females. When we divide Gini's share by group, we get an exact subgroup decomposition (p. 644).

3 THE GINI INDEX: A MODERN MEASURE OF INEQUALITY

Table 3 Alternative Gini formulations

Gini index	Individual diversity	Alleged original proponent	Form
$G^{I} = \frac{1}{n^{2}\mu_{Y}}\sum_{i=1}^{n}\frac{(n+1-2i)(y_{n-i+1}-y_{i})}{2}$	$g_{i}^{I} = \frac{(n+1-2i)(y_{n-i+1}-y_{i})}{2}$	Gini (1912, 1914)	Original
$G^{II} = \frac{1}{n^{2}\mu_{Y}}\sum_{i=1}^{n}2(i-M)(y_{i}-y_{M})$	$g_{i}^{II} = 2(i-M)(y_{i}-y_{M})$	Gini (1912)	In terms of distances from the median
$G^{III} = \frac{1}{n^{2}\mu_{Y}}\sum_{i=1}^{n}\sum_{j=1}^{n}\frac{|y_{i}-y_{j}|}{2}$	$g_{i}^{III} = \sum_{j=1}^{n}\frac{|y_{i}-y_{j}|}{2}$	Kendall and Stuart (1958)	Adjusted Gini
$G^{IV} = \frac{1}{n^{2}\mu_{Y}}\sum_{i=1}^{n}(n+1)\mu_{Y}-2(n+1-i)y_{i}$	$g_{i}^{IV} = \mu_{Y} - 2(n+1-i)y_{i}$	Sen (1973)	Geometric
$G^{V} = \frac{1}{n^{2}\mu_{Y}}\sum_{i=1}^{n}\sum_{j>i}(y_{j}-y_{i})$	$g_{i}^{V} = \sum_{j>i}(y_{j}-y_{i})$	Yitzhaki (1979)	Deprivation
$G^{VI} = \frac{1}{n^{2}\mu_{Y}}\sum_{i=1}^{n}2iy_{i}-(n+1)\mu_{Y}$	$g_{i}^{VI} = 2iy_{i}-(n+1)\mu_{Y}$	Anand (1983)	Covariance
$G^{VII} = \frac{1}{n^{2}\mu_{Y}}\sum_{i=1}^{n}(2i-n-1)y_{i}$	$g_{i}^{VII} = (2i-n-1)y_{i}$	Silber (1989)	Matrix
$G^{VIII} = \frac{1}{n^{2}\mu_{Y}}\sum_{i=1}^{n}2i(y_{i}-\mu_{y})$	$g_{i}^{VIII} = 2i(y_{i}-\mu_{Y})$	Shorrocks (2013)	In terms of distances from the mean

Source Ceriani and Verme (2015, p. 640)

It is worth pointing out that there exists a long-standing stream of literature discussing how to decompose the Gini index, although such treatment is outside the scope of the present manuscript. For example, more recently, Sarntisart (2020) proposed a novel method that divides the Gini index into *within-subgroup* and *across-subgroup* components, which was then applied to the case of Thailand during the years 2009–2017.

2.2.3   Limitations and Difficulties Related to the Construction and Interpretation of the Gini Index

A relevant question that gets asked and over which there is still debate going on among specialists is: when is the Gini index big enough to represent a "high" level of inequality? "Because summary measures of inequality are not associated mathematically with probability functions, or theoretically with sampling distributions, their magnitude and change can only be interpreted using subjectively defined criteria. Once we are satisfied that differences in Gini ratios cannot be attributed to methodological choices, we are left with no objective, scientific method to assess whether these differences in measured inequality are 'statistically significant'—large enough to rule out measurement error, sampling error, or random chance—or whether they are 'substantively meaningful'—large enough to signal a material shift in the way society distributes income" (Moran, 2003, p. 365).

Moran (2003) goes on to state that "like other statistics involving subjective interpretation, the magnitude of inequality represented by Gini can only be assessed in relation to the Gini ratio of other units, and even in these situations, we can only imprecisely conclude which Gini ratios fall towards the 'high' or 'low' end historically. In the presence of intersecting Lorenz curves, even this comparison can at times be problematic" (p. 365).

3   Traditional Views and Applications of the Gini Index

As previously stated, inequality measures have been used in the economics field ever since the seminal study conducted by Gini (1912), which proposed an income inequality index. A substantial part of the literature, therefore, is dedicated to what can be called the "traditional Gini index".

Below, we explore some of the most recent literature in this regard, across countries.

For example, Chauhan et al. (2016) aimed to provide a comparable estimate of poverty and inequality in the regions of India over the past two decades. The unit data from three quinquennial rounds of consumption expenditure survey, *i.e.*, 1993–1994, 2004–2005, and 2011–2012, were used in the analysis. Thus, the authors estimated the extent of money metric poverty and inequality in the regions of India, based on these three quinquennial rounds. The Gini index, rich–poor ratio, and regression analyses were used in the process to understand the extent of economic inequality in the regions of India (pp. 1249, 1253). The comparable estimates were provided for 81 regions of India to the extent possible for rural and urban areas as well otherwise for overall areas (p. 1253). Results indicated that although the extent of poverty declined, economic inequality increased in the regions of India. By contrast to poverty estimates, the Gini index decreased in 20 regions and increased in 61 regions. Based on these findings, the authors suggested that the regions with persistently high poverty be accorded priority in the poverty alleviation programme, while also exploring the factors leading to increasing economic inequality (pp. 1249–1250).

The work by Osabohien et al. (2020) measured inequality using the Gini index and examined how social protection policies and programmes can help in poverty and inequality reduction in Africa (p. 575). The study covered 38 African countries and engaged the fixed and random effects models utilising data sourced from the World Development Indicators, International Country Risk Guide, and the Country Policy and Institutional Assessment, for the period 2005–2017 (pp. 575, 581, 585). Results showed that a 1% increase in the provision of social protection would decrease poverty and inequality by 58 and 26%, respectively. The authors also showed that the type of social protection policies may need to differ from one region to the other (p. 575).

Zaborskis et al. (2019) aimed to compare socio-economic inequality in adolescent life satisfaction across countries employing different measures, as well as to determine the correlations between outcomes of tested measures and country-level socio-economic indices (*e.g.*, Gross National Income, Gini index, and so on; p. 1058). The paper introduced several methods for measuring family affluence inequality in adolescent life satisfaction and assessed its relationship with macro-level indices (p. 1055). The Gini index served as an indicator of country-level economic inequality. The data were collected in 2013/2014 in 39 European countries, Canada, and Israel, and were obtained from the Health Behavior in School-aged Children study, a cross-national survey with support from the World Health Organization (pp. 1055–1056, 1058). The 11-, 13-, and 15-year olds were surveyed by means of self-report anonymous questionnaires. Fifteen methods controlling for confounders (family structure, gender, and age were regarded as confounders) were tested to measure social inequality in adolescent life satisfaction (pp. 1056, 1072). The study found that gender, age, and family structure all played a role in defining inequities in adolescent life satisfaction, though to a lesser extent than family affluence (p. 1072). All metrics in each country showed that adolescents from more affluent homes were happier with their lives than those from less affluent families.

According to Poisson regression estimates, adolescents in Malta have the lowest level of life satisfaction inequality, whereas adolescents in Hungary have the highest level of life happiness disparity (p. 1056). The ratio between the mean values of the life satisfaction score at the extremes of family affluence (Relative Index of Inequality) derived from regression-based models is notable for its positive correlation with the Gini index and negative correlation with Gross National Income, Human Development Index, and the mean Overall Life Satisfaction score. From a cross-national viewpoint, the measure permitted the in-depth examination of the interplay between individual and macro-socio-economic determinants affecting adolescent well-being (p. 1056).

In their paper, Panzera and Postiglione (2020) introduced a new measure that facilitates the assessment of the relative contribution of spatial patterns to overall inequality. The proposed index is based on the Gini correlation measure, accounts for both inequality and spatial autocorrelation, and introduces regional importance weighting in the analysis, which distinguishes the regional contributions to overall inequality (p. 379). In the approach of this paper, the spatial Gini is based upon the correlation between the value that is observed for the reference unit and the values that are observed for the neighbouring regions (p. 384). The Gini correlation is a measure of association between two random variables, which is based on the covariance between one variable and its cumulative distribution function (p. 384). The Gini correlation between two variables is expressed as the ratio of two covariances. The covariance in the numerator is computed between one variable and the cumulative distribution function of the other, and it corresponds to the Gini covariance between the variables. The covariance in the denominator is computed between the variable and its cumulative distribution function and represents a measure of variability (p. 385). The paper introduces a measure that is defined as the Gini correlation between the variable Y and its spatial lag WY, where Y denotes the regional GDP per capita and W is a row-standardised spatial weight matrix that summarises the proximity relationship between regional units. The spatially lagged variable expresses a weighted average of the values of Y that are observed for neighbouring regions (p. 386). When the ranking of WY is identical to the original ranking of Y, the overall inequality is completely explained by the given pattern of spatial dependence. As the ranking of the regional GDPs (*i.e.*, Y) becomes more dissimilar to the ranking of average GDPs in neighbour regions (*i.e.*, WY), the spatial component of inequality decreases. When Y and WY are uncorrelated, the overall inequality is completely explained by its non-spatial component (p. 388). The proposed measure is demonstrated through empirical research of income inequality in Italian provinces that correspond to the NUTS 3 level of the official EU classification. The authors looked at regional GDP per capita data from the EUROSTAT database from 2000 to 2015 (p. 388).

The spatial component of the Gini index is slightly greater than the non-spatial component for any specifications of the spatial weight matrix. This means that both of these factors account for nearly the same amount of global inequality in Italian provinces (p. 389).

Moreover, these findings show that a positive spatial autocorrelation increases inequality by forming clusters of similar incomes (p. 390). The ability to determine the role of the spatial dependence relationship in generating income inequality at fine geographical scales is critical for providing meaningful information for location-based policies targeted at lowering income inequality (Márquez et al., 2019, cited in Panzera & Postiglione, 2020, p. 393).

The above are certainly not the only examples, and interested readers may wish to explore other studies.

4 Modern Views and Applications of the Gini Index

Originally defined as a standardised measure of statistical dispersion intended to understand income distribution, it comes as no surprise that the Gini index has been most widely used in the field of economics.

Interestingly enough, however, in time, the Gini index has evolved into quantifying inequity in all kinds of distributions of wealth, energies, masses, temperatures, city sizes, and pollution levels, gender parity, access to education and health services, environmental policies, and so on (Mukhopadhyay & Sengupta, 2021). This is because while the Gini index was devised in order to measure socio-economic inequality, it is actually a "measure of *statistical variability* that is applicable to *size distributions* at large" (Eliazar, 2016, p. 67). As mentioned previously, fields as diverse as sociology, health science, ecology, engineering, and agriculture have thus also benefited from Gini's work (Sadras & Bongiovanni, 2004). This has given birth to a plethora of modern views and applications of the Gini Index, some of which we explore below.

For example, in engineering, the Gini index has been used to assess the fairness achieved by Internet routers in scheduling packet transmissions from different flows of traffic (Shi & Sethu, 2003). In health, the Gini index has been employed as a measure of health-related quality of life inequality in a population (Asada, 2005). Using race as an example, the study dissected the overall Gini index into the between-group, within-group, and overlap Gini indices to reflect health inequality by the group. In addition to the absolute mean differences across groups, the researchers looked at how much the overlap Gini index contributed to the overall Gini index. In chemistry, it has been used to describe the selectivity of protein kinase inhibitors against a panel of kinases (Graczyk, 2007). In education, it has been used as a measure of the inequality of universities (Halffman & Leydesdorff, 2010). The Gini index has even been applied to examine inequality on dating apps (Kopf, 2017; Worst-Online-Dater, 2015).

In ecology, it has been used as a measure of biodiversity, where the cumulative proportion of species is plotted against cumulative proportion of individuals (Wittebolle et al., 2009). In this sense, linear models have been used to evaluate the impacts of stress, the Gini index, the relative abundance of the dominant species, and that of their interactions on the ecosystem functionality.

In China, the environmental Gini index is widely used for the allocation of regional water pollutant emissions and for the inequality analysis of urban water use. To build this environmental Gini index model, the cumulative proportion of various water pollutant emissions is generally used as the vertical axis and the cumulative proportion of the GDP or ecological capacity as the horizontal axis to establish the environmental

Lorenz curve (Zhou et al., 2015, p. 1047). Specifically, Zhou et al. (2015, pp. 1049–1052, 1054) studied the application of an environmental Gini index optimisation model to the industrial wastewater chemical oxygen demand (COD) discharge in seven cities in the Taihu Lake Basin, China, in order to improve the equality of water governance responsibility allocation and optimise water pollutant emissions and water governance inputs. The research found that three cities displayed inequality factors and were adjusted to reduce the water pollutant emissions and to increase the water governance inputs (Zhou et al., 2015, p. 1047).

More recently, the Gini index has been used to measure the inequality in greenspace exposure of a city, with an application to 303 major Chinese cities; interestingly enough, the study leveraged multi-source geospatial big data and a modified urban greenspace exposure inequality assessment framework (Song et al., 2021).

In credit risk management, the Gini index is sometimes used to assess the discriminating power of rating systems (Christodoulakis & Satchell, 2007). The applications of the Gini methodology to financial theory are relevant whenever one is interested in decision-making under risk (Yitzhaki & Schechtman, 2013, p. 365). Specifically, the Gini methodology has been applied to portfolio theory, which aims to find a combination of safe and risky assets that maximises the expected utility of the investor (Yitzhaki & Schechtman, 2013, p. 372). For instance, if we denote the absolute Lorenz curve (ALC) of a safe asset by LSA (the line of safe asset), then one can express the same expected return and its ALC: the farther the LSA from the ALC is, the greater the risk assumed by the portfolio. Thus, one possible measure of risk is the Gini mean difference of the portfolio which is obtained from the distance between the LSA and the ALC (Yitzhaki & Schechtman, 2013, p. 385).

In agriculture, Sadras and Bongiovanni (2004) explored the applicability of Lorenz curves and Gini indices to characterise the magnitude of the variation in grain yield. The agronomic relevance of the Gini index was summarised in an inverse relationship with yield. Lorenz curves seemed particularly apt to present crop heterogeneity in terms of inequality, and to highlight the relative contribution of low- and high-yielding sections of the field to total paddock yield. As assessed by the authors, the Lorenz curves and Gini indices provide a potentially useful extension tool, a complement to yield maps and other statistical indices of yield variation, and further contact points between site-specific management, economics, and ecology.

In business, Morais and Kakabadse (2014, pp. 393–394) considered that the Corporate Gini Index (CGI) is a valuable measure of corporate income inequality, urging regulators around the world to consider the CGI as a measure that should be disclosed in proxy statements, by introducing amendments to existing regulation. It is worth mentioning that Morais and Kakabadse (2014, p. 387) computed the CGI by collecting income distributions for six basic categories of pay for a company. These basic categories of pay were Executive Board, Top Management, Regional Directors/Deputy Directors, District Managers, Store Managers, and Equivalent.

The Gini index has further been used in genetics for assessing the inequality of the contribution of different marked effects to genetic variability (Gianola et al., 2003), and in astronomy for providing a quantitative measure of the inequality with which a galaxy's light is distributed among its constituent pixels (Abraham et al., 2003).

Although, not exhaustive in nature, the above-mentioned studies demonstrate the breadth of applications of the Gini index, justifying its status as a modern measure of inequality.

All in all, it is interesting to note how scientists and researchers across many fields have found occasions to apply the Gini index.

5 Implications for Economic Diplomacy and Future Research Directions

In this work, we have aimed to present the original Gini index, as well as the various existent alternative Gini formulations, while also exploring various traditional and modern applications of the index in different settings, at national and international levels. In this section, we briefly discuss the overall implications of the Gini index for international economic diplomacy and policymaking (therefore, taking the more traditional view of the index into account) and conclude with some future research directions.

Without a doubt, the problem of inequality among people has become more salient in recent years. Indeed, data and research show that the degree of inequality has increased in most countries around the world, which in turn, has generated concerns both from the perspective of the sustainability of economic growth, as well as from the perspective of social cohesion and well-being.

The Gini index is not without criticism. And some of it is justified, to some extent. For example, the fact that the Gini index, as a single statistical measure cannot capture the nature of inequality among people. Although nor should it be expected to do so in the first place. The Gini index is not a perfect measure and it is insufficient on its own, so much so that, if not properly understood in view of its limitations, it can turn out to be misleading. And that is exactly the point. One should never rely on a single summary statistic, be it the Gini index or any other index. To get a more comprehensive and accurate picture of any given socio-economic reality, any index needs to be complemented with insights obtained from other composite indices of well-being. In this sense, the Gini index remains a powerful inequality measure and the most popular of all to help understand the economic diversity of an area, especially when used along with additional data on income, education, and poverty, among others. For example, Pandey and Nathwani (1996) presented a new method for measuring the socio-economic inequality using a composite social indicator, Life-Quality Index, derived from two principal indicators of development, namely, the Real Gross Domestic Product per person and the life expectancy at birth. To account for the observed differences in life-quality of distinct quintiles of the population, income inequality and the accompanying life expectancy variations were combined into a quality-adjusted income (QAI). The Gini coefficient of the distribution of QAI was introduced as a measure of socio-economic inequality (Pandey & Nathwani, 1996, p. 187).

Preventing and reducing inequality is a multi-stakeholder effort, requiring an efficient social and civil dialogue between various interested groups (Charles et al., 2019), although it depends largely on the actions and reforms taken by the countries' governments. In this sense, then, the role and responsibility of the governments is to support policies and initiatives in the field of social inclusion and social protection by providing policy guidelines and budgetary support for reform implementation. Of course, policy responses will be dependent on the careful interpretation of the factors that determine inequality in each country, as well as in view of country-specific factors such as unemployment rate, economic sectoral composition, labour market institutions, and the design of the social protection system (European Commission, 2017).

More recently, efforts have also been made to enhance the Gini index with insights from big data-driven approaches. Because the potential to exploit location to generate insights to understand relationships across different levels of geography is rising, geospatial analysis plays an essential role here. For example, Haithcoat et al. (2021) used big data geospatial analytics to examine ways that income inequality is associated with a range of health and health-related outcomes among individuals. In the authors' words, "the development of spatially enabled big data that integrates sociodemographic, environmental, cultural, economic, and infrastructural variables within a common framework has the potential to transform social research. Using geostatistical approaches to create new information from data captured through topology, intersection, and complex queries among data sets allows researchers to more fully explore context. Quantifying this 'context' is fundamental to understanding disparity and inequality" (p. 547). In turn, this has important implications for international economic diplomacy and policymaking, as such insights "may be used to inform state-level relationships underpinning social and structural variables that may associate with the Gini coefficient itself" (p. 547).

The arrival of big data has indeed opened up new opportunities (Charles & Gherman, 2013; Charles et al., 2015, 2021). And it remains an important direction for future research, which calls for more cross- and inter-disciplinary empirically grounded research, more specifically, for new research approaches to study people and practice in truly insightful and impactful ways [for an example, please see Charles and Gherman (2018); Gherman (2018)], which can then translate into the creation of better, more comprehensive composite indices, in general (Charles et al., 2022).

The Gini index can, thus, help governments in their efforts to track inequality and poverty levels, but this is not the only use for the index. Studies (e.g., Gurr, 1970) have shown that increased inequality increases the likelihood of violent conflict and violent social conflict. Therefore, another practical use of the Gini index is in policy support on conflict prevention by means of reducing economic inequality through various policy interventions. In other words, supporting socio-economic development through aid programmes and diplomacy. As Tadjoeddin et al. (2021) elegantly stated, "local governments at sub-national level must have a clear understanding of the taxonomy of collective violence (ethnic and routine) and inequality (vertical and horizontal), and more importantly, have an ability to closely monitor both variables and take necessary measures" (p. 566).

6 Conclusions

The Gini index is a prominent measure of income or wealth inequality, with relevancy at both national and international levels. For policymakers, the Gini index plays a vital role, as it can assist in determining where resources and support are most needed. All in all, the Gini index is more relevant today than ever before, being a powerful inequality measure and the most popular of all to help understand the economic diversity of an area, especially when used along with additional data on income, education, and poverty, among others.

Although originally developed to be a standardised measure of statistical dispersion intended to understand income distribution, mainly used in the field of economics, the Gini index has evolved in time into a means of quantifying inequity in all kinds of distributions of wealth, gender parity, access to education and health services, and environmental policies, among others. Fields as diverse as sociology, health science, ecology, engineering, and agriculture have also benefited from Gini's work, and the existing literature stands as evidence of the breadth of applications of the Gini index.

Today, growing complexities of markets and states, enterprises and governments alike, coupled with technological developments, call for improved Gini indices. In this sense, it is necessary not only to make methodological improvements, but also to nurture an extended network of experts who can engage in constructive dialogue, with greater collaboration among a broader range of stakeholders, including scholars, data scientists, regulators and politicians, business leaders, and representatives of civil society, just to name a few. We, therefore, join calls for more cross- and inter-disciplinary research that can translate into more comprehensive, impactful Gini indices.

Acknowledgements The authors are grateful to the referees for their valuable comments on the previous version of this work.

References

Abraham, R., van den Bergh, S., & Nair, P. (2003). A new approach to galaxy morphology, I: Analysis of the Sloan digital sky survey early data release. *Astrophysical Journal, 588,* 218–229.

Adeleye, N. (2018, May). *Financial reforms, credit growth and income inequality in sub-Saharan Africa.* A Ph.D. Thesis Presented to the Department of Economics and Development Studies, Covenant University, Ota, Nigeria.

Allison, P. D. (1978). Measures of inequality. *American Sociological Review, 43*(6), 865–880.

Anand, S. (1983). *Inequality and poverty in Malaysia: Measurement and decomposition.* Oxford University Press.

Asada, Y. (2005). Assessment of the health of Americans: The average health-related quality of life and its inequality across individuals and groups. *Population Health Metrics, 3,* Article 7.

Castillo, L. E. (2020). *Regional dynamics of income inequality in Peru* (Working Paper N° 2020-004). Central Reserve Bank of Peru.

Ceriani, L., & Verme, P. (2015). Individual diversity and the Gini decomposition. *Social Indicators Research, 121*(3), 637–646.

Charles, V., & Gherman, T. (2013). Achieving competitive advantage through big data: Strategic implications. *Middle-East Journal of Scientific Research, 16*(8), 1069–1074.

Charles, V., & Gherman, T. (2018). Big data and ethnography: Together for the greater good. In A. Emrouznejad & V. Charles (Eds.), *Big data for the greater good* (pp. 19–34). Springer.

Charles, V., Gherman, T., & Emrouznejad, A. (2022). The role of composite indices in international economic diplomacy. In V. Charles & A. Emrouznejad (Eds.), *Modern indices for international economic diplomacy.* Springer-Palgrave Macmillan (Forthcoming).

Charles, V., Gherman, T., & Paliza, J. C. (2019). Stakeholder involvement for public sector productivity enhancement: Strategic considerations. *ICPE Public Enterprise Half-Yearly Journal, 24*(1), 77–86.

Charles, V., Emrouznejad, A., & Gherman, T. (2021). Strategy formulation and service operations in the big data age: The essentialness of technology, people, and ethics. In A. Emrouznejad & V. Charles (Eds.), *Big data for service operations management* (pp. 1–30). Springer's International Series in Studies in Big Data. Springer-Verlag, UK. (Forthcoming).

Charles, V., Tavana, M., & Gherman, T. (2015). The right to be forgotten—Is privacy sold out in the big data age? *International Journal of Society Systems Science, 7*(4), 283–298.

Chauhan, R. K., Mohanty, S. K., Subramanian, S. V., Parida, J. K., & Padhi, B. (2016). Regional estimates of poverty and inequality in India, 1993–2012. *Social Indicators Research, 127*(3), 1249–1296.

Christodoulakis, G. A., & Satchell, S. E. (Eds.). (2007). The validity of credit risk model validation methods. In *The Analytics of Risk Model Validation*. Elsevier Finance.

Eliazar, I. (2016). Visualizing inequality. *Physica A: Statistical Mechanics and Its Applications, 454*, 66–80.

European Commission. (2017). European semester thematic factsheet. *Addressing Inequalities*. Available at https://ec.europa.eu/info/sites/default/files/file_import/european-semester_thematic-factsheet_addressinginequalities_en_0.pdf

EUROSTAT. (2021). *Gini coefficient of equivalised disposable income—EU-SILC survey*. EUROSTAT [cited on August 12, 2021]. Retrieved from https://ec.europa.eu/eurostat/web/products-datasets/-/ilc_di12

Foster, J. E., & Wolfson, M. C. (2010). Polarization and the decline of the middle class: Canada and the U.S. *The Journal of Economic Inequality, 8*(2), 247–273.

Furman, E., Kye, Y., & Su, J. (2019, December). Computing the Gini index: A note. *Economics Letters, 185*, 108753.

Gherman, T. (2018). Machine learning and ethnography: A marriage made in heaven. *Informs OR/MS Tomorrow*, Spring/Summer 2018 Issue (pp. 12–13).

Gianola, D., Perez-Enciso, M., & Toro, M. A. (2003). On marker-assisted prediction of genetic value: Beyond the ridge. *Genetics, 163*, 347–365.

Gimpelson, V., & Treisman, D. (2018). Misperceiving inequality. *Economics & Politics, 30*(1), 27–54.

Gini, C. (1912). Variabilitá e mutabilitá: Contributo allo studio delle distribuzioni e delle relazioni statistiche. *Studi Economico-giuridici della Regia Facolt'a Giurisprudenza, 3*(2), 3–159.

Gini, C. (1914). Sulla Misura della Concentrazione e della Variabilità dei Caratteri. *Atti del Reale Istituto Veneto di Scienze, Lettere ed Arti, 73*(2), 1203–1248.

Graczyk, P. (2007). Gini coefficient: A new way to express selectivity of Kinase inhibitors against a family of Kinases. *Journal of Medicinal Chemistry, 50*(23), 5773–5779.

Gurr, T. R. (1970). *Why men rebel*. Princeton University Press.

Haithcoat, T. L., Avery, E. E., Bowers, K. A., Hammer, R. D., & Shyu, C.-R. (2021). Income inequality and health: Expanding our understanding of state-level effects by using a geospatial big data approach. *Social Science Computer Review, 39*(4), 543–561.

Halffman, W., & Leydesdorff, L. (2010). Is inequality among universities increasing? Gini coefficients and the elusive rise of elite universities. *Minerva, 48*(1), 55–72.

Imedio-Olmedo, L. J., Parrado-Gallardo, E. M., & Bárcena-Martín, E. (2012). Income inequality indices interpreted as measures of relative deprivation/satisfaction. *Social Indicators Research, 109*, 471–491.

INEI. (2018). Evolución de la Pobreza Monetaria, 2007–2017. *Informe Técnico*. Instituto Nacional de Estadística e Informática. INEI.

Kendall, M. G., & Stuart, A. (1958). *The advanced theory of statistics* (1st ed., Vol. 1). Hafner Publishing Company.

Kokko, H., Mackenzie, A., Reynolds, J. D., Lindström, J., & Sutherland, W. J. (1999). Measures of inequality are not equal. *The American Naturalist, 154*(3), 358–382.

Kopf, D. (2017). These statistics show why it's so hard to be an average man on dating apps. *Quartz*. Retrieved April 28, 2021, from https://qz.com/1051462/these-statistics-show-why-its-so-hard-to-be-an-average-man-on-dating-apps/

Krebs, C. J. (1989). *Ecological methodology*. Harper & Row.

Liao, T. F. (2006). Measuring and analyzing class inequality with the Gini index informed by model-based clustering. *Sociological Methodology, 36*(1), 201–224.

Liu, Y., & Gastwirth, J. L. (2020). On the capacity of the Gini index to represent income distributions. *METRON, 78*, 61–69.

Luebker, M. (2010). *Inequality, income shares and poverty: The practical meaning of Gini coefficients* (TRAVAIL Policy Brief N° 3). International Labour Office.

Márquez, M. A., Lasarte-Navamuel, E., & Lufin, M. (2019). The role of neighborhood in the analysis of spatial economic inequality. *Social Indicators Research, 141*(1), 245–273.

Morais, F., & Kakabadse, N. K. (2014). The Corporate Gini Index (CGI) determinants and advantages: Lessons from a multinational retail company case study. *International Journal of Disclosure and Governance, 11*(4), 380–397.

Moran, T. P. (2003). On the theoretical and methodological context of cross-national inequality data. *International Sociology, 18*, 351–378.

Mukhopadhyay, N., & Sengupta, P. P. (2021). *Gini inequality index: Methods and applications*. Routledge.

Osabohien, R., Matthew, O., Ohalete, P., & Osabuohien, E. (2020). Population-poverty-inequality nexus and social protection in Africa. *Social Indicators Research, 151*, 575–598.

Osberg, L. (2017). On the limitations of some current usages of the Gini Index. *Review of Income and Wealth, 63*(3), 574–584.

PAHO. (2019). *PAHO budget policy*. 57th Directing Council, 71st Session of the Regional Committee of WHO for the Americas. Pan American Health Organization, 30 September–4 October 2019. PAHO [cited on August 10th, 2021]. https://www3.paho.org/hq/index.php?option=com_docman&view=

download&alias=49746-cd57-5-e-budget-policy&category_slug=cd57-en&Itemid=270&lang=en

Pandey, M. D., & Nathwani, J. S. (1996). Measurement of socio-economic inequality using the life-quality index. *Social Indicators Research, 39*, 187–202.

Panzera, D., & Postiglione, P. (2020). Measuring the spatial dimension of regional inequality: An approach based on the Gini correlation measure. *Social Indicators Research, 148*, 379–394.

Sadras, V. O., & Bongiovanni, R. (2004). Use of Lorenz curves and Gini coefficients to assess yield inequality within paddocks. *Field Crops Research, 90*(2–3), 303–310.

Sarntisart, I. (2020). Income inequality and conflicts: A Gini decomposition analysis. *The Economics of Peace & Security Journal, 15*(2).

Sen, A. K. (1973). *On economic inequality*. Clarendon Press.

Shi, H., & Sethu, H. (2003). Greedy fair queueing: A goal-oriented strategy for fair real-time packet scheduling. In *Proceedings of the 24th IEEE Real-Time Systems Symposium, IEEE Computer Society* (pp. 345–356). ISBN 978-0-7695-2044-5.

Shorrocks, A. F. (2013). Decomposition procedures for distributional analysis: A unified framework based on the Shapley value. *The Journal of Economic Inequality, 11*(1), 99–126.

Silber, J. (1989). Factor components, population subgroups and the computation of the Gini index of inequality. *Review of Economics and Statistics, 71*(1), 107–115.

Song, Y., et al. (2021). Observed inequality in urban greenspace exposure in China. *Environment International, 156*, 106778.

Stefanescu, S. (2011). About the accuracy of Gini index for measuring the poverty. *Romanian Journal of Economic Forecasting, 3*, 255–266.

Székely, M., & Mendoza, P. (2015). Is the decline in inequality in Latin America here to stay. *Journal of Human Development and Capabilities, 16*(3), 397–419.

Tadjoeddin, M. Z., Yumna, A., Gultom, S. E., Fajar Rakhmadi, M., & Suryahadi, A. (2021). Inequality and violent conflict: New evidence from selected provinces in Post-Soeharto Indonesia. *Journal of the Asia Pacific Economy, 26*(3), 552–573.

Tammaru, T., Marcinczak, S., Aunap, R., van Ham, M., & Janssen, H. (2020). Relationship between income inequality and residential segregation of socioeconomic groups. *Regional Studies, 54*(4), 450–461.

Temkin, L. S. (1986). Inequality. *Philosophy & Public Affairs, 15*, 99–121.

Temkin, L. S. (1993). *Inequality*. Oxford University Press.

Theil, H. (1967). *Economics and information theory*. Rand McNally.

Tsuji, K., & Tsuji, N. (1998). Indices of reproductive skew depend on average reproductive success. *Evolutionary Ecology, 12*, 141–152.

Wittebolle, L., Marzorati, M., Clement, L., Balloi, A., Daffonchio, D., Heylen, K., De Vos, P., Verstraete, W., & Boon, N. (2009). Initial community evenness favours functionality under selective stress. *Nature, 458*, 623–626.

Worst-Online-Dater. (2015, March 25). Tinder experiments II: Guys, unless you are really hot you are probably better off not wasting your time on Tinder—A quantitative socio-economic study. *Medium*. Retrieved October 10, 2021, from https://medium.com/@worstonlinedater/tinder-experiments-ii-guys-unless-you-are-really-hot-you-are-probably-better-off-not-wasting-your-2ddf370a6e9a

Wu, W.-C., & Chang, Y.-T. (2019). Income inequality, distributive unfairness, and support for democracy: Evidence from East Asia and Latin America. *Democratization, 26*(8), 1475–1492.

Yamada, G., Castro, J. F., & Oviedo, N. (2016). *Revisitando el coeficiente de Gini en el Perú: El Rol de las Políticas Públicas en la Evolución de la Desigualdad* (Working Paper N° 16-06). Centro de Investigación de la Universidad del Pacífico.

Yitzhaki, S. (1979). Relative deprivation and the Gini coefficient. *Quarterly Journal of Economics, 93*, 321–324.

Yitzhaki, S., & Schechtman, E. (2013). *The Gini methodology: A primer on a statistical methodology*. Springer Series in Statistics 272. Springer Science + Business Media.

Zaborskis, A., Grincaite, M., Lenzi, M., Tesler, R., Moreno-Maldonado, C., & Mazur, J. (2019). Social inequality in adolescent life satisfaction: Comparison of measure approaches and correlation with macro-level indices in 41 countries. *Social Indicators Research, 141*, 1055–1079.

Zhou, S., Du, A., & Bai, M. (2015). Application of the environmental Gini coefficient in allocating water governance responsibilities: A case study in Taihu Lake Basin China. *Water Science & Technology, 71*(7), 1047–1055.

CHAPTER 4

The Gender Inequality Index Through the Prism of Social Innovation

Vanina Farber and Patrick Reichert

1 Introduction

Gender inequality has been, and still is, one of the most debated issues in contemporary society. Promoting gender equality and empowering women in the socio-economic arena are therefore core policy priorities and business issues in countries around the world. To this end, gender-sensitive statistics are critical pieces of information that enable governmental policy-makers and private-sector practitioners to make decisions. Gender-sensitive statistics ensure data collection on specific issues that disproportionately affect women in society and the workplace. These indicators help to benchmark the progress made and inform strategies

---

V. Farber (✉) · P. Reichert (✉)
Elea Center for Social Innovation, International Institute for Management Development, Lausanne, Switzerland
e-mail: Vanina.Farber@imd.org

P. Reichert
e-mail: Patrick.Reichert@imd.org

© The Author(s), under exclusive license to Springer Nature Switzerland AG 2022
V. Charles and A. Emrouznejad (eds.), *Modern Indices for International Economic Diplomacy*, https://doi.org/10.1007/978-3-030-84535-3_4

to realize gender equality and the empowerment of women and girls throughout the world.

To measure gender inequality, the United Nations Development Programme (UNDP) created the Gender Inequality Index (GII) in 2010 to replace its two predecessors, the Gender-related Development Index (GDI) and the Gender Empowerment Measure (GEM). The GII measures gender inequalities across three important aspects of human development: (1) reproductive health measured by maternal mortality ratio and adolescent birth rates; (2) empowerment, measured by the share of parliamentary seats occupied by females and educational attainment at the secondary level by gender; and (3) economic opportunity measured by the labour force participation rates of females and males (UNDP, 2019).

According to the GII website, the index "sheds new light on the position of women in 160 countries; it yields insights in gender gaps in major areas of human development. The component indicators highlight areas in need of critical policy intervention and it stimulates proactive thinking and public policy to overcome systematic disadvantages of women" (UNDP, 2019). Although imperfect, the advantage of producing a single measure to capture gender inequality has several implications for the coordinated efforts of various actors, including international public and non-profit bodies, national and local governments and businesses in the private sector.

As globalization continues to increase the complexity of international economic relations, countries not only compete with each other using traditional tools of economic diplomacy such as attracting foreign-direct investment, negotiating market access for their national companies or attempting to protect domestic markets through trade barriers but also face increasing sway from non-state actors in economic policy debates (Saner & Yiu, 2003). At the same time, countries are deepening their cooperation for rule setting (e.g. WTO, ITU) and regional economic integration (e.g. NAFTA, EU, FTAA). Along these lines, the United Nations (UN) 2030 Agenda for the Sustainable Development Goals (SDGs) is an important political consensus document declaring the intention of UN Member States to work collectively towards sustainable development. Given that the UN estimates an additional $2.5 trillion a year of investment is needed to achieve the goals in developing countries alone (UNCTAD, 2014), the 2030 Agenda encourages dialogue and collaboration between the private sector, civil society and governmental bodies to address the most serious challenges to sustainable development facing humanity today (UN General Assembly, 2015). Introduced as one of the 17 core objectives (Goal 5: Gender Equality), reducing gender inequality can also serve as an effective foreign policy tool in the frame of International Economic Diplomacy.

In short, the 2030 SDG Agenda offers a framework for building global resilience to meet some of the significant challenges facing the world today, such as gender equality, and the GII provides policy-makers and practitioners a tool to assess the progress being made. The implementation of effective projects and responses to gender gaps also requires the disaggregation of the GII into its sub-components. As a result, gender data needs to be analysed based on the specific purposes and issues that are under consideration of government policy-makers and practitioners. Wicked problems such as gender inequality require multilateralism, and all tools within the diplomatic toolbox should be made available: diplomacy, partnerships, mediation, political dialogue, financing and global governance (Carius et al., 2018). As scholars in social innovation, our aim in this chapter is to highlight successful examples of projects and entrepreneurial approaches that have helped in reducing gender inequality around the world.

In the chapter, we delve into the GII and its components. We review some criticism that has been levied towards the GII and identify other measures and indices that have been developed to capture gender inequality. We illustrate how the GII informs concrete actions that empower women and reduce gender-based discrimination and inequality. To conclude, we offer a discussion of how social innovation can help government, non-profit and business actors move towards the 2030 SDG goal of gender equality.

2 Construction of the Gender Inequality Index (GII)

To understand whether progress is being made towards the policy objective of gender equality, relevant indicators and monitoring are required. This task is surprisingly difficult, not only due to conceptual complexities and deficient data but also since many dimensions of gender inequality do not lend themselves to quantitative measurement (Gaye et al., 2010). Since there is no universally accepted measure of gender inequality, most studies focus on specific elements of gender inequality to measure gaps in health, education, labour force participation and political activity.

At the Fourth World Conference on Women in 1995, the UNDP created the GDI and the GEM as first attempts to develop a comprehensive measure of gender inequality. However, most of the indicators to construct the GDI and GEM were ultimately found to be more suitable for developed countries and several indicators were not available in developing countries due to data constraints (Bardhan & Klasen, 1999, 2000; Dijkstra, 2002, 2006; Dijkstra & Hanmer, 2000; Klasen, 2006; Schüler, 2006). As a result, the UNDP made several improvements to both indices that eventually led to the creation of the Gender Inequality Index (GII) in 2010 (Gonzales et al., 2015). In the process, the new GII came to replace the GDI and GEM indices as the primary measure of gender inequality.

Gathering quality data at the global level introduces important trade-offs between data relevance and geographical coverage. Despite these constraints, the GII designers were able to identify relevant indicators for a reasonably large set of countries (138 countries in 2010) that cover most regions of the world (Permanyer, 2013).

The GII is a composite measure of gender inequality across three dimensions: reproductive health, empowerment and economic opportunity (or labour market). Indicators were selected based on their conceptual and practical relevance, data reliability, international comparability, reasonable country coverage and frequency of availability (Gonzales et al., 2015). The index uses five indicators across these dimensions, shown graphically in Fig. 1 (UNDP, 2019). Reproductive health indicators are captured by the maternal mortality ratio and the adolescent fertility rate. Empowerment is also measured by two indicators: (1) female and male shares of parliamentary seats, and (2) educational attainment at the secondary level (% of females and males aged 25 and older). Finally, economic opportunity is captured by a single indicator, i.e. labour force participation (UNDP, 2019).

The GII calculation method does not report absolute development achievement, but rather assesses a country's gender achievement and distance from the baseline of gender equality (Gaye et al., 2010). Ideal outcomes are set at zero for the adverse reproductive health outcomes (i.e. adolescent fertility and maternal mortality rates) and at parity with male achievements across the education, political and economic measures. According to the GII's development team, "the score can thus be interpreted as characterizing where a country lies in reference to normative

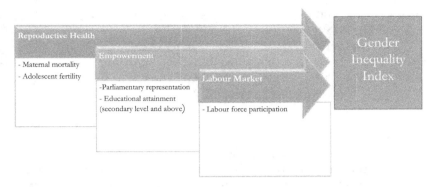

Fig. 1 Gender inequality index

ideals for key indicators of women's health, empowerment, and economic status" (Gaye et al., 2010, p. 9).

GII values range between 0 and 1: values closer to 1 indicate greater gender inequality. While not directly mapped to the Human Development Index (HDI), higher GII values can be interpreted to indicate a loss in human development (Gaye et al., 2010). Below each dimension of the index is explored in more detail.

2.1 Reproductive Health

Reproductive health is an important dimension to evaluate individual well-being levels that are typically absent in other UNDP composite indices such as the HDI, the Human Poverty Index (HPI), the GDI and the GEM. Reproductive health is captured by two measures: maternal mortality and adolescent fertility.

Maternal mortality. The maternal mortality ratio (MMR), defined as the number of women who die from pregnancy-related causes while pregnant or within 42 days of pregnancy termination per 100,000 live births, captures a leading cause of death and disability among women of reproductive age in developing countries. The data are estimated with a regression model using information on the proportion of maternal deaths among non-AIDS deaths in women ages 15–49, fertility, birth attendants and GDP. Current global estimates of maternal mortality suggest that more than 500,000 women die each year because of complications related to childbirth (UNICEF, 2008).

Adolescent fertility. Since women that have children at such young ages see their health and future economic opportunities diminished, the GII captures the risk of childbearing among adolescent women using the adolescent fertility rate (AFR), defined as the number of births per 1000 women aged 15–19.

Adolescence is a period of key transitions in life within a short period of time. Chief among these transitions for many girls is the start of sexual activity, marriage and childbearing. Concerns about adolescent childbearing include its association with heightened health risks for mothers and their infants and lower educational attainment and increased risk of poverty among women who become mothers during adolescence.

Sexual activity at an early age, before girls have adequate information on potential health risks, self-protection skills or access to reproductive health services, puts girls at an elevated risk of sexual and reproductive health and childbearing problems. Furthermore, young women are particularly vulnerable to sexual violence and coerced sex (Andersson et al., 2012; Song & Ji, 2010), unintended and unwanted pregnancy and abortion (Gómez et al., 2008; Murray et al., 2006). The start of childbearing in adolescence is closely tied to early marriage. Adolescent females who marry early are likely to participate in arranged marriages, to marry older men, to have less decision-making power and communication with their husbands and to be in polygamous unions (Santhya et al., 2010). Marriage can also exert pressures and expectations upon adolescents, including the expectation of immediate pregnancy upon marriage. Adolescents who marry early are also less likely to use contraceptives to delay a first pregnancy (Santhya et al., 2010) and are generally less likely than unmarried adolescents to use modern contraceptives (Blanc et al., 2009).

2.2 *Empowerment*

The women's empowerment movement has gained widespread momentum since the 1994 International Population Conference held in Cairo and has been gradually incorporated into the everyday parlance of national and international institutions. Although there are a number of critical elements related to empowerment, such as violence against women (inside and outside of the home), data availability and the lack of internationally consistent and comparable measures make empowerment difficult to measure (Gaye et al., 2010). As a result, the GII focusses on two widely available and important indicators: parliamentary representation and educational attainment.

Parliamentary representation. The political arena has historically been discriminatory to women across the world throughout all levels of government. Although measures in this area are admittedly sparse and provide a relatively crude measure of women's access to levers of power, estimates for parliamentary representation at the national level are suggestive of women's visibility in political leadership and society more generally (Permanyer, 2013). The measure represents the extent to which women can hold high offices and is measured by the percentage of parliamentary seats in a single or lower chamber held by women. While this measure has the broadest country coverage, it excludes political participation at the community and local levels.

Educational attainment. Education is widely perceived as an indicator of the status of women and perhaps even more importantly, as an agent for the empowerment of women. Although the gap between boys and girls is closing for secondary education, substantial differences in graduation rates persist across many countries (Duflo, 2012). Education, especially higher levels of attainment, fosters empowerment since it is associated with an individual's capacity to reflect, question and take action concerning their life circumstances. Educated women are thought to be more likely to engage in rewarding career options, use their voices in public debate and/or care for their health and that of their family. As such, education is particularly important in strengthening the agency of women (Permanyer, 2013). Educational attainment is measured as the percentage of people who completed education at the secondary level (female and male).

2.3 Labour Market

Labour force participation rate. To measure economic activity, the GII uses gender-specific labour force participation rates. This measure has come to replace the problematic gender-specific earned income component that was used both in the GDI and GEM, which were imputed based on questionable assumptions that led to misleading international comparisons (Bardhan & Klasen, 1999). While imperfect, the measurement of the labour force participation rate is much more reliable. One important caveat of using labour force participation rates is that it ignores the unpaid work contributions of women, which can be substantial in many economies (Gaye et al., 2010).

2.4 Criticism of the GII and Alternative Gender Inequality Measures

The GII is not without criticism. Notably, the GII integrates indicators that compare men and women with other indicators that pertain only to women. As a result, the health status of men is completely disregarded in the evaluation of gender inequality levels measured by the GII. Even if the GII designers claim that a value of 1 must be interpreted as the ideal achievement of MMR and AFR to attain gender equality, the practical implication is that men's health is artificially fixed at the highest possible level (Permanyer, 2013). Indeed, as illustrated in Permanyer (2013), countries with high MMR and AFR are strongly associated with lower life expectancies of men. It's therefore likely that the inclusion of men's health status variables would narrow the gender gaps observed in the GII. This argument does not diminish the importance of reproductive health variables, but rather emphasizes that the omission of men's health variables inevitably penalizes countries with high MMR and AFR scores (which also have lower levels of GDP per capita).

Other indices have also emerged from international organizations in recent years that attempt to measure gender inequality across countries. Although the GII is preferable to alternatives such as the GDI in which one of the main components is imputed rather than observed, other widely recognized indices propose a range of potential indicators that inform the gender inequality debate (Table 1).

The Global Gender Gap Index (GGGI) was created in 2006 by the World Economic Forum. The index covers four domains (economy, education, health and politics) through 14 indicators. Values range between 0 and 1 and higher scores indicate more unequal gender relations. Index values may be interpreted as a percentage that reveals how much of the gender gap has been closed in a given country. As of the 2018 report, data was available for 149 countries (WEF, 2018).

The Social Institutions and Gender Index (SIGI) was developed in 2010 using the Gender and Institutions Database by the OECD. The index covers five categories: family code, physical integrity, son preference,

Table 1 An overview of gender inequality indices and their indicators

Gender Inequality Index (UNDP)	Global Gender Gap Index (WEF)	Social Institutions and Gender Index (OECD)
Reproductive health	**Economic participation and opportunity**	**Family code**
Maternal mortality	Labour force participation*	Early marriage
Adolescent fertility	Ratio of wages for similar work	Polygamy
Empowerment	Ratio of earned income	Parental authority
Educational attainment (secondary and above)*	Ratio of legislators, senior officials and managers	Inheritance
Parliamentary representation*	Ratio of professional and technical workers	**Physical integrity**
Labor Market	**Educational attainment**	Female genital mutilation
Labour force participation*	Ratio of literacy rate	Violence against women
	Ratio of net primary school enrolment	**Son preference**
	Ratio of net secondary school enrolment	Missing women
	Ratio of gross tertiary school enrolment	**Civil liberties**
	Health and survival	Freedom of movement
	Sex ratio at birth	Freedom of dress
	Ratio in healthy life expectancy	**Ownership rights**
	Political empowerment	Access to land
	Ratio of seats in parliament*	Access to bank loans
	Ratio of ministerial level positions	Access to property
	Ratio of years with a female head of state (last 50 years)	

Note *denote overlap with other indices

civil liberties and ownership rights. These five domains cover a total of 12 indicators. They concern both formal institutions—rights and laws—and informal institutions—social and cultural practices. Each of the five categories is equally weighted but in-category weights differ due to the nonlinearity of indicators. Like the GGGI, values range from 0 to 1 and higher scores indicate more unequal gender relations. As of the 2019 report, data was available for 120 countries (OECD, 2019).

As illustrated in Table 1, three of the five GII indicators overlap with the GGGI. A recent study comparing these gender indices found that country rankings tend to have considerable overlap at the top and bottom but vary considerably in terms of indicator overlap. Methodological differences concern variation in indicator weighting, capping and aggregation of categories (Van Staveren, 2013). These differences lead the author to suggest that the GII is particularly well-suited to measure outcomes of various gender equality improvements across and within countries. In the next section, we assess GII outcomes and identify some of the innovative solutions driving the trend towards gender parity.

3 View and Applications

In this section, we examine the GII and its sub-components in detail and highlight several applications that stakeholders have developed in recent years to improve gender equality throughout the world. All analysis is based on publicly available source data downloaded from the UNDP Human Development Reports (http://hdr.undp.org/en/data). We cluster countries by region based on The World Bank classification (World Bank, 2019).

To avoid bias in the interpretation of the data, we report both absolute and percentage change. In short, an indicator with a large absolute change may not necessarily have a large relative change and vice versa. Hence in analysing relative change figures for different groups, it would be useful to also look at the absolute change or the initial value from which the changes were computed, to reach a more balanced conclusion on how the indicators have changed over time.

3.1 GII Empirical Overview

Of the 122 countries for which the necessary data was available to generate a GII score for the years 1995 and 2017, the GII global average has been reduced from 0.47 to 0.33, a reduction of 29.7% (see Table 2). As illustrated by Fig. 2, with the exception of Papua New Guinea, every country has made some improvement over the 22-year timeframe. According to the GII, the most gender-equal countries in 2017 were Switzerland, Denmark and Sweden/Netherlands (tied for third). In contrast, the bottom three countries were Papua New Guinea, Mali and Central African Republic.

Table 2 GII by region

Region	n	1995 average	2017 average	Absolute change	Percentage change
East Asia and Pacific	12	0.48	0.36	(0.12)	−25.9
Eastern Europe and Central Asia	22	0.39	0.21	(0.18)	−46.4
Latin America and Caribbean	20	0.51	0.38	(0.12)	−24.4
Middle East and North Africa	11	0.58	0.36	(0.21)	−36.8
Western Europe and Other Developed	22	0.17	0.08	(0.09)	−53.5
South Asia	7	0.67	0.46	(0.20)	−30.3
Sub-Saharan Africa	25	0.65	0.54	(0.11)	−17.0
Global GII	**122**	**0.47**	**0.33**	**(0.14)**	**−29.7**

Note Table constructed by authors based on source data from the UNDP Human Development Reports n = number of countries

As shown in Table 2, on a percentage basis, Western Europe & Other Developed countries (i.e. United States, Japan, Australia, Canada and New Zealand) have made the most improvements, lowering gender inequality by 53.5% on average. In absolute terms, the Middle East and North Africa (MENA) and South Asia regions have made the most progress towards gender equality during the observed time period, reducing gender inequality by 0.21 and 0.20, respectively.

Country performance is highlighted in Table 3. The top three performers in terms of absolute reduction in gender inequality are United Arab Emirates, Turkey and Kuwait. By contrast, the bottom three included Syria, Thailand and Papua New Guinea. The top three countries by percentage change during the observed period include Slovenia, South Korea and Cyprus, while the bottom three remained the same as in the absolute change case (see Table 3).

Despite marginal improvements in recent years, results from the GII illustrate that gender inequality has been an enduring issue for both emerging markets and developed economies. Current estimates suggest

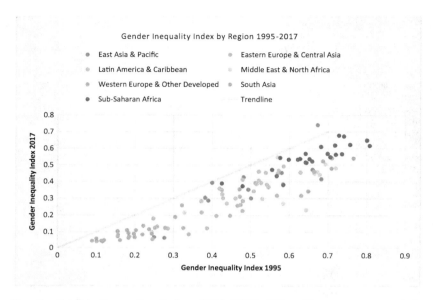

Fig. 2 Gender Inequality Index 1995–2017 (*Note* Figure constructed by authors based on source data from the UNDP Human Development Reports)

that at the current rate of change, the global gender gap will take 108 years to close; economic parity remains some 202 years off (Cann, 2018). Given the slow rate of progress to date, the 2030 SDG objective of gender parity is likely going to be difficult to achieve.

The SDG goals serve as a useful framework to categorize and describe the world's greatest challenges and their fulfilment depends on multi-sector partnerships involving government, the private sector and civil society. The United Nations estimates an additional $2.5 trillion a year of investment is needed to achieve the goals in developing countries (UNCTAD, 2014). As a result, development aid and public-sector support alone are likely inadequate to meet the SDG 2030 goals. Instead, the application of novel solutions that change the underlying dynamics of society to create a more level playing field of incentives to innovate, educate and invest is therefore likely to play a large role in transforming gender dynamics and helping to achieve gender parity. In this vein, social innovation provides one potential avenue to leapfrog the current pace of change and kickstart rapid systemic change.

Table 3 Top and worst performing countries

Top and worst performers (country)	1995 average	2017 average	Absolute change	Percentage change
Top 3 performers (Absolute Change)				
United Arab Emirates	0.64	0.23	(0.41)	−64.0
Turkey	0.63	0.32	(0.31)	−49.8
Kuwait	0.58	0.27	(0.31)	−53.8
Bottom 3 performers (Absolute Change)				
Syria	0.57	0.55	(0.02)	−3.9
Thailand	0.40	0.39	(0.01)	−1.8
Papua New Guinea	0.67	0.74	0.07	10.1
Top 3 performers (Percentage Change)				
Slovenia	0.25	0.05	(0.19)	−78.0
South Korea	0.28	0.06	(0.21)	−77.3
Cyprus	0.34	0.09	(0.26)	−75.0
Bottom 3 performers (Percentage Change)				
Syria	0.57	0.55	(0.02)	−3.9
Thailand	0.40	0.39	(0.01)	−1.8
Papua New Guinea	0.67	0.74	0.07	10.1

Note Table constructed by authors based on source data from the UNDP Human Development Reports

We follow van Wijk et al. (2019, p. 889) who define social innovation as "the agentic, relational, situated, and multilevel process to develop, promote, and implement novel solutions to social problems in ways that are directed toward producing profound change in institutional contexts … who view social innovation as embedded and self-reflective, and that it may be coordinated and collaborative, or that it may be the emergent product of accumulation, collective bricolage and muddling through daily work."

Often, social innovation takes the form of applying novel market solutions to global social and environmental problems by creating or improving products, services, processes, business models and markets to more effectively and efficiently respond to unmet societal needs (Nicholls & Murdock, 2012). The value created accrues primarily to society as a whole rather than private individuals and focusses on actions that have the potential for systemic transformation (Phills et al., 2008).

Social innovation embodies a mindset driven by purpose, openness, partnership, innovation and accountability to develop solutions that allow excluded people to participate in the economy while conserving and replenishing natural capital (Moore et al., 2014).

What has gender equality got to do with social innovation? The rapid development and diffusion of innovation, including digital technologies, are challenging the systems and capacity of traditional societal institutions. The testing and scaling of innovation and technology require agile thinking, continuously learning from research and constant adaptation. How can we better harness socially innovative ideas and methods to advance gender equality? In this section, we explore this question by looking at specific interventions that pertain to GII indicators and tie them to three dimensions of gender equality: (1) resources, (2) attitudes, and (3) power.

3.2 Reproductive Health

3.2.1 Mother Mortality

The GII data indicate that the average rate of mother mortality has decreased from 341.3 deaths per 100,000 live births to 169.5 deaths over the 1990–2015 timeframe, a reduction of 50.3%. Compared to the trendline in Fig. 3, nearly every country reduced the incidence of mother morality from 1990 to 2015.

In absolute numbers, South Asian and Sub-Saharan African countries made the biggest strides over the 1990–2015 timeframe (Table 4). At the regional level, South Asia transitioned from an average of 624.1 deaths per 100,000 live births to 161.4, corresponding to an impressive reduction of 462.7 deaths per 100,000 births in the 25-year timeframe. Similarly, the Sub-Saharan African country average improved from an

Fig. 3 Mother mortality rate by region 1990–2015 (*Note* Figure constructed by authors based on source data from the UNDP Human Development Reports)

Table 4 Mother mortality rate by region

Region	n	1995 average	2017 average	Absolute change	Percentage change
East Asia and Pacific	23	283.0	91.5	(191.6)	−67.7
Eastern Europe and Central Asia	31	43.9	18.8	(25.1)	−57.1
Latin America and Caribbean	30	139.5	87.4	(52.1)	−37.4
Middle East and North Africa	20	129.2	64.8	(64.4)	−49.8
Western Europe and Other Developed	22	10.2	6.7	(3.5)	−34.7
South Asia	9	624.1	161.4	(462.7)	−74.1
Sub-Saharan Africa	47	886.0	482.0	(404.0)	−45.6
Global MMR	**182**	**341.3**	**169.5**	**171.8**	**50.3**

Note Table constructed by authors based on source data from the UNDP Human Development Reports n = number of countries initial average of 886.0 deaths per 100,000 live births to 482.0 over the same duration.

By country, the top three performers in terms of absolute reduction in mother mortality are Sierra Leone, Eritrea and Rwanda. By contrast, the bottom three included Bahamas, Tonga and Guyana. The top three countries by percentage change during the observed period include Maldives, Belarus and Kazakhstan, while the bottom three remained the same as in the absolute change case (see Table 5).

Table 5 Top and worst performing countries (Mother mortality rate)

Top and worst performers (country)	1995 average	2017 average	Absolute change	Percentage change
Top 3 performers (Absolute Change)				
Sierra Leone	2630	1360	(1270)	−48.3
Eritrea	1590	501	(1089)	−68.5
Rwanda	1300	290	(1010)	−77.7
Bottom 3 performers (Absolute Change)				
Bahamas	46	80	34	73.9
Tonga	75	124	49	65.3
Guyana	171	229	58	33.9
Top 3 performers (Percentage Change)				
Maldives	677	68	(609)	−90.0
Belarus	33	4	(29)	−87.9
Kazakhstan	78	12	(66)	−84.6
Bottom 3 performers (Percentage Change)				
Guyana	171	229	58	33.9
Tonga	75	124	49	65.3
Bahamas	46	80	34	73.9

Note Table constructed by authors based on source data from the UNDP Human Development Reports

With 1360 mothers dying per 100,000 live births, Sierra Leone has the highest MMR in the world. According to the latest estimates from 2015, 1 in 17 mothers in Sierra Leone has a lifetime risk of death associated with childbirth (Mason, 2016). Although Sierra Leone still has the highest MMR worldwide, the country has made tremendous progress since 1990, when the MMR of 2630 deaths per 100,000 births was nearly double the current value. To further reduce the MMR and achieve the SDG 2030 target of less than 70 deaths per 100,000 live births, a wide range of actors have been engaged to create equitable access to high-quality care by skilled staff during pregnancy and childbirth.

International bodies working in partnership to tackle the issue include UNICEF and the European Union. With EU funds, UNICEF has been supporting the training health workers and increasing their capacity. The support further invests in the provision of equipment and supplies that are needed to deliver quality health care and improve maternal and new-born health services. The programme is also establishing a network or care centres to facilitate the shift away from Traditional Birth Attendants (TBAs), typically senior women from the community, who are not skilled to address the major killers of mothers (Mason, 2016). To this end, the partnership is providing financial support for doctors, including obstetricians and gynaecologists, to undertake further studies in nearby Ghana to further develop skills and knowledge in the birth delivery process and post-natal care. Finally, the programme also intends to build basic health infrastructure by funding the construction of 16 facilities, 5 of which will be dedicated for Basic Emergency Obstetrical and Neonatal Care (BEmONC) (Mason, 2016).

A project from Concern Worldwide, an international NGO, also takes a pragmatic approach to tackle the crisis in Sierra Leone. Since 2014, Concern Worldwide, with funding from the Bill and Melinda Gates Foundation, has trained more than 200 TBAs and rebranded them as MNHPs (maternal and new-born health promoters) (Young, 2016). Rather than delivering babies in isolation, MNHPs are trained to counsel mothers on prenatal care, check for danger signs and refer at-risk mothers to healthcare facilities. The programme also included a complementary business model to incentivize MNHPs in their new roles. Half of the MNHPs received business training and a loan in the form of a start-up basket of health and baby products, valued at approximately USD30, to sell during their home visits (Concern Worldwide, 2016). During monthly meetings, MNHPs made loan payments and had the opportunity to purchase more products to build their businesses. An initial evaluation of the programme suggests positive effects on three post-delivery outcomes: breastfeeding initiation, post-natal care for the mother and post-natal care for the infant. The programme also indicates that providing a business case for MNHPs and incentivizing MNHP visits are more likely to refer women showing signs of risk to health facilities (Concern Worldwide, 2016).

3.2.2 Adolescent Fertility Ratio

At the global level, GII data indicate that the average rate of adolescent fertility has decreased from 80.4 births per 1000 women aged 15–19 to 46.9 births over the 1990–2016 timeframe, corresponding to a reduction of 41.7%. As illustrated in Fig. 4, nearly every country has reduced the incidence of adolescent fertility over the timeframe.

Table 6 reports changes in AFR by region. The largest reduction at the regional level (in both absolute terms and on a percentage basis) came from South Asia, where the AFR fell from 121.2 to 37.1 (a reduction of 69.4%). In absolute terms, Sub-Saharan Africa reported the second largest reduction in AFR, from 141.4 in 1990 to 94.7 in 2017. Regardless

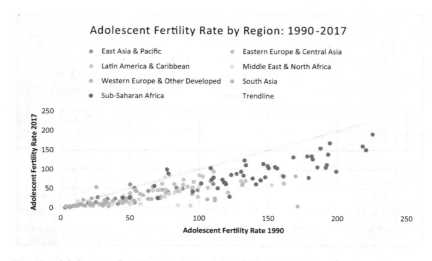

Fig. 4 Adolescent fertility rate by region 1990–2017 (*Note* Figure constructed by authors based on source data from the UNDP Human Development Reports)

Table 6 Adolescent fertility rate by region

Region	n	1990 average	2017 average	Absolute change	Percentage change
East Asia and Pacific	24	47.5	28.7	(18.8)	−39.7
Eastern Europe and Central Asia	31	44.7	21.0	(23.6)	−52.9
Latin America and Caribbean	31	93.0	57.3	(35.7)	−38.4
Middle East and North Africa	20	59.4	24.7	(34.7)	−58.4
Western Europe and Other Developed	22	18.4	8.1	(10.2)	−55.6
South Asia	9	121.2	37.1	(84.1)	−69.4
Sub-Saharan Africa	48	141.4	94.7	(46.7)	−33.0
Global Adolescent Fertility Rate	**185**	**80.4**	**46.9**	**(33.6)**	**−41.7**

Note Table constructed by authors based on source data from the UNDP Human Development Reports n = number of countries

of starting point, every global region reduced the AFR by at least one-third over the 1990–2017 timeframe, illustrating the problem's global reach and need for continued support to ensure the 2030 target to ensure universal access to sexual and reproductive health-care services.

By country, the top three performers in terms of absolute reduction in adolescent fertility are Maldives Gabon and Gambia. By contrast, the bottom three included Lesotho, Somalia and Azerbaijan. The top three countries by percentage change during the observed period include Maldives, Oman and Saudi Arabia while the bottom three are Somalia, Malta and Azerbaijan (see Table 7).

Reducing adolescent fertility and addressing the multiple factors underlying it are essential for improving sexual and reproductive health and the social and economic well-being of adolescents. Underlying factors typically include early marriage, the timing and context of first sex, contraceptive use and education. Development goals emphasize the reduction

Table 7 Top and worst performing countries (Adolescent fertility rate)

Top and worst performers (country)	1990 average	2017 average	Absolute change	Percentage change
Top 3 performers (Absolute Change)				
Maldives	171.3	5.8	(165.5)	−96.6
Gabon	199.1	95.3	(103.8)	−52.1
Gambia	179.2	79.2	(100.0)	−55.8
Bottom 3 performers (Absolute Change)				
Lesotho	77.7	89.5	11.8	15.2
Somalia	76.7	100.1	23.4	30.5
Azerbaijan	25.7	53.5	27.8	108.2
Top 3 performers (Percentage Change)				
Maldives	171.3	5.8	(165.5)	−96.6
Oman	93.9	7.1	(86.8)	−92.4
Saudi Arabia	84.7	7.8	(76.9)	−90.8
Bottom 3 performers (Percentage Change)				
Somalia	76.7	100.1	23.4	30.5
Malta	12.4	16.6	4.2	33.9
Azerbaijan	25.7	53.5	27.8	108.2

Note Table constructed by authors based on source data from the UNDP Human Development Reports

of early childbearing, the expansion of access to reproductive health and investing in the human capital of youth, especially girls.

Given the complexity of adolescent fertility, social innovations to reduce the incidence of adolescent fertility have emerged from a wide range of actors through a range of implementation strategies. To combat sexual violence against women at a global scale, the Center for Women's Global Leadership (CWGL) launched the 16 Days of Activism Against Gender Violence in 1991, a campaign that has since run every year from

25 November, the International Day for the Elimination of Violence against Women, to 10 December, Human Rights Day (Thompson, 2017). In the first 20 years alone, more than 3700 organizations have participated across 164 countries (Thompson, 2017). The campaign aims to complement the local and national actions and campaigns and change attitudes at a more global, systemic level, while contributing to a global feminist solidarity around a shared goal to end violence against women.

3.3 Empowerment

3.3.1 Parliamentary Representation

Globally, the GII data indicate that women have increased their percentage of parliamentary seats from an average of 15.6% in 2005 to 21.4% in 2017, an increase of 5.8 absolute percentage points equivalent to growth of 36.9% over the 12-year timeframe (see Table 8). Although female participation in country-level politics has increased substantially

Table 8 Parliamentary representation by region (reports percentage of women in parliament)

Region	n	2005 average	2017 average	Absolute change	Percentage change
East Asia and Pacific	25	9.8	14.1	4.3	43.4
Eastern Europe and Central Asia	29	14.2	20.8	6.6	46.4
Latin America and Caribbean	33	18.3	25.1	6.7	36.8
Middle East and North Africa	17	6.8	14.9	8.1	118.2
Western Europe and Other Developed	26	26.2	31.5	5.3	20.3
South Asia	9	11.9	15.0	3.1	25.6
Sub-Saharan Africa	46	15.8	21.1	5.3	33.8
Global Female Parliamentary Representation	**185**	**15.6**	**21.4**	**5.8**	**36.9**

Note Table constructed by authors based on source data from the UNDP Human Development Reports n = number of countries when aggregated, progress is far from universal as 32 countries (nearly one-fifth of the 185 countries on which data is available) saw the percentage of women in parliament decrease over the time period (see Fig. 5).

Table 8 reports parliamentary representation by region. Aggregation at the regional level suggest that Western Europe and Other Developed countries have the highest absolute participation of women in parliament, on average making up 31.5% of representatives. Latin American countries are not far behind, with 25.1% on average. On a percentage basis, MENA, Eastern Europe & Central Asia and East Asia & Pacific regions have made the most progress with increases of 118.2, 46.4 and 43.4%, respectively.

The use of gender quotas appears to be an important mechanism to increase the participation of women in national parliaments. An interesting case is that of the Western Balkans, illustrated graphically in Fig. 6. Since the early 2000s, throughout the Western Balkans, gender quotas require political parties to include at least 30% women in their lists of

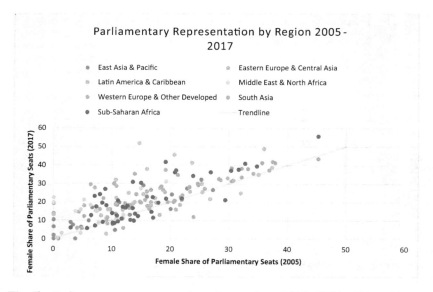

Fig. 5 Parliamentary representation by region 2005–2017 (*Note* Figure constructed by authors based on source data from the UNDP Human Development Reports)

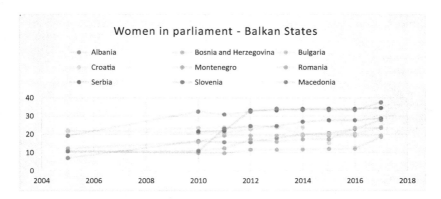

Fig. 6 Parliamentary representation in Balkan States (*Note* Figure constructed by authors based on source data from the UNDP Human Development Reports)

candidates (40% in Macedonia & Bosnia and Herzegovina), although the quotas are not always strictly followed (Duhaček et al., 2019). Although representation does not automatically imply that gender equality and women's rights are promoted and defended, it does appear that women in the Western Balkans have more decision-making power and influence than ever before, as their representation in parliaments has grown.

In terms of visibility, the European Parliament (EP) has repeatedly drawn attention to the situation of women in the Western Balkans. In 2008, the EP adopted a resolution, stressing the importance of NGOs and women's organizations in finding adequate solutions and contributing to the democratic processes in the region (Lilyanova, 2018). Additionally, the EP called on the European Commission to ensure that its policy for strengthening Western Balkan NGOs should be particularly focussed on the empowerment of women's participation in civil society, even advancing a 2013 resolution that called for measures to increase awareness through the media, public campaigns and education programmes to eliminate gender stereotypes and promote women's active participation in all spheres of life (Lilyanova, 2018).

The three countries with the highest female participation in parliament include Rwanda, Bolivia and Cuba, which have rates of 49% or more. Top performers by absolute change and percentage change are reported in Table 9. By country, the top three performers in terms of absolute reduction in parliamentary representation are Bolivia, Nicaragua and Nepal.

Table 9 Top and worst performing countries (parliamentary representation)

Top and worst performers (country)	2005 average	2017 average	Absolute change	Percentage change
Top 3 performers (Absolute Change)				
Bolivia	14.7	51.8	37.1	252.4
Nicaragua	20.7	45.7	25.0	120.8
Nepal	6.4	29.6	23.2	362.5
Bottom 3 performers (Absolute Change)				
Grenada	32.1	25.0	(7.1)	−22.1
Seychelles	29.4	21.2	(8.2)	−27.9
Liechtenstein	24.0	12.0	(12.0)	−50.0
Top 3 performers (Percentage Change)				
United Arab Emirates	0.1	22.5	22.4	22,400.0
Saudi Arabia	0.1	19.9	19.8	19,800.0
Kyrgyzstan	0.1	19.2	19.1	19,100.0
Bottom 3 performers (Percentage Change)				
Vanuatu	3.8	0.1	(3.7)	−97.4
Papua New Guinea	0.9	0.1	(0.8)	−88.9
Haiti	9.1	2.7	(6.4)	−70.3

Note Table constructed by authors based on source data from the UNDP Human Development Reports

By contrast, the bottom three included Grenada, Seychelles and Lichtenstein. The top three countries by percentage change during the observed period include United Arab Emirates, Saudi Arabia and Kyrgyzstan while the bottom three are Vanuatu, Papua New Guinea and Haiti.

The South American country of Bolivia offers another particularly successful example of gender quotas. Bolivia has increased its female parliamentary representation from 14.7% in 2005 to 51.8% in 2017. Origins of this seismic shift began with the passing of the "Quotas Act" passed in March 1997, which established an obligation for political parties to include women candidates for at least 30% of elective posts. The measures were formally adopted in The Political Parties Act (1999), which states the same principle of affirmative action in paragraph 4 of Article 19, "...the parties shall establish a quota of at least thirty percent women on all the party's decision-making levels and as regards the candidates for representative office." As Bolivia adopted a new constitution in 2009, a new provision formalized and guaranteed the principle of parity and alternation between male and female candidates in national, departmental, municipal and judicial electoral processes. The 2009 Constitution enshrined these progressive values from the point of view of gender and ethnicity, leading to unprecedented female participation in the political system.

From 1982 to 2009, only 83 of 910 deputies (9%) and only 9 of 182 senators (5%) were elected women (UNDP, 2014). In 1993, prior to the introduction of the electoral quotas, women representation reached a historical high of just under 9%. In 1997, with the application of the 30% quota of women on candidate lists, women's participation rose to 13 incumbents and 28 substitute deputies, or 11.5% of the parliament. By 2009, under the parity and alternation principles, over 30% of the parliament (both chambers) was composed of women, which has continued to the present day where gender equality (at least in terms of representation) has been achieved.

3.3.2 Educational Attainment

Globally, the GII data indicate that the gender gap related to secondary education has been reduced from 6.3% in 2000 to 3.6% in 2017, a decrease of 43.2% over the 17-year timeframe. Although these figures illustrate substantial progress in evening the playing field between men and women in terms of educational attainment, more work is needed to ensure universal access to secondary education. As of 2017, only 62.6% of women and 66.2% of men had completed some secondary education.

Figure 7 illustrates how the gender gap has changed for countries from 2000 to 2017. To put the gender gap in perspective, each observation (i.e. size of the bubble) is scaled by the total educational achievement within a given country. For countries on the left side of the y-axis, the rate of female secondary education outpaced that of their male counterparts

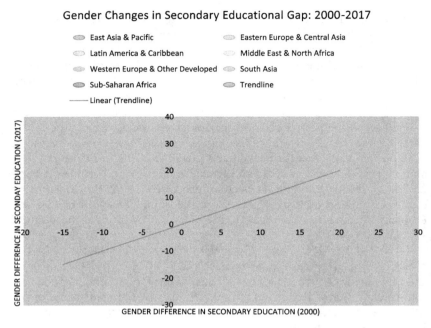

Fig. 7 Education gender gap (*Note* Figure constructed by authors based on source data from the UNDP Human Development Reports)

in the year 2000. Similarly, for countries below the x-axis, women educational rates were higher than male educational rates for the year 2017. Most countries fall into the upper right quadrant of the graph, illustrating that a significant gender gap still exists at the global level, although most countries fall below the trendline, indicating that progress has been made over the 2000–2017 time period.

Results at the regional level indicate that Latin America & Caribbean and Western Europe & Other Developed countries have the lowest gender gap in educational outcomes (Table 10). Indeed, Latin America even shows higher educational outcomes for women relative to men in 2017. To put gender differences in perspective, the total educational achievement is also presented in Table 10 (a maximum score of 200 indicates that 100% of women and 100% of men attain some secondary education). In terms of progress in reducing the gender gap, the MENA, East Asia & Pacific and Eastern Europe appear to have made the most

Table 10 Education gap by region

Region	n	2000 average	2017 average	Absolute change	Percentage change	Total educational achievement
East Asia and Pacific	18	7.0	3.0	(4.1)	−58.0	127.46
Eastern Europe and Central Asia	26	6.7	2.8	(3.9)	−58.4	184.20
Latin America and Caribbean	27	1.1	(0.7)	(1.8)	−159.6	121.39
Middle East and North Africa	18	8.1	2.0	(6.1)	−75.3	117.46
Western Europe and Other Developed	23	4.4	1.1	(3.2)	−73.9	178.54
South Asia	8	11.1	12.5	1.4	12.6	98.04
Sub-Saharan Africa	32	9.1	8.6	(0.5)	−5.9	69.36
Global Education Gap	152	6.3	3.6	(2.7)	−43.2	128.85

Note Table constructed by authors based on source data from the UNDP Human Development Reports n = number of countries

progress on an absolute basis, with absolute reductions in the gender gap ranging from 3.9 to 6.1%. On a percentage basis, Latin American & Caribbean, MENA and Western Europe and Other Developed countries have made the most progress, reducing the gender gap by 159.6, 75.3, and 73.9%, respectively (Table 11).

By 2017, six countries (Austria, Canada, Estonia, Finland, Iceland and Luxembourg) had achieved universal secondary educational outcomes for both men and women (i.e. 100% of boys and girls acquire at least some secondary education). Furthermore, during the observation period, 31 countries were able to achieve gender parity in terms of secondary educational achievement. Countries with the largest educational gender gap today, all with a gap of more than 20%, include: DRC Congo, Togo, Afghanistan, India, Turkey, Liberia and Pakistan.

Table 11 Labour force participation gap by region

Region	n	1990 average	2017 average	Absolute change	Percentage change	Total labour force participation
East Asia and Pacific	22	22.5	18.2	(4.3)	−19.0	130.58
Eastern Europe and Central Asia	31	19.4	16.9	(2.5)	−12.7	116.70
Latin America and Caribbean	29	36.5	24.6	(11.8)	−32.5	130.80
Middle East and North Africa	20	54.0	45.7	(8.3)	−15.4	105.69
Western Europe and Other Developed	22	22.8	11.1	(11.7)	−51.3	123.36
South Asia	9	50.5	41.7	(8.7)	−17.3	117.32
Sub-Saharan Africa	47	19.0	13.2	(5.8)	−30.6	134.75
Labour Force Participation Gap	**180**	**28.2**	**21.1**	**(7.2)**	**−25.4**	**125.00**

Note Table constructed by authors based on source data from the UNDP Human Development Reports n = number of countries

One of the most challenging times for students is puberty, when the body goes through multiple changes as it makes the transition to adulthood. These developments can be accompanied by the added pressure of cultural expectations for starting a family life. A 2014 United Nations Educational, Scientific and Cultural Organization (UNESCO) report estimates that one in ten girls in Sub-Saharan Africa misses school during their menstrual cycle (UNESCO, 2014). By some estimates, this amounts to 20% of a given school year. Worse still, many girls drop out of school altogether once they begin menstruating (Sommer, 2010).

As a result, students (and young women in particular) need access to information on hygiene and sanitation. The information that students often receive is selective and shaped by taboos. In many cases, the education sector avoids the issue by considering it a private matter or a problem to be addressed within the family. It may come as no surprise then to learn that over 300 million women in India do not use sanitary pads and that 71% of girls in the country report having no knowledge of menstruation before their first period (Dasra & USAID, 2014).

In this context, Mumbai-based Aakar Innovations was established in 2010. Driven by a mission to provide access to affordable, biodegradable sanitary pads and menstrual health education to women and girls in rural India, Aakar developed India's first certified 100% compostable sanitary pad (Aakar, 2019). The sanitary pads are manufactured by women self-groups who then also distribute them among other women in the village. Aakar also raises awareness and intends to boost confidence, ease pain, save lives and increase the social and economic opportunities for girls and women. Their business model works as a platform integrator by selling machines to women Self Help Groups and ensuring the timely availability of raw materials at the low cost and best prices. Aakar also has a non-profit arm that engages with villages to generate community awareness, build the capacity of village micro-entrepreneurs and ensure distribution to the last mile.

3.4 Labour Market

3.4.1 Labour Force Participation

Women have been steadily increasing their participation in economic affairs and the workplace. Globally, GII data indicate that the gender gap related to labour force participation has been reduced from 28.2% in 1990 to 22.1% in 2017, a decrease of 25.4% over the timeframe. Although these figures illustrate the rising role of women in the workforce, critical measures such as compensation and activity in the informal sector are not captured by the GII indicator. With that caveat, as of 2017, 52% of women and 73% of men were active in the labour force as of 2017.

Figure 8 illustrates country-level changes for the gender gap related to labour force participation between 1990 and 2017. To put the gender gap in perspective, each observation (i.e. size of the bubble) is scaled by the total labour force participation within a given country. For countries on the left side of the y-axis, the rate of women in the labour force outpaced that of their male counterparts in the year 1990. Similarly, for countries below the x-axis, the labour force participation of women was higher than men in 2017. Most countries fall into the upper right quadrant of the graph, illustrating that a significant gender gap still exists at the global

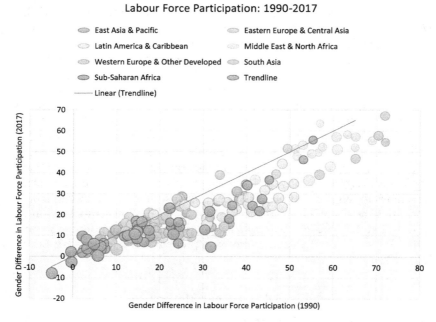

Fig. 8 Labour force participation gender gap (*Note* Figure constructed by authors based on source data from the UNDP Human Development Reports)

level, although most countries fall below the trendline, indicating that progress has been made over the 1990–2017 time period.

Aggregation at the regional level suggests that Western Europe & Other Developed countries and Sub-Saharan Africa have the lowest gender gap in terms of labour force participation, with gaps of 11.1 and 13.2%, respectively. The highest gender gaps in workforce exist in MENA and South Asia, with 2017 averages of 45.7 and 41.7%, respectively. On a percentage basis, Western Europe & Other Developed countries, Latin America & Caribbean and Sub-Saharan Africa regions have made the most progress with decreases of 51.3, 32.5, and 30.6%, respectively, from 1990 to 2017.

At the country level, only three countries achieved gender parity in labour force participation: Mozambique, Burundi and Rwanda. By contrast, 15 countries (all from South Asia and MENA) reported a gender gap of 50 percentage points or more for labour force participation. Syria, Afghanistan and Yemen reported the highest gender gaps.

One company trying to change this paradigm in the Arab world is Glowork, a start-up that integrates women into the workforce. Started in 2011 by Khalid Alkhudair, a former KPMG auditor, Glowork is attempting to break down barriers about the types of jobs for women. Leading these changes can result in pushback from more conservative parties in Saudi Arabia. In 2010, a year before starting Glowork, Alkhudair advised a client to hire 11 cashiers at Panda supermarkets in Jeddah (Glowork, 2019). This led to a prominent religious cleric calling for a boycott against the stores. Although women working as cashiers is now a more common sight in Saudi Arabia, Glowork also has focussed on "virtual offices" that allow women to work from home, a benefit in linking rural areas to the labour market (Glowork, 2019).

Integrating women into the workforce is also a considerable challenge in even the most developed economies. A common barrier to increasing women participation in the workforce is childbirth and early childcare, where women are much more likely to take time off to raise children. To help women "relaunch" their careers, Anne Zacharias created iRelaunch in 2007. The company provides career re-entry strategies for professionals returning to work after a career break. Similar to Glowork, iRelaunch serves as a bridge between professionals looking to re-enter the workforce and companies looking for qualified workers. The company also facilitates access to career coaches and experienced resume writers and has built a supportive online community where job seekers encourage each other and provide advice and potential leads. iRelaunch only charges job seekers for its "Return to Work Roadmap" programme, a five-phase programme that offers a structured step-by-step guide to re-entering the workforce (iRelaunch, 2019).

4 Discussion

In this chapter, we have examined one measure of the progress being made towards gender equality, the UNDP's Gender Inequality Index. We examined the theoretical underpinnings of the GII's sub-components and how these indicators are practically constructed. We then illustrated some of the shortcomings of the GII and highlighted two additional indices that inform the debate on gender inequality. Finally, we illustrated where gender inequality has been reduced according to GII measures and offered some examples of concrete actions that are attempting to reduce gender inequality.

In terms of improving the index, we believe the GII should drop (absolute) "women-only" indicators (i.e. MMR and AFR) and only include (relative) "men-versus-women" indicators. As already covered in our criticism of the GII, we argue that the inclusion of MMR and AFR penalize poorer countries where health outcomes are worse for both men and women. Thus, we suggest, in line with Benería and Permanyer (2010) and Klasen and Schüler (2011), to replace MMR and AFR with the gender-specific life expectancies at birth—a widely used indicator in previous global gender inequality assessments. Realizing that reproductive health conditions affect women and men differently, it is a conceptual and methodological challenge to identify and construct gender-specific variables that can easily be integrated into gender inequality indices.

Overall, the GII indicates that gender inequality is being reduced, albeit too slowly to achieve the current 2030 SDG targets of gender parity. Of the 122 countries for which the necessary data was available to generate a GII score for the years 1995 and 2017, the GII global average was reduced by 29.7%, from 0.47 to 0.33. Performance across each sub-indicator also showed measurable progress to the goal of gender equality, with considerable progress being made with respect to the reproductive health indicators of mother mortality and adolescent fertility.

For each indicator, we identified some key social innovations taking place that aim to reduce gender inequality. These innovations sometimes operate through activist and political action, such as the imposition of gender quotas to increase the political power of women in national governments. Other times, social innovations may stem from bottom-up approaches, such as the start-up ventures that aim to reintegrate women into the workplace or empower women to take control over their financial situations. Social innovations can also originate from the integrated actions of development agencies with local communities, such as the re-tooling and training of Traditional Birth Attendants who now offer women in Sierra Leone modern medical advice and can refer women to well-equipped medical facilities in case of any problems during pregnancy or post-natal care.

Finding solutions to achieve the 2030 goal of gender parity requires collaboration and dialogue between many actors. We hope that this chapter has illustrated a few of the ways that these stakeholders are coming together to organize responses to gender inequality. We believe that social innovation provides several tools for public bodies to engage civil society and the private business sector, which ultimately can crowd-in resources that would otherwise be unavailable to tackle global challenges such as gender inequality. Rather than a focus on traditional economic diplomacy instruments such as large-scale development projects, trade tariffs or foreign-direct investment, we suggest that seeding and scaling local changemakers and social entrepreneurs can serve as an additional economic diplomacy tool that change local attitudes and behaviours, create access to improved health services and influence gender paradigms that prohibit the economic and political engagement of women.

Gender equity is an intrinsic dimension of human development. Women and girls represent half of the world's population and, therefore, also half of its potential. If girls and women are systematically denied freedoms and opportunities, our societies will never reach their full human potential. Additionally, empowering women also has been linked to greater economic prosperity and development. Although gender equality has now been at the forefront of the global agenda for some decades, further investments in women and girls are required to promote long-term opportunities for growth prospects and human development.

References

Aakar. (2019). Aakar website. Retrieved September 4, 2019, from https://aakarinnovations.com/

Andersson, N., Paredes-Solís, S., & Milne, D. (2012). Prevalence and risk factors for forced or coerced sex among school-going youth: National cross-sectional studies in 10 southern African countries in 2003 and 2007. *British Medical Journal Open, 2*(2), 1–9.

Bardhan, K., & Klasen, S. (1999). UNDP's gender-related indices: A critical review. *World Development, 27*(6), 985–1010.

Bardhan, K., & Klasen, S. (2000). On UNDP's revisions to the Gender-Related Development Index. *Journal of Human Development, 1*(2), 191–195.

Benería, L., & Permanyer, I. (2010). The measurement of socio-economic gender inequality revisited. *Development and Change, 41*(3), 375–399.

Blanc, A. K., Tsui, A. O., Croft, T. N., & Trevitt, J. L. (2009). Patterns and trends in adolescents' contraceptive use and discontinuation in developing countries and comparisons with adult women. *International Perspectives on Sexual and Reproductive Health, 35*(2), 63–71.

Cann, O. (2018, December 18). *108 years: Wait for gender equality gets longer as women's share of workforce, politics drops*. World Economic Forum. Retrieved September 4, 2019, from https://www.weforum.org/press/2018/12/108-years-wait-for-gender-equality-gets-longer-as-women-s-share-of-workforce-politics-drops/

Carius, A., Ivleva, D., Pohl, B., Ruttinger, L., Schaller, S., Tanszler, D., & Vivekananda. (2018). *A foreign policy perspective on the SDGs: Climate diplomacy brief*. Retrieved September 11, 2019, from https://www.adelphi.de/en/publication/foreign-policy-perspective-sustainable-development-goals

Concern Worldwide. (2016). *Essential Newborn Care Corps: Evaluation of program to rebrand traditional birth attendants as health promoters in Sierra Leone*. Concern Worldwide. Retrieved September 4, 2019, from https://www.concern.net/insights/essential-newborn-care-corps

Dasra, Kiawah Trust, & USAID. (2014). *Spot on! Improving menstrual health and hygiene in India*. Retrieved September 4, 2019, from https://www.dasra.org/resource/improving-menstrual-health-and-hygiene

Dijkstra, A. G. (2002). Revisiting UNDP's GDI and GEM: Towards an alternative. *Social Indicators Research, 57*(3), 301–338.

Dijkstra, A. G. (2006). Towards a fresh start in measuring gender equality: A contribution to the debate. *Journal of Human Development, 7*(2), 275–283.

Dijkstra, A. G., & Hanmer, L. C. (2000). Measuring socio-economic gender inequality: Toward an alternative to the UNDP Gender-Related Development Index. *Feminist Economics, 6*(2), 41–75.

Duflo, E. (2012). Women empowerment and economic development. *Journal of Economic Literature, 50*(4), 1051–1079.

Duhaček, D., Brankovic, B., & Mirazic, M. (2019). *Women's rights in Western Balkans*. European Parliament. Retrieved September 4, 2019, from http://www.europarl.europa.eu/RegData/etudes/STUD/2019/608852/IPOL_STU(2019)608852_EN.pdf

Gaye, A., Klugman, J., Kovacevic, M., Twigg, S., & Zambrano, E. (2010). *Measuring key disparities in human development: The gender inequality index*. Human Development Research Paper 2010/46. United Nations Development Programme.

Glowork. (2019). *Glowork website*. Retrieved September 4, 2019, from https://www.glowork.net/

Gómez, A. M., Speizer, I. S., Reynolds, H., Murray, N., & Beauvais, H. (2008). Age differences at sexual debut and subsequent reproductive health: Is there a link? *Reproductive Health, 5*(1), 8.

Gonzales, C., Jain-Chandra, S., Kochhar, K., Newiak, M., & Zeinullayev, T. (2015). *Catalyst for change: Empowering women and tackling income inequality*. IMF Staff Discussion Note, SDN 15/20. IMF.

iRelaunch. (2019). iRelaunch website. Retrieved September 4, 2019, from https://www.irelaunch.com/

Klasen, S. (2006). UNDP's gender-related measures: Some conceptual problems and possible solutions. *Journal of Human Development, 7*(2), 243–274.

Klasen, S., & Schüler, D. (2011). Reforming the gender-related index and the gender empowerment measure: Implementing some specific proposals. *Feminist Economics, 17*(1), 1–30.

Lilyanova, V. (2018). *Women in the Western Balkans: Gender equality in the EU accession process*. European Parliamentary Research Service. Retrieved September 4, 2019, from http://www.europarl.europa.eu/thinktank/en/document.html?reference=EPRS_BRI(2018)625139

Mason, H. (2016, May 26). *Making strides to improve maternal health in Sierra Leone*. UNICEF Newsline. Retrieved September 4, 2019, from https://www.unicef.org/infobycountry/sierraleone_91206.html

Moore, M. L., Tjornbo, O., Enfors, E., Knapp, C., Hodbod, J., Baggio, J. A., Norstrom, A., Olsson, P., & Biggs, D. (2014). Studying the complexity of change: Toward an analytical framework for understanding deliberate social-ecological transformations. *Ecology and Society, 19*(4), 54.

Murray, N., Winfrey, W., Chatterji, M., Moreland, S., Dougherty, L., & Okonofua, F. (2006). Factors related to induced abortion among young women in Edo State, Nigeria. *Studies in Family Planning, 37*(4), 251–268.

Nicholls, A., & Murdock, A. (Eds.). (2012). *Social innovation: Blurring boundaries to reconfigure markets*. Palgrave Macmillan. http://dx.doi.org/https://doi.org/10.1057/9780230367098

OECD. (2019). *SIGI 2019 global report: Transforming challenges into opportunities, social institutions and gender index*. OECD Publishing. https://doi.org/10.1787/bc56d212-en

Permanyer, I. (2013). A critical assessment of the UNDP's gender inequality index. *Feminist Economics, 19*(2), 1–32.

Phills, J. A., Deiglmeier, K., & Miller, D. T. (2008). Rediscovering social innovation. *Stanford Social Innovation Review, 6*(4), 34–43.

Saner, R., & Yiu, L. (2003). International economic diplomacy: Mutations in post-modern times. *Discussion Papers in Diplomacy, 84*, 1–31.

Santhya, K. G., Ram, U., Acharya, R., Jejeebhoy, S. J., Ram, F., & Singh, A. (2010). Associations between early marriage and young women's marital and reproductive health outcomes: Evidence from India. *International Perspectives on Sexual and Reproductive Health, 36*(3), 132–139.

Schüler, D. (2006). The uses and misuses of the Gender-Related Development Index and Gender Empowerment Measure: A review of the literature. *Journal of Human Development, 7*(2), 161–181.

Sommer, M. (2010). Where the education system and women's bodies collide: The social and health impact of girls' experiences of menstruation and schooling in Tanzania. *Journal of Adolescence, 33*(4), 521–529.

Song, Y., & Ji, C.-Y. (2010). Sexual intercourse and high-risk sexual behaviours among a national sample of urban adolescents in China. *Journal of Public Health, 32*(3), 312–321.

Thompson, C. (2017). *A life of its own an assessment of the 16 days of activism against gender-based violence campaign*. Center for Women's Global Leadership. Retrieved September 4, 2019, from https://16dayscampaign.org/wp-content/uploads/2018/11/16-Days-Campaign-Assessment.pdf

UN General Assembly. (2015). *Transforming our world: The 2030 agenda for sustainable development*. Resolution adopted by the General Assembly on 25 September 2015. A/RES/70/1. United Nations.

UNCTAD. (2014). *World investment report 2014: Investing in the SDGs: An action plan*. Retrieved September 9, 2019, from https://unctad.org/en/PublicationsLibrary/wir2014_en.pdf

UNDP. (2014). *Promoting gender equality in electoral assistance: Lessons learned in comparative perspective: Country report for Bolivia*. Retrieved September 4, 2019, from https://www.undp.org/content/dam/undp/library/Democratic%20Governance/Electoral%20Systems%20and%20Processes/2122-UNDP-GE-bolivia.pdf

UNDP. (2019). *Gender Inequality Index (GII)*. Retrieved September 4, 2019, from http://hdr.undp.org/en/content/gender-inequality-index-gii

UNESCO. (2014). *Puberty education & menstrual hygiene management*. Good Policy and Practice in Health Education Booklet 9. United Nations Educational, Scientific and Cultural Organization. Retrieved September 4, 2019, from https://unesdoc.unesco.org/ark:/48223/pf0000226792

UNICEF. (2008). *Progress for children: A report card on maternal mortality*. United Nations.

Van Staveren, I. (2013). To measure is to know? A comparative analysis of gender indices. *Review of Social Economy, 71*(3), 339–372.

van Wijk, J., Zietsma, C., Dorado, S., de Bakker, F. G., & Martí, I. (2019). Social innovation: Integrating micro, meso, and macro level insights from institutional theory. *Business & Society, 58*(5), 887–918.

WEF. (2018). *The global gender gap report 2018*. World Economic Forum.

World Bank. (2012). *World development report 2012: Gender equality and development*. World Bank.

World Bank. (2019). *World Bank country and lending groups*. Retrieved September 12, 2019, from https://datahelpdesk.worldbank.org/knowledgebase/articles/906519-world-bank-country-and-lending-groups

Young, F. (2016, November 17). *The slow road to progress: Why is Sierra Leone's maternal mortality rate so high?* Financial Times. Retrieved September 4, 2019, from https://www.ft.com/content/8205b21e-7b44-11e6-ae24-f193b105145e

CHAPTER 5

Gender Equality Index for Country Regions (GEICR)

Beatrice Avolio and Luis del Carpio

1 Introduction

Gender equality is a fundamental aspect for building a prosperous and sustainable world (United Nations [UN], 2016). Gender equality means that both women and men "enjoy the same status and have equal opportunity to realize their human rights and potential to contribute to national, political, economic, social and cultural development, and to benefit from the results" (United Nations Educational, Scientific and Cultural Organization [UNESCO], 2017a, para. 2). The right to equality and non-discrimination is part of the international system for

---

B. Avolio (✉) · L. del Carpio
CENTRUM Católica Graduate Business School, Lima, Peru
e-mail: bavolio@pucp.pe

L. del Carpio
e-mail: ldelcarpio@pucp.edu.pe

Pontificia Universidad Católica del Perú, Lima, Peru

© The Author(s), under exclusive license to Springer Nature Switzerland AG 2022
V. Charles and A. Emrouznejad (eds.), *Modern Indices for International Economic Diplomacy*, https://doi.org/10.1007/978-3-030-84535-3_5

the protection of human rights and is also evident in various international instruments such as the Charter of the United Nations (1945) and the Universal Declaration of Human Rights (1948) (UN, n.d.). Likewise, the United Nations has several documents focused on women's human rights, such as: The Convention on the Elimination of All Forms of Discrimination against Women (CEDAW), the Fourth World Conference on Women in Beijing (1995), the Millennium Declaration and the CEDAW Resolutions.

Despite this, there are still troubling gender inequalities in the world that need to be addressed. According to the World Economic Forum (2020), from 2006 to 2018, the gap in health, education, and political and economic opportunities between men and women decreased by 4%. Likewise, although men and women have managed to almost double their salaries between 2006 and 2015, women are 10 years behind in salaries, i.e., only in 2015 women managed to receive the same remuneration that a man received in 2006. Similarly, although the political world has made great progress, women are still politically underrepresented (women represent 25% of parliamentarians and 21% of the world's cabinet ministers). In addition, it has been proven that there is no direct ratio between: the number of women in universities, female skilled workers and female leaders. All things being equal, with current trends, the overall global gender gap can be closed in 99.5 years (World Economic Forum, 2020).

The United Nations Population Fund (UNFPA) (2014) points out that gender equality will only be achieved when men and women can meet in an environment where there is an equal distribution of power, but also when both can enjoy the same opportunities, rights and obligations, reflected in economic independence, education and achievement of their personal ambitions. Under this context, the Regional Gender Equality Index (GEICR) was created. The GEICR is a proposal that is aligned with global goals and aims to make the reality of men and women visible by analyzing the different factors that influence the sub-national level of a country. The index provides more information on the impact of the differentiated access of men and women to resources and how much progress needs to be made in each of the different dimensions. This proposal is intended to reduce differences and improve the general condition of a country's inhabitants. It is also intended to serve as a useful tool in the development of public policies and to be part of the tools used to strategically guide social investment. The proposed GEICR includes 4 pillars, 12 factors and 32 indicators, which have been analyzed by gender in each region of the country. For this purpose, the index was created based on the concept of gender equality and region, also known as sub-national level.

The development linked to gender equality implies "breaking apart the culture, values and traditional gender roles that reproduce and maintain the subordination of women" (Economic Commission for Latin America and the Caribbean [ECLAC], 2010, p. 16). The concept of gender equality recognizes that women have been historically discriminated, so it is necessary to take actions to eliminate inequalities and close the gaps between women and men. In this sense, equal opportunities between men and women are considered a vital element for the political, social and economic construction of any democratic society (Castro & Álvarez, 2011).

Based on the review of previous literature, the proposed definition of regional gender equality for this study is the equality of duties, rights, responsibilities and opportunities for men and women in the different aspects of life, recognizing the peculiarities of both and without diminishing them by their gender. It also involves the construction of a panorama of access and a fair use of resources that are the fundamental basis for the complete development of the individual and the democratic societies. Gender equality has a global priority, but the analysis and understanding of inequalities is based on a study at a country and regional (also called sub-national) level. The regional divisions of a country are based on its geography, as well as its demographics, history, culture, economy, climate, ideology, etc. factors that determine the particularity of each region within a country. Therefore, gender equality in each area has its own characteristics.

1.1 Role of the Gender Equality Index in International Economic Diplomacy

International Economic Diplomacy requires tools that allow design policies at national and international levels. In this regard, the GEICR can be used by policymakers and other relevant stakeholders for policy and strategy design and development. In the first place, the GEICR overcame one of the main criticisms of early indicators, which is the inability to separate gender equality from local development. The decision to split the scores for men and women makes the index a useful tool to identify gender gaps, independently from the level of development in an area.

Likewise, it is based on measuring results rather than on processes, which makes it a tool for measuring progress in the implementation of gender-differentiated policies. Furthermore, a major problem in Latin American region is the centralization and large regional differences, so this tool allows capturing regional differences and makes it easier to understand the current situation of a country through the national score. The information that otherwise would be unavailable becomes visible. Also, by tanking into account several dimensions, it allows focusing public and private efforts on those aspects of lesser development. This is particularly important because the index makes it possible to visualize how some regions may have greater social development, but at the same time, large gender differences. In other words, the social development of the regions does not necessarily imply equality between men and women, and the same environment does not necessarily provide the same quality of life for men and women. Finally, having this information allows the strategic allocation of resources to the regions in a more effective way.

2 Main Indexes Analyzing Gender Equality

In recent years, the awareness of the importance of gender equality has increased, recognizing it as a positive element for the personal, economic and social growth of all countries. For this reason, different organizations have carried out researches to find instruments to measure progress and setbacks in gender issues, initiating the development of indexes that reflect the situation of men and women.

The indicators appeared several years ago, however, they were focused on economic areas, particularly economic growth and infrastructure development. During the 1970s, the search for indicators that evaluate other aspects besides economic growth started, which led to the generation of social indicators that could investigate aspects such as health, education and social progress. Later on, in the 1980s, a concern for the construction of gender measurement instruments arose, seeking indicators disaggregated by gender and indicators that show their respective realities (Dávila, 2004).

The first gender indexes were presented by the United Nations Development Program (UNDP) in the Human Development Report in 1995. The indexes presented were: The Gender Development Index (GDI) and the Gender Empowerment Measure (GEM). The first investigated inequality based on the same dimensions of the Human Development

Index (HDI), and the second focused on the analysis of political participation, economic participation and ownership of economic resources. The fundamental criticisms of these indexes centered on questioning the combination of absolute and relative achievement, i.e., taking income into account, so that even if a country scored well in terms of gender equality, it was deficient because of its low income. Likewise, the GEM was criticized for using indicators that were more in line with the reality of developed countries and not the rest of the countries (United Nations Development Program [UNDP], 2010).

There are currently other gender gap indexes, the most important have been prepared by the World Economic Forum and the United Nations Development Program (UNDP). These indexes have gained relevance due to the number of countries included, as well as the quantity and quality of the data they present. Since 2006, the World Economic Forum has annually presented the Global Gender Gap Index, which quantifies and rates the distribution of resources and opportunities between men and women. This index analyzes four dimensions: economic participation and opportunity, educational attainment, health and survival, and political empowerment. Each of the dimensions is made up of a set of indicators. The number of indicators in this index is 14. The Global Gender Gap Index Report 2020 included a total of 153 countries (World Economic Forum, 2020).

The United Nations Development Program (UNDP), after overcoming the criticisms made of its first indexes, has annually presented the Gender Inequality Index (GII) since 2010, and the Gender Development Index since 2014. The Gender Inequality Index includes three dimensions: reproductive health, empowerment and labor market. Unlike the first gender indexes (the Gender Development Index and the Gender Empowerment Measure presented in the Human Development Report in 1995), the Gender Inequality Index does not rely on imputations. This means that this index does not apply any method to add missing data and none of the indicators are directly related to a country's economic growth. Similarly, the Gender Development Index measures gender differences with regard to the HDI, calculating the same HDI values: health, knowledge and standard of living, for men and women separately. The higher the value, the smaller the difference between men and women. The Human Development Report (where the Gender Development Index and the Gender Inequality Index are located) presented in 2015 counted a total of 188 countries (United Nations Development Program [UNDP], 2015).

In addition, there are other indicators that, although they do not measure gender differences, do include it as one of their variables. This is the case of the Social Progress Index developed by the Social Progress Imperative. This index measures the capacity of a society to satisfy basic needs, increase the quality of life and generate conditions and opportunities to achieve the potential of its population. The index combines three dimensions: basic human needs, opportunities for progress and fundamental wellbeing. These dimensions are disaggregated into 12 components and one of them is framed in the gender category.

The three indexes mentioned above measure gender inequalities by integrating different variables (Table 1). They also present rankings of the countries studied. The gender gap of these indexes ranges from 0 to 1, where 0 represents perfect equality and 1 represents perfect inequality. It is based on data provided by the main international sources. The Global Gender Gap Index draws on information from the International Labour Organization (ILO), the United Nations Educational, Scientific and Cultural Organization (UNESCO), among others. Likewise, for the Gender Development Index and the Gender Inequality Index they use the World Health Organization (WHO), the United Nations Population Fund (UNFPA) and the World Bank, among others, as a data base. Finally, for the Social Progress Index, for the gender aspect, it uses information from UNESCO.

3 Constructing an Index

For the Organisation for Economic Co-operation and Development (OECD) and the Joint Research Center (JRC), developing indicators involves a solid theoretical framework, a structure of the subgroups of the phenomenon, and a list of the selection criteria for the underlying variables (OECD & JRC, 2008). The theoretical framework should provide a clear definition of what is measured, the sub-components and the underlying indicators. In addition, multidimensional concepts can be divided into several sub-groups and the connections should be described theoretically or empirically (OECD & JRC, 2008). The selection criteria for underlying indicators can be similarly developed and should serve as a guide to determine whether or not a variable should be included. A composite indicator is the sum of its parts; therefore, the variables must

Table 1 Gender indexes

Index	Global gender gap index	Gender development index	Gender inequality index	Social progress index
Author	World Economic Forum	United Nations Development Programme		Social Progress Imperative
Name of the report	Global gender gap report	Human development report		Social progress index report
Publication frequency	Annual	Annual		Annual
Number of countries included in the study	153 (year 2020)	162 (year 2020)		163 (year 2020)
Objective	Describe the performance of countries regarding the gap between women and men in order to understand if the countries distribute equally the resources and opportunities, regardless of the levels of national general revenue	Measure the Human Development Index (HDI) for men and women	Measure gender inequality without taking into account the variables related to economic growth	Evaluate the effectiveness with which a country's economic success translates into social progress
Dimensions	• Economic participation and opportunity • Educational attainment • Health and survival • Political empowerment	• Long and healthy life • Knowledge • Standard of living	• Reproductive health • Empowerment • Economic status	• Basic human needs • Foundations of wellbeing • Opportunity
Components	Economic participation and opportunity educational attainment Health and survival Political empowerment	Long and healthy life Knowledge Standard of living	Reproductive health Empowerment Economic status	Basic human needs Foundations of wellbeing Opportunity

(continued)

Table 1 (continued)

Index	Global gender gap index	Gender development index	Gender inequality index	Social progress index
Methodology	The data are converted into proportions between women and men and were subsequently made equal to a benchmark (1). This means equal numbers for men and women in all indicators, except for the two health indicators since they have a different approach. Then, a weighted average is calculated in each dimension (the score in each indicator and the weights). The value of the dimension ranges from 0 to 1, where 0 is perfect inequality and 1 perfect equality	The index is calculated separately for men and women. The same methodology included in the HDI is used. Each dimension has the same weight. The same points of reference included in the HDI are used to transform the dimensions on a scale that ranged from 0 and 1	The index includes three dimensions different from those included in the HDI, and these cannot be interpreted as a loss in the HDI. The index scores range from 0 to 1. The higher the value, the higher the levels of inequality	The index includes three elements: 3 dimensions, 12 components, and 50 indicators. The factor analysis statistically determined the weights. The scores ranged from 0 to 100, where 100 is the highest score and 0 the lowest score

Source Developed based on the World Economic Forum (2020), the United Nations Development Programme (2020), and Social Progress Imperative (2020) be selected by identifying the characteristics related to relevance, soundness, timeliness, accessibility, among others. Finally, even though a proper theoretical framework can lead to a sound indicator, the data used to build it is subjectively selected. The quality and accuracy of composite indicators benefit greatly from improvements in data collection and availability (OECD & JRC, 2008). Figure 1 shows the "operationalizing" process, which is developed based on the scheme proposed by Lazarsfeld (1958).

The adequacy of an indicator lies on its ability to collect part of the information related to a real phenomenon (Dávila, 2004). In order to achieve this, the indicator should comply with several basic conditions

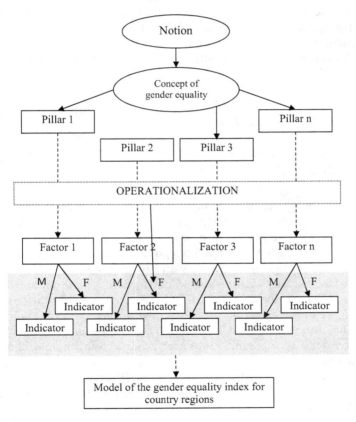

Fig. 1 Indicator's operationalization process

(a) validity, i.e., to show the actual differences of the characteristics that are measured; (b) reliability, i.e., the differences are not chance results or random errors; (c) sensitivity, i.e., the results must show finite distinctions of what is measured, and must be precise enough to reflect changes; (d) clarity, i.e., results should be easily interpreted to provide coherent information; and (e) accessibility, i.e., to obtain information and make calculations in an agile way (Dávila, 2004).

Gender indicators use the gender approach in statistics. The various factors that influence men and women differently were considered (Economic Commission for Latin America and the Caribbean [ECLAC], 2016); thus, ECLAC noted that the gender approach in statistics is necessary because it shows different roles, activities, tasks and responsibilities for both genders (Milosavljevic, 2007). The first step in the statistical construction of the index was the standardization of the data collected, as the information is measured differently in each indicator. This was done with the following formula (1):

$$\frac{(Xi - \overline{X})}{(Standard\ deviation)} = INDICATOR_i \qquad (1)$$

Xi: Score of the indicator i
$\overline{X}$: Average of the indicator i

The following step was testing the variables of interest using Cronbach's alpha. This allows estimating the internal consistency of the factors within each pillar. The OECD suggests a minimum threshold of 0.70 as an acceptable measure of reliability (2008). When the model was validated after verifying the consistency and suitability of the indicators, the weights had to be calculated—based on the Principal Component Analysis—in order to obtain the GEICR. Therefore, the resulting index is the weighted average of the value obtained in one region in each of the three dimensions. The GEICR applies to men and women independently, which creates a general ranking for each group. This technique allows the combination of indicators in a component that captures the maximum value in data variance and reduces any redundancy among the indicators, thus leaving only the most important variables with weights according to their significance.

Then, Min–Max method (OECD & JCR, 2008) was used to convert each variable into a score from 0 to 100. To achieve this, the best-case scenario and the worst-case scenario, the utopia, and dystopia, respectively, were used to benchmark each region and allow an effective comparison. In addition, the score is easy to interpret by both policymakers and interested citizens, making the progress of women and men in each region readable at a glance. This method is represented as follows (2):

$$\frac{(INDICATOR_i - Worst\,case\,scenario)}{(Best\,scenario - Worst\,case\,scenario)} \quad (2)$$

With the information already normalized and with solid verifications of internal consistency and goodness of fit, the last step is the aggregation of information. The GEICR is aggregated as follows, with each pillar having equal relevance in the Eq. (3):

$$GEIR = \frac{1}{4} * \sum_d PILAR_p \quad (3)$$

$Pillar_p$: Every pillar in the index

Each pillar includes factors that represent independent concepts related to the pillar, since they have equal significance for the GEICR, the weight is the same (4):

$$Pillar_p = \frac{1}{3} * \sum_f CFACTOR_f \quad (4)$$

$Pillar_p$: Every pillar in the index
$CFACTOR_f$: Factor f within the pillar p

Similarly, the factor is the sum of i weighted indicators determined by the principal component analysis (5):

$$FACTOR_f = \sum_i (W_i * INDICATOR_i) \quad (5)$$

$FACTOR_f$: Factor f within the pillar p

$INDICATOR_i$: Indicator i within the factor f
W_i: Weight of each indicator i within the factor f

After this, the Kaiser–Meyer–Olkin (KMO) test was used to verify the goodness of fit. In general, this value should exceed the 0.5 threshold (Porter & Scott, 2018). Therefore, all factors with a KMO value equal to or greater than 0.50 were selected.

4 Proposal for a Regional Gender Social Development Index

4.1 GEICR Description

The Gender Equality Index for Country Regions (GEICR) seeks the social, economic and political improvement of countries. The GEICR is a tool that makes it possible to measure, through a holistic and integrative approach, the current situation of access to resources by men and women in different dimensions in each region. The GEICR is a social indicator because it is "a statistical measure related to the amount or magnitude of a set of parameters or attributes of a society" (Benzaquen et al., 2010, p. 76). Specifically, it measures current access to resources for both men and women in various dimensions in each region. Social indicators can be classified according to the measurement objective. These can be impact, effect and compliance indicators (Bobadilla et al., 1998). The GEICR is an impact index because it measures the social progress of gender equality at the end of a period.

The GEICR is independent of the overall development of a country, it measures the relative levels of regions in relation to gender differences in access to resources, independently of elements such as GDP, infrastructure, competitiveness, social progress, etc. In this sense, the fact that a region is positioned at the top of the ranking because of the value given to it, according to the analysis of the index, does not determine that it has good conditions in reality, but rather that it is better positioned than the other regions. Likewise, regions with high levels of economic development and/or social progress will not necessarily have high values for the female and/or male index.

The GEICR shows an index for men, an index for women and their difference. The same methodology was used, with the same dimensions, components and indicators, independently for men and women.

Furthermore, a higher value in the index for women does not necessarily correspond to a smaller difference with regard to men in the region, or vice versa, since the score presented by each of the genders varies with regard to the reality they have had in the region, independently from women and men. In addition, the index evaluates results and not processes. The GEICR measures the real and current characteristics of the situation of access to resources for men and women in different dimensions and in each of the regions. The index shows, based on accurate and reliable data, the results of past actions reflected in the present; it measures current results and not the processes that have taken place in each of the dimensions studied.

The GEICR considers the use of time as one of its elements. A pioneering component of this index is the use of time, which has not been taken into account in any other previous index. Paid work has traditionally been considered as a source of income; however, the valuation of unpaid work, mainly performed by women, both in domestic and care work, has been invisible in the published indexes. The fact that this population tends to work double shifts or two jobs presents adverse effects on the workforce, such as unequal job opportunities, economic compensation and also affects their personal and social development, takes away leisure time and increases their stress and physical fatigue. In this sense, it is considered an important component that clearly shows the differences in access to opportunities between men and women.

4.2 GEICR Documentation

The GEICR was created by analyzing key international documents that serve as guidelines and the most important national and international indexes on gender issues, as well as studies related to the areas addressed by the GEICR. In particular, the Platform for Action of the Fourth World Conference on Women held in Beijing (United Nations [UN], 1995) is one of the main references. It defined a global platform of action for the empowerment of women, reaffirming the commitment of the different countries to fully develop women's potential and establishing as a strategic objective the preparation and dissemination of aspects that have to do with the realities of women (Economic Commission for Latin America and the Caribbean [ECLAC], 2004). Likewise, the *Millennium Development Goals* outlined in 2000 at the United Nations Millennium Summit is another important document that promotes gender equality and women's empowerment (United Nations [UN], 2015). Likewise, it is also important the "Sustainable Development Goals" agreed in 2015 by the multilateral system of the United Nations, where emphasis is placed on achieving gender equality and empowering women and girls, eradicating discrimination and violence against women, recognizing unpaid work, making women's participation in decision-making spaces viable, ensuring their sexual and reproductive health, generating reforms that contribute to generate equal rights in economic resources, property, land, services; in addition to generating policies and laws that promote gender equality and the empowerment of women and girls (United Nations [UN], 2016).

During the analysis of international indexes and their structure, different studies were observed such as the one proposed by the World Economic Forum (2020) with the Global Gender Gap Index which uses the variables of economic participation and opportunity, educational attainment, health and survival and political empowerment; also the UNDP with the Gender Inequality Index which uses variables such as health, empowerment and labor market; and the Gender Development Index with variables such as long and healthy life, knowledge and standard of living (United Nations Development Program [UNDP], 2015).

4.3 GEICR Pillars, Factors and Indicators

Based on the literature review, the GEICR is composed of 4 pillars, 12 factors and 32 indicators analyzed by gender in each of the country regions. These pillars are education, health, autonomy and opportunity. Each pillar has three factors. The education pillar includes the following factors: (a) primary education, (b) high-school education and (c) educational attainment; the health pillar: (a) access, (b) morbidity and (c) basic care; the autonomy pillar: (a) economic autonomy, (b) physical autonomy and (c) decision-making autonomy; and the opportunities pillar: (a) access to higher education, (b) employment and (c) time use. These variables were chosen due to their theoretical relevance in gender equality and social progress in the literature review.

Similarly, each factor is disaggregated into indicators that aim to explain its relevance. There is a variation in the number of indicators per component, even two and three indicators per component may be included in order to explain the latter as accurately as possible. Tables 2, 3, 4 and 5 show the pillars, factors and indicators of the model as well as the

Table 2 Factors, indicators, variables, unit and objectives of the education pillar

Factors	Indicator	Variable	Unit	Objective
Educational attainment	Literacy	Literacy of men/women (+15 years old)	Percentage	Do women and men have equal access to primary education?
	Years of study	Years of study completed by men/women (+15 years old)	Years	
Primary education	Attendance at primary school	Attendance at primary education (boys/girls from 6 to 11 years old)	Percentage	Do women and men have equal access to secondary education?
	Primary school enrollment	Primary school enrollment (boys/girls from 6 to 11 years old)	Percentage	
Secondary education	Attendance at secondary school	Attendance at secondary education (male/female teenagers from 12 to 16 years old)	Percentage	What are men's and women's achievements with regard to the level of literacy and total years of study?
	Secondary school enrollment	Attendance at secondary education (male/female teenagers from 12 to 16 years old)	Percentage	

questions that are the basis for explaining the importance of each of the components of each dimension. Each question shows a global perspective that is considered to develop the index, and what is to be measured with it.

(a) *Education*

The education pillar analyzes different aspects involving the scope of educational levels. It takes into account primary and high-school education, considering enrollment, attendance and educational attainment,

Table 3 Factors, indicators, variables, unit and objectives of the health pillar

Factors	Indicator	Variable	Unit	Objective
Access to health	Distance to the health care center	Men/women do not receive medical care due to the remoteness to health care facilities	Percentage	What is women's and men's access level to health services?
	National Identity Card	Men/women with a national identity card	Variation % over the years	
	Health insurance	Men/women with some type of health insurance different from comprehensive health insurance (public and free)	Percentage	
Morbidity	Hospitalizations	Hospitalized men/women	Percentage	What is the difference between men's and women's life expectancy and health conditions?
	Chronic conditions	Men/women reported suffering from a chronic disease	The percentage in relation to the total of men/women in the region	
Basic care	Medical attention at public health centers	Number of outpatient medical attention (men/women)	Total cases per 1000 habitants	How often do men and women come to public health centers?
	Medicine reception	Men/women who receive medicine	Percentage	

covering literacy level and years of completed studies. The pillar is linked to the Millennium Development Goals where emphasis has been placed on guaranteeing people's education, particularly in Objectives 2 and 3 that propose achieving universal primary education and promoting gender equality and the autonomy of women (United Nations [UN], 2015).

Additionally, this pillar is included because the access to education and higher levels of schooling are the main accomplishments achieved by women. However, those accomplishments are not directly proportional to the economic equality and empowerment level of that population

Table 4 Factors, indicators, variables, unit and objectives of the autonomy pillar

Factors	Indicator	Variable	Unit	Objective
Economic	Economic dependence	Men/women without own income	The percentage in relation to the total of men/women in the region	What are the economic factors that represent men's and women's autonomy?
	Labor income	Men/women's average monthly income	Current PEN	
	Unpaid work	Unpaid family workers	Percentage	
Physical	Adult sexual abuse	+18-year-old men/women rape victims	Total registered cases per 10,000 habitants	Is men's and women's physical integrity valued and respected equally?
	Child sexual abuse	Men/women rape victims under 18 years old	Total registered cases per 10,000 habitants	
	Human trafficking	Men/women alleged victims of human trafficking	Total registered cases per 10,000 habitants	
	Family violence	Registered cases of family and/or sexual violence	Total registered cases per 10,000 habitants	
Decision-making	Councilors	Number of councilmen/councilwomen	Total cases per 10,000 habitants	How do men and women participate in democracy and politics in their regions?
	Municipal governments	Number of men/women mayors	Total cases per 10,000 habitants	
	Parliament	Number of men/women parliamentarians	Total cases per 10,000 habitants	

Table 5 Factors, indicators, variables, unit and objectives of the opportunities pillar

Factors	Indicator	Variable	Unit	Objective
Access to higher education	University enrollment	Men/women between 17 and 24 years old enrolled at university	Percentage	What is the highest level of education achieved by women and men?
	Enrollment in art higher education	Men/women at artistic training centers	Total enrollments per 10,000 habitants	
	Enrollment in technological higher education	Men/women at technological training centers	Total enrollments per 10,000 habitants	
Employment	Informality	Male/female informality	Percentage	Are there equal opportunities to enter the labor market for women and men?
	Participation in the labor market	Economically active men/women in an economically active population	Percentage	
	Underemployment	Economically active underemployed men/women	Percentage	
Use of time	Time used in paid labor	Average hours per week men/women spent doing paid activities	Hours per week	How do men and women distribute their time?
	Employer	Men/women who employ others in a registered business	Percentage	
	Weekend labor	Total hours of labor during the weekend by men/women	Hours per weekend	

(Milosavljevic, 2007). UNESCO (2017b) estimates that globally two-thirds of illiterate adults are women and that 16 million girls will never go to school. Educational gaps are going to limit women's access to information and opportunities (United Nations Population Fund [UNFPA], 2014). In addition, different studies point to the significant positive effects of a mother's education on her children and on the reduction of factors linked to poverty (Milosavljevic, 2007). Empowering women's education, not only becomes an individual but also a collective benefit, more education is related to lower fertility and infant mortality, and to better results for their descendants (United Nations Population Fund [UNFPA], 2014).

When relating gender equality to education, in terms of learning achievement and access to education, girls are the least favored in certain regions due to their level of poverty, violence, culture, among other reasons. In terms of the academic performance of school children, gender gaps are also evident. This is explained by the characteristics of the home (which in turn are related to the low level of education of the mother compared to the father) for the integral development of the child, regardless of whether the child studies in a public or private school. In addition, these performance gaps are more evident when they are observed by region and considering the ethnicity of the student (Giménez & Castro, 2015). These previous studies show that efforts should focus on the reduction of gender gaps since equity in education is an important piece within the educational policy, because any measure outlined will achieve its effectiveness in the long term in the search for income equality and consequently in greater social cohesion (Giménez & Castro, 2015).

(b) *Health*

The health pillar analyzes access to health instruments, morbidity and basic care. The Pan American Health Organization (2009) promotes gender equity in health so that men and women can enjoy good health, without becoming ill, disabled or dying from causes that are both unfair and preventable. For the individual, enjoying good health requires greater purchasing power, and is therefore correlated with the level of wealth.

According to Rodríguez (2016), in developing countries such as Colombia, it is shown that socioeconomic status is a fundamental determinant of the population's perception of health and that this varies according to income inequality by region. On the other hand, in countries such as Spain, where a study was applied to infants and adolescents to determine self-perceived health and quality of life by gender, it was found that women were twice as likely to have poorer health and a lower quality of life as men (Vélez et al., 2009).

The United Nations (n.d.) points out that women have less opportunity to access material resources to obtain health services and are the ones who demand more health care throughout their lives due to their reproductive function and the role of motherhood. Reduced access to knowledge, nutrition, employment and income brings fewer opportunities for women to enjoy good health. Empowered women contribute to the health and productivity of their families and communities. Furthermore, it is essential for the women's reproductive health along with the ability to control their own fertility, as well as access to information and services that improve their health (United Nations Population Fund [UNFPA], 2014). State intervention in public policy on health acts on public spending and transfers, though the effect of this inequality would obtain greater results for the households (Rodríguez, 2016).

(c) *Autonomy*

In the autonomy pillar, three factors are analyzed: economic, physical integrity and decision making. These three components consolidate important aspects in order to measure the person's capacity for action as an individual and as part of society and the factors that limit this development. These factors are consistent with the three-dimensional autonomy proposal presented by ECLAC (2010). According to ECLAC (2010), physical autonomy refers to women's reproductive rights and gender violence; autonomy in decision-making refers to the presence of women in decision-making in different political positions as well as to actions aimed at promoting their participation under equal conditions; while economic autonomy is "understood as women's capacity to generate their own income and resources, based on access to paid work under equal conditions as men" (p. 23).

Global labor markets present inequalities between men and women in terms of opportunities, treatment and outcomes. In general, women are more likely to be unemployed and remain that way with fewer opportunities to participate in the labor force (International Labour Organization [ILO], 2016).

Economic autonomy is explained as the capacity of women to generate their own income and resources through access to paid work on equal terms as men. It considers the use of time and the contribution of women to the economy (Economic Commission for Latin America and the Caribbean [ECLAC], 2016). On economic empowerment, it is recognized that six out of ten of the world's poorest people are women and economic inequalities are reflected in women's unpaid work. In general, women continue to be discriminated in the economic sphere (United Nations Population Fund [UNFPA], 2014).

Physical autonomy is expressed in two dimensions that account for relevant social issues in the region: respect for women's reproductive rights and gender-based violence (Economic Commission for Latin America and the Caribbean [ECLAC], 2016). In relation to gender-based violence, high rates of violence against women are found worldwide. The World Health Organization defines this violence as an act that results in physical, sexual or psychological harm to women, including threats of such acts or arbitrary deprivation of liberty. On average, one in three women in the world have suffered physical and/or sexual violence and most cases have been carried out by their partners (World Health Organization [WHO], 2016).

Autonomy in decision-making refers to the presence of women at the different levels of the branches of government and measures aimed at promoting their full and equal participation (Economic Commission for Latin America and the Caribbean [ECLAC], 2016). Regarding leadership and political participation, it was found that women are underrepresented in management positions, elected positions, public administration, etc. This is due to structural barriers that are represented in discriminatory laws and institutions that limit women's options to vote or represent themselves; and also relative gaps, which are linked to other factors, such as having education, contacts, resources, among other elements to be able to be leaders (UN, 2012). However, the few social movements represented and led by a woman have had an impact on the achievement of welfare indicators for the benefit of the population, demonstrating the qualities of leadership and the ability to relate to others (Tabbush & Caminotti, 2015).

Furthermore, gender equality cannot be achieved without the support of social and judicial institutions, access to or control of resources, and social or political participation (United Nations Population Fund [UNFPA], 2014). The actions taken to diminish these problems are recorded in the Convention on the Elimination of All Forms of Discrimination against Women, the Beijing Platform for Action and the Millennium Development Goals and the Sustainable Development Goals, among others.

(d) *Opportunity*

The opportunity pillar shares areas linked to the factors of the other pillars. It is characterized by the idea of openness to options related to education, employment and time management. Higher education creates knowledge, teaches specific competencies and promotes values; however, there are inequalities in the access to studies. Despite the fact that higher education has increased around the world and there are more students, male predominance in bachelor's degree programs is still present in different regions of the world and the gap widens further in doctoral degree programs (United Nations Educational, Scientific and Cultural Organization [UNESCO], 2017b).

In terms of work, Kanter (1977) described the incorporation of women into the labor market as the most important silent social revolution of the twentieth century. This has resulted in profound transformations in the labor market, educational achievements, a reduction in the female fertility rate, changes in family relationships and greater access to decision-making (Economic Commission for Latin America and the Caribbean [ECLAC], 2004). Despite this, there are still great challenges related to the equal participation of women in economic activities. Women and youth are both overrepresented in the informal economy and in all employment categories women's earnings are lower (International Labour Organization [ILO], 2013).

In terms of time management, it has been found that around the world women work less time than men in paid work and assume the majority of unpaid care work and housework that involves much of their time (International Labour Organization [ILO], 2016).

5 The Gender Equality Index for Country Regions: The Peruvian Case

5.1 Background

The ongoing cultural processes in Peru called for the GEICR. The extreme centralization during most of Peruvian history led to the regions' underdevelopment. In recent years, several attempts to reform the political, tax and administrative centralization were made. Despite the mixed results of these policies, the transfer of resources to subnational governments increased as a result of the sustained economic growth, but it is still the backbone of decentralization and regional budgets regardless of the recent deceleration of economic growth. Therefore, a major factor in the future development of the country is the subnational governments' ability to optimize public spending according to cultural and tax constraints. In addition, in the last decade, there is a marked and increasing societal interest in gender issues. In 2007, the member states of the ECLAC requested the constitution of a gender equality observatory during a Regional Conference held in Quito (Economic Commission for Latin America and the Caribbean [ECLAC], 2019). Then, the creation of the SDGs (UN) in 2015 included gender equality as goal number 5.

As these decentralization and gender gap awareness processes develop, the need for a better progress indicator and a better summary of interesting variables for policymakers becomes more evident. Thus, we created the GEICR as a tool to evaluate the needs of each region and to assist the local authorities to make strategic spending according to those needs. This would represent a significant improvement in contrast to the current indicators used by the Peruvian government, which mostly reward the execution of the scheduled budget regardless of the result. Instead, the GEICR helps measuring the ability of subnational governments to translate the economic growth into social progress (CENTRUM PUCP, 2019), taking into account that the effects of this progress might not be homogenous for women and men. Hence, this index presents different results for each and emphasizes the difference between the scores of men and women at the national and regional level.

5.2 Results

Accuracy depends on the quality of the data used to create any index. The GEICR has statistical information collected from secondary sources and it also includes primary information collected from specific surveys conducted in all the regions of the country. The secondary sources are official statistics published mostly by the National Institute of Statistics and Data Processing (INEI), with specific data from the Ministry of Education (MINEDU, 2014), the Ministry of Health (MINSA), the Office of the Attorney General (2014) and the National Vital Statistics and Civil Registry Office (RENIEC), the entity responsible for the registry of identified population. The indicators—health, education, autonomy and opportunities—were selected based on these sources of information. In addition, the government has taken measures to ensure the transparency and usefulness of the data for policy-making and scientific research by aligning the INEI's standards to those of the United Nations and EUROSTAT (National Institute of Statistics and Data Processing [INEI], 2012).

With the required information to create the index, the next step was standardizing the data, and verifying its suitability. Table 6 shows the results of Cronbach's Alpha and KMO for each factor of the GEICR with both tests above their recommended thresholds in all cases; thus,

Table 6 Statistical analysis by dimension—Peruvian GEICR

Pillar	Factor	Cronbach's Alpha	KMO
Education	Primary education	0.9667	0.5000
	Secondary education	0.9737	0.5000
	Educational attainment	0.8176	0.5000
Health	Access to health	0.8247	0.6916
	Morbidity	0.7164	0.5000
	Basic care	0.8357	0.5000
Autonomy	Economic	0.8505	0.6395
	Physical	0.9944	0.7911
	Decision-making	0.8485	0.5591
Opportunity	Access to higher education	0.8124	0.7134
	Employment	0.9453	0.7597
	Use of time	0.8211	0.6548

validating the internal consistency of the variables within each factor and the goodness of fit.

The following step was the principal component analysis (Appendix 1) and setting the utopias and dystopias for every indicator. The use of the Min–Max method allows to assign each pillar a value from 0 to 100 depending on the level of achievement. In order to show the progress of each gender in every region of Peru, and facilitate the comparison, a 7-point scale was used. It ranges from: extremely low (25–34 points), very low (35–44 points), low (45–54 points), medium–low (55–64 points), medium–high (65–74 points), high (75–84 points) and very high (85–100 points).

Table 7 shows the results for men and women, along with the existing gender gap by region, the results by dimension of the women index, the men index and the gender gap can be reviewed in Appendixes 2–4. In the case of Peru, the results obtained reflect a very worrisome situation regarding the differences between men and women, as well as large differences in different regions of the country. The main results, as well as the policy implications for the Peruvian regions in view of each pillar, are presented below.

(a) Results show that none of the regions were able to score higher than medium–low social development, a worrying situation for the country. The highest scores were obtained in the coastal regions of the country, particularly the capital and southern coast, a historically better developed area. Meanwhile, most regions in the Andes and the Amazon have very low development for men and women, and the gender gap is also large, with the notable exception in Ucayali. However, it should be noted that having relatively high development does not mean less gender inequality, Moquegua has one of the largest breaches in gender equality and very high scores for men's index and women's index, being first and fourth, respectively. An inverse situation can be observed in Loreto, ranking 25th and 18th with the third smallest breach.

(b) The results of the index reveal that the same environment does not necessarily provide the same quality of life for men and women. Also, the leading regions in social development for women are different from those for men. Taking into account a scale from 0 to 100, the regions with the highest scores for women were Ica

Table 7 General results of the Peruvian GEICR—2019

Region	Women index	Ranking	Men index	Ranking	Gender gap
Piura	37.0	13	44.8	19	−7.9
Ucayali	39.5	10	47.6	16	−8.0
Loreto	32.7	18	41.3	25	−8.6
Lima (city)	47.9	2	56.7	4	−8.7
Ica	48.5	1	57.7	3	−9.2
Tumbes	42.5	6	52.6	8	−10.1
PERU	37.9	12	48.4	14	−10.5
Lambayeque	39.1	11	49.6	12	−10.5
La Libertad	36.5	14	47.9	15	−11.4
Lima (provinces)	40.2	9	51.8	11	−11.6
San Martín	29.7	21	41.4	24	−11.7
Huánuco	28.4	23	40.7	26	−12.3
Callao	42.6	5	55.2	5	−12.7
Junín	35.3	16	48.6	13	−13.3
Amazonas	30.6	20	44.3	21	−13.7
Cajamarca	25.1	27	39.0	27	−14.0
Madre de Dios	40.7	7	55.0	6	−14.3
Tacna	40.3	8	54.7	7	−14.4
Puno	32.7	19	47.3	18	−14.6
Ayacucho	27.3	24	42.6	23	−15.2
Arequipa	43.8	3	59.2	2	−15.4
Cusco	28.9	22	44.4	20	−15.5
Ancash	36.3	15	52.0	10	−15.6
Moquegua	42.7	4	59.9	1	−17.1
Pasco	35.0	17	52.4	9	−17.3
Huancavelica	26.1	25	43.7	22	−17.6
Apurímac	25.7	26	47.3	17	−21.6

(48.5) and Metropolitan Lima (47.9), while for men, they were Moquegua (59.9) and Arequipa (59.2).

(c) Regarding the gender gap, in 2019, women have 10.5 points less in development than men in Peru. In addition, the figures show there is a significant gender gap in all the regions of the country. Despite the troubling breach, not all pillars have a large gap, and the situation can vary greatly among the regions. If we look at it by dimensions, the gender gap in favor of men is present in the four dimensions of the index.

(d) Another interesting result is the size of the gap in all the dimensions, especially in the opportunity pillar and autonomy pillar since they have the worst gaps. The latter has by far the largest gender gap, with an average national difference of −26.8 as shown in Appendix 4. Only in the education dimension, there is a gap in favor of women in 5 of the 26 regions, compared to the other 21 regions where men are favored. In addition to the mixed result in the education dimension, a result close to the "equilibrium" is recorded in the health dimension. These two dimensions contrast significantly with the dimension of autonomy and opportunity, which are the areas where the gap in favor of men is significantly higher.

(e) If we analyze it by component, we can see that the gap in favor of women is relatively large in aspects related to education and basic health care. However, this situation is not correlated in components such as economic autonomy, decision making, employment or time management, where the gap exceeds 40% in favor of men's social development.

These results present a series of policy implications. While important advances in the areas of health and education can be observed and should continue in the future, efforts should be mainly oriented to the dimensions of autonomy and opportunity. Autonomy is related to women's economic participation in productive activities (economic autonomy), participation in decision-making positions and, above all, physical autonomy. The latter, in particular, is a priority agenda item in the country, given the very high levels of female violence in the country; regarding the opportunities, access to higher education, access to quality employment (women currently occupy the most vulnerable positions in terms of employment) and women's time management (where they are primarily responsible for the care economy). These results clearly show us the need to reduce the gaps between men and women in Peru, at a regional level.

6 Conclusions

In recent decades, there has been a series of positive changes that contribute to generating more egalitarian societies. Within this process, gender equality has become an internationally recognized and promoted concept, since it is part of the foundations that contribute to the development of countries and the world. In order to solve the problems caused by inequalities between men and women, different national and international organizations have shown a growing interest in the generation of indicators that show the real situation of access to resources disaggregated by gender, with the aim of obtaining more specific information on this phenomenon. The construction of gender-sensitive indexes is a modern proposal based on public and private initiatives. Gender mainstreaming in the indexes is aimed at recognizing inequalities between men and women and seeking strategic ways to promote equality between both groups.

The GEICR is part of this process of building tools that help to visualize the differences and overcome them. GEICR is a pioneering initiative that looks into the reality of each of the regions of a country and provides specific knowledge to work in a focused manner, recognizing the differences in access to resources for each gender in a particular area. Its status as a relative indicator provides a referential view of gender equality in a given region based on the analysis of different dimensions. Likewise, the index recognizes and overcomes the criticisms made of the pioneering international indexes; therefore, it is constructed independently of the general development of each region. In addition, it integrates time use as a variable. These characteristics make the index a strategically constructed tool for environmental analysis.

The GEICR is composed of statistical information from secondary sources and may also include primary information from specific surveys in all regions of the country. From these sources of information, we selected the indicators that shape the four dimensions that make up the index: health, education, autonomy and opportunities. For each of these dimensions, four components and their respective indicators were identified. The selected indicators undergo a standardization process to consolidate the units of measurement, in order to finally obtain three types of results: the global result, the partial results for each of the regions and the partial results of the ICR for each of the dimensions. Each aspect considered in the elaboration of the index has been constructed taking into account the literature review, the critical analysis of other experiences, but above all, clearly understanding the concept of equality to be measured.

The GEICR can be used by policymakers and other relevant stakeholders for policy and strategy design and development at the national and international levels, making it an important tool for International Economic Diplomacy. The GEICR enables strategic targeting of social investment and provides the necessary resources to contribute to the design of policies aimed at reducing the negative differences between men and women and improving the overall condition of a country's regions. The GEICR should not be taken as a complete and final index, but instead as a part of the development process of necessary tools to identify inequalities.

One aspect of the index that could be improved in the future is the inclusion of an instrument with specific questions to obtain primary information for the index. This recommendation is based on the fact that the availability and quality of secondary data in Latin American regions is an important constraint for developing indexes. This is a major issue for applying the GEICR in other countries, since the index requires different data of every region. Only the Government can collect this kind of information, which means that it is necessary to have cooperation agreements between the academic organizations that create the index and the Government. This might even allow including specific questions in the yearly surveys made by most governments, which could give valuable information for new GEICRs.

Appendix 1

The Gender Equality Index for Peruvian Regions—Weights Used.

Pillar	Factor	Indicator	Weight
Education	Educational attainment	Literacy	0.50
		Years of study	0.50
	Primary Education	Attendance at primary school	0.50
		Primary school enrollment	0.50
	Secondary education	Attendance at secondary school	0.50
		Secondary school enrollment	0.50
Health	Access to health	Distance to the health care center	0.34
		National Identity Card	0.34
		Health insurance	0.31
	Morbidity	Hospitalizations	0.50
		Chronic conditions	0.50
	Basic care	Medical attention at public health centers	0.50
		Medicine reception	0.50
Autonomy	Economic	Economic dependence	0.35
		Labor income	0.36
		Unpaid work	0.30

(continued)

(continued)

Pillar	Factor	Indicator	Weight
	Physical	Adult sexual abuse	0.25
		Child sexual abuse	0.25
		Human trafficking	0.25
		Family violence	0.25
	Decision-making	Councilors	0.37
		Municipal governments	0.26
		Parliament	0.37
Opportunity	Access to higher education	University enrollment	0.34
		Enrollment in art higher education	0.34
		Enrollment in technological higher education	0.33
	Employment	Informality	0.33
		Participation in the labor market	0.33
		Underemployment	0.34
	Use of time	Time used in paid labor	0.36
		Employer	0.30
		Weekend labor	0.34

Appendix 2

The Gender Equality Index for Peruvian Regions—Women's Index by Dimension 2019.

Region	General	Education	Health	Autonomy	Opportunity
Ica	48.5	50.2	49.8	32.2	61.9
Lima (city)	47.9	56.3	39.8	41.9	53.7
Arequipa	43.8	53.9	37.9	31.0	52.6
Moquegua	42.7	50.1	38.9	34.2	47.7
Callao	42.6	46.9	43.7	42.2	37.5
Tumbes	42.5	47.1	39.7	36.2	47.0
Madre de Dios	40.7	43.0	45.6	29.9	44.1
Tacna	40.3	55.7	35.1	28.5	41.7
Lima (provinces)	40.2	48.3	48.8	31.7	31.9
Ucayali	39.5	38.9	45.7	36.3	37.1
Lambayeque	39.1	37.9	47.2	41.0	30.1
PERU	37.9	40.2	39.7	34.4	37.4

(continued)

(continued)

Region	General	Education	Health	Autonomy	Opportunity
Piura	37.0	37.4	44.2	39.6	26.7
La Libertad	36.5	37.2	38.2	39.7	30.9
Áncash	36.3	38.8	39.0	38.0	29.5
Junín	35.3	38.6	40.1	29.3	33.1
Pasco	35.0	39.1	39.0	30.9	31.2
Loreto	32.7	21.5	39.4	36.6	33.3
Puno	32.7	39.3	30.3	34.8	26.3
Amazonas	30.6	27.0	36.5	35.7	23.2
San Martín	29.7	20.8	40.0	34.8	23.2
Cusco	28.9	24.3	28.0	28.7	34.7
Huánuco	28.4	17.5	42.5	29.7	23.9
Ayacucho	27.3	14.3	37.8	30.2	27.0
Huancavelica	26.1	15.4	40.3	31.5	17.0
Apurímac	25.7	19.3	30.6	29.7	23.2
Cajamarca	25.1	13.4	37.8	32.2	16.8

Appendix 3

The Gender Equality Index for Peruvian Regions—Men's Index by Dimension 2019.

Region	General	Education	Health	Autonomy	Opportunity
Moquegua	59.9	51.4	45.7	76.4	66.1
Arequipa	59.2	57.9	40.6	66.4	71.9
Ica	57.7	45.9	52.1	64.5	68.3
Lima (city)	56.7	52.4	42.3	64.2	67.7
Callao	55.2	55.3	46.1	62.8	56.7
Madre de Dios	55.0	53.0	50.1	68.4	48.5
Tacna	54.7	58.6	38.4	66.6	55.0
Tumbes	52.6	53.5	42.6	62.4	51.9
Pasco	52.4	47.3	44.5	67.9	49.9
Áncash	52.0	52.6	44.4	66.6	44.3
Lima (provinces)	51.8	45.4	50.0	67.1	44.8
Lambayeque	49.6	38.6	47.5	61.1	51.2
Junín	48.6	40.6	44.1	63.9	45.9
PERU	48.4	41.3	42.4	61.2	48.8
La Libertad	47.9	41.5	41.2	62.0	46.9
Ucayali	47.6	31.7	48.1	59.6	50.8

(continued)

(continued)

Region	General	Education	Health	Autonomy	Opportunity
Apurímac	47.3	44.1	35.3	71.8	38.1
Puno	47.3	55.0	34.2	62.5	37.3
Piura	44.8	35.6	45.3	59.2	39.1
Cusco	44.4	36.3	31.6	59.5	50.5
Amazonas	44.3	36.7	36.8	69.7	34.0
Huancavelica	43.7	30.7	42.4	74.1	27.6
Ayacucho	42.6	28.9	42.0	68.3	31.0
San Martín	41.4	27.9	41.6	62.8	33.3
Loreto	41.3	27.3	40.2	57.6	40.1
Huánuco	40.7	26.1	45.7	62.9	28.1
Cajamarca	39.0	26.5	41.0	60.4	28.2

Appendix 4

The Gender Equality Index for Peruvian Regions—Gender Gap by Dimension 2019.

Region	General	Education	Health	Autonomy	Opportunity
Piura	−7.9	1.8	−1.1	−19.6	−12.4
Ucayali	−8.0	7.2	−2.4	−23.3	−13.7
Loreto	−8.6	−5.8	−0.8	−21.0	−6.8
Lima (city)	−8.7	3.9	−2.5	−22.4	−14.0
Ica	−9.2	4.3	−2.3	−32.3	−6.5
Tumbes	−10.1	−6.4	−2.9	−26.2	−4.9
PERU	−10.5	−1.1	−2.7	−26.8	−11.4
Lambayeque	−10.5	−0.7	−0.2	−20.1	−21.1
La Libertad	−11.4	−4.3	−3.1	−22.3	−16.0
Lima (provinces)	−11.6	2.8	−1.2	−35.3	−12.8
San Martín	−11.7	−7.1	−1.5	−28.0	−10.2
Huánuco	−12.3	−8.6	−3.3	−33.2	−4.2
Callao	−12.7	−8.4	−2.3	−20.6	−19.2
Junín	−13.3	−1.9	−4.0	−34.6	−12.8
Amazonas	−13.7	−9.6	−0.4	−34.0	−10.8
Cajamarca	−14.0	−13.0	−3.2	−28.2	−11.4
Madre de Dios	−14.3	−9.9	−4.5	−38.5	−4.4
Tacna	−14.4	−2.9	−3.3	−38.0	−13.3
Puno	−14.6	−15.7	−3.9	−27.7	−10.9
Ayacucho	−15.2	−14.6	−4.2	−38.1	−4.0

(continued)

(continued)

Region	General	Education	Health	Autonomy	Opportunity
Arequipa	−15.4	−4.0	−2.7	−35.4	−19.3
Cusco	−15.5	−12.0	−3.6	−30.7	−15.8
Áncash	−15.6	−13.7	−5.4	−28.5	−14.8
Moquegua	−17.1	−1.3	−6.7	−42.2	−18.4
Pasco	−17.3	−8.2	−5.5	−37.0	−18.7
Huancavelica	−17.6	−15.3	−2.1	−42.5	−10.6
Apurímac	−21.6	−24.8	−4.7	−42.2	−14.8

References

Benzaquen, J., Del Carpio, L., Zegarra, L., & Valdivia, C. (2010). A competitiveness index for the regions of a country. *CEPAL Review, 2010*(102), 67–84. https://doi.org/10.18356/7781698b-en

Bobadilla, P., Del Aguila, L., & Morgan, M. (1998). *Diseño y evaluación de proyectos de desarrollo* [Design and evaluation of development projects]. PACT-PERU.

Castro, C., & Álvarez, B. (2011). *La igualdad en la responsabilidad social de las empresas* [Equality in corporate social responsibility]. http://www.castello.es/web20/archivos/contenidos/61/D021_Igualdad_RSE.pdf

CENTRUM PUCP. (2019). *Índice de progreso social regional del Perú 2019* [Peru regional social progress index 2017]. CENTRUM PUCP. https://www.centrumbusinesspublishing.org/product-page/%C3%ADndice-del-progreso-social-de-regional-del-per%C3%BA-2019

Dávila, M. (2004). *Indicadores de género:* guía práctica [Gender indicators: A practical guide]. Andalusian Women's Institute. Consejería de igualdad y políticas sociales. http://www.juntadeandalucia.es/iamindex.php/recursos-y-servicios/2013-04-19-11-45-20/func-startdown/616/

Economic Commission for Latin America and the Caribbean [ECLAC]. (2004). *Caminos hacia la equidad de género en América Latina y el Caribe* [Pathways to gender equity in Latin America and the Caribbean]. Author. https://repositorio.cepal.org/bitstream/handle/11362/16577/S2004062_es.pdf

Economic Commission for Latin America and the Caribbean [ECLAC]. (2010). *Manual de uso del observatorio de igualdad de género de América Latina y el Caribe* [User's manual for the gender equality observatory for Latin America and the Caribbean]. CEPAL. https://repositorio.cepal.org/bitstream/handle/11362/2966/1/lcl3223.pdf

Economic Commission for Latin America and the Caribbean [ECLAC]. (2016). *Incorporar la perspectiva de género en la producción estadística supone interrogar sobre cómo impactan de forma diferenciar determinados fenómenos a hombres y mujeres* [Incorporating a gender perspective in statistical production involves asking how certain phenomena impact men and women differently]. CEPAL. http://www.cepal.org/es/notas/incorporar-la-perspectiva-genero-la-produccion-estadistica-supone-interrogar-como-impactan

Economic Commission for Latin America and the Caribbean [ECLAC]. (2019). *About the observatory.* Gender Equality Observatory. https://oig.cepal.org/en/about-observatory

Giménez, G., & Castro, G. (2015). *¿Por qué los estudiantes de colegios públicos y privados de Costa Rica obtienen distintos resultados académicos?* [Why do students from public and private schools in Costa Rica obtain different academic results?]. *Perfiles Latinoamericanos, 49,* 195–223. http://www.scielo.org.mx/pdf/perlat/v25n49/0188-7653-perlat-25-49-00195.pdf

International Labour Organization [ILO]. (2013). *La economía informal y el trabajo decente: Una guía de recursos sobre políticas apoyando a transición hacia la formalidad* [The informal economy and decent work: A resource guide on policies supporting the transition to formality]. Author. http://www.ilo.org/wcmsp5/groups/public/@ed_emp/@emp_policy/documents/publication/wcms_229429.pdf

International Labour Organization [ILO]. (2016). *Women in the workplace.* Author. http://www.ilo.org/wcmsp5/groups/piloublic/---dgreports/---dcomm/---publ/documents/publication/wcms_483214.pdf

Kanter, R. (1977). *Men and women in corporations.* Basic Books.

Lazarsfeld, P. F. (1958). Evidence and inference in social research. *American Academy of Arts & Sciences, 87*(4). American Academy of Arts & Sciences.

Milosavljevic, V. (2007). *Estadísticas para la equidad de género. Magnitudes y tendencias en América Latina* [Statistics for gender equity: Magnitudes and trends in Latin America]. UNESCO. https://www.cepal.org/es/publicaciones/27843-estadisticas-la-equidad-genero-magnitudes-tendencias-america-latina

Ministry of Education [MINEDU]. (2014). *Encuesta nacional a egresados universitarios y universidades* [National survey of university graduates and universities]. https://www.inei.gob.pe/media/MenuRecursivo/publicaciones_digitales/Est/Lib1298/Libro.pdf

National Institute of Statistics and Data Processing [INEI]. (2012). *Código de buenas prácticas estadísticas* [Statistical code of practice]. https://www.inei.gob.pe/media/buenas-practicas/Codigo_Buenas_Practicas.pdf

Office of the Attorney General. (2014). *Observatorio de criminalidad* [Observatory of criminality]. https://portal.mpfn.gob.pe/boletininformativo/infotratadepersonas

Organization for Economic Co-operation and Development [OECD], & Joint Research Center [JRC]. (2008). *Handbook on constructing composite indicators: Methodology and user guide*. OECD.
Pan American Health Organization [PAHO]. (2009, May 24). *Equidad de género en salud. Programa mujer, salud y desarrollo* [Gender equity in health. Women, health and development program]. http://www1.paho.org/Spanish/AD/GE/GenderEquityinHealthsp.pdf
Porter, M., & Scott, A. (2018). *2018 Social progress index: Methodology summary*. Social Progress Imperative. https://www2.deloitte.com/content/dam/Deloitte/ec/Documents/deloitte-analytics/Estudios/2018-Social-Progress-Index-brief.pdf
Rodríguez, S. (2016). La desigualdad de ingresos y salud en Colombia [Income and health inequality in Colombia]. *Perfiles Latinoamericanos, 24*(48), 265–296. https://doi.org/10.18504/pl2448-011-2016
Social Progress Imperative (2020). *2020 Social progress index executive summary*. Washington, DC: Social Progress Imperative. https://www.socialprogress.org/static/8dace0a5624097333c2a57e29c2d7ad9/2020-global-spi-findings.pdf
Tabbush, C., & Caminotti, M. (2015). Igualdad de género y movimientos sociales en la Argentina posneoliberal: La organización Barrial Tupac Amaru [Gender equality and social movements in post-neoliberal Argentina: The organización barrial Tupac Amaru]. *Perfiles Latinoamericanos, 23*(46), 147–171. http://www.scielo.org.mx/pdf/perlat/v23n46/v23n46a6.pdf
United Nations [UN]. (1995). *Fourth world conference on women Beijing declaration*. http://www.un.org/womenwatch/daw/beijing/platform/declar.htm
United Nations [UN]. (2012). *Leadership and political participation*. UN Women. http://www.unwomen.org/es/what-we-do/leadership-and-political-participation
United Nations [UN]. (2015). *Objetivos de desarrollo del milenio Peru: The United Nations System of Peru*. http://onu.org.pe/que-son-los-odm/
United Nations [UN]. (2016). *2030 Agenda and the sustainable development goals*. http://www.sela.org/mean/2262361/agenda-2030-and-the-objectives-of-development-sustainable-development.pdf
United Nations [UN]. (n.d.). *Women's human rights and gender equality*. Author. http://www.ohchr.org/SP/Pages/Home.aspx
United Nations Development Programme [UNDP]. (2010). *Informe sobre desarrollo humano 2010* [Human development report 2010]. http://hdr.undp.org/sites/default/files/hdr_2010_es_complete_reprint.pdf
United Nations Development Programme [UNDP]. (2015). *Informe sobre desarrollo humano 2015* [Human development report 2015]. http://hdr.undp.org/sites/default/files/2015_human_development_report_overview_-_es.pdf

United Nations Development Programme [UNDP]. (2020). *What does the GII measure and how is it calculated?* http://hdr.undp.org/sites/default/files/hdr2020_technical_notes.pdf

United Nations Educational, Scientific and Cultural Organization [UNESCO]. (2017a). *Gender equality.* Author. http://www.unesco.org/new/es/havana/areas-of-action/igualdad-de-genero/

United Nations Educational, Scientific and Cultural Organization [UNESCO]. (2017b). *Seis maneras de asegurar que la educación superior no deje a nadie atrás* [Six ways to ensure that higher education leaves no one behind]. Author. http://unesdoc.unesco.org/images/0024/002478/247862S.pdf

United Nations Population Fund [UNFPA]. (2014). *Igualdad entre los géneros* [Gender equality]. http://www.unfpa.org/es/igualdad-entre-los-g%C3%A9neros

Vélez, R., López, S., & Rajmil, L. (2009). Género y salud percibida en la infancia y la adolescencia en España [Gender and self-perceived health in childhood and adolescence in Spain]. *Gaceta Sanitaria, 23*(5), 433–439. https://doi.org/10.1016/j.gaceta.2009.01.014

World Economic Forum. (2020). *The global gender gap report 2020.* http://www3.weforum.org/docs/WEF_GGGR_2020.pdf

World Health Organization [WHO]. (2016). *Violence against women.* World Health Organization. http://www.who.int/mediacentre/factsheets/fs239/es/

CHAPTER 6

International Energy Security Risk Index and Energy Diplomacy

Mohga Bassim and Vincent Charles

1 Introduction

Energy has long been recognised as a core requirement for economic growth and development, prosperity, well-being, and strategic priority, probably only after air, water and food. Energy is essential for all economic activities, including transportation of goods and people and generating the electrical energy necessary for homes, services, and production.

M. Bassim (✉)
Department of Economics and International Studies,
Faculty of Business, Humanities, and Social Sciences, The University of Buckingham, Buckingham, UK
e-mail: mohga.bassim@buckingham.ac.uk

V. Charles
CENTRUM Católica Graduate Business School, Lima, Peru
e-mail: vcharles@pucp.pe

Pontifical Catholic University of Peru, Lima, Peru

© The Author(s), under exclusive license to Springer Nature Switzerland AG 2022
V. Charles and A. Emrouznejad (eds.), *Modern Indices for International Economic Diplomacy*, https://doi.org/10.1007/978-3-030-84535-3_6

The increase in world energy consumption due to the large increase in population, economic growth, and the increase in prosperity and well-being led to increases in the trade competition for energy resources between developed, developing and economies in transition.

This chapter focuses on the energy security risks, threats, evaluation, mitigation policies, energy diplomacy, and its broader impact on importers and producers' economies rather than its impact on a specific country or disadvantaged group. The risk management process described here is based on risk management standards and practices not adequately found in the energy security literature.

The increase in world population and the needs for economic growth drive the increase in energy consumption. The world population increased by 202% in the period from 1971 to 2018 (World Bank Data, 2021). Over the same period, the energy demand has grown by 260% (IEA, 2020) to meet the increase in population, economic growth, prosperity, and living standards. The population is expected to increase from 7.8 Billion to 9.74 Billion in the period from 2020 to 2050 (UN, 2019), i.e. approx. 24.9%, whereas British Petroleum expects energy use to increase by approx. 27 and part of the energy will be offset by improvements in energy intensity and efficiency (British Petroleum, 2020). The increase is expected to continue, but at reduced rates, up to the end of the century.

Increases in demand and trade competitions between countries for energy are considered the main sources of energy security risks, among other human-made and natural phenomena challenges. The importance of energy security dates back to World War I timed when Churchill ordered imported oil in place of the secured locally produced coal to make the British Navy ships faster (Yergin, 2006). The energy security term was initially used after the supply shock in the 1970s and gained broader use in the 2000s (Szulecki, 2020). The definitions of energy security in the 1970s considered "availability and affordability", and these are still in the IEA definitions. "Accessibility and acceptability" were introduced to energy security in the early 2000s (Cherp & Jewell, 2014). More recently, the United Nations adopted "access to affordable, reliable, sustainable and modern energy" as the goal number seven of the Sustainable Development Goals (SDGs) for 2030 (UNDP, 2020). National and international bodies, including the World Bank (2019) and United Nations, Economic and Social Council (2019), monitor the UNDP goals.

Along with the strategic necessity for energy security for growth and well-being comes the need to fight against the devastating impact of

CO_2 emission on climate changes and the consequences of environmental degradation on growth and the life on earth.

Energy security affects developing and developed countries, whether these countries are producing, consuming, or transit countries. A balance among the energy security objectives of the different countries needs to be found and has been attempted (Energy Charter Secretariat, 2015).

Different international organisations have defined energy security; however, these definitions are covered in the subsequent UN SDGs definition. For example, the Asia Pacific Energy Research Centre (APERC) defines that "energy security is the ability of an economy to guarantee the availability of energy resource supply in a sustainable and timely manner with the energy price being at a level that will not adversely affect the economic performance of the economy" and the IEA defines it as "uninterrupted availability of sources at an affordable price". There are some differences in the exact meanings of terms in the academic interpretations of researchers; however, in this work, we will concentrate on the basic accepted definitions.

Several published studies for different countries evaluated energy security with some differences in indicators, metrics, indexes, and interpretation of their meanings. Energy security is also discussed in the overall context of national security, as detailed in Sect. 2.

There have been several severe energy security events in the past 70 years including, the Iranian nationalisation of the Anglo-Persian Oil Company in 1951 and the oil embargo supply shock in 1973. The discontent of oil-exporting countries with the distribution of wealth from oil led to the formation of the Organisation of Petroleum Exporting Countries (OPEC) in 1960. OPEC coordinates the production of oil and trading prices. The IEA was established in 1974 by OECD countries, initially to coordinate response to major disruptions in oil supply, which was subsequently extended to include energy security, economic development, and environmental awareness, with a worldwide engagement.

The oil supply events and shocks continued, the Iraq-Iran war in the late seventies resulting in an oil price increase of more than three folds, invasion of Kuwait in 1990 and the gulf war, US and international coalition 2003 invasion of Iraq, which at the time ranked 2nd in proven oil reserve, and the repeated Russia-Ukraine gas crises which affected EU gas supply in 2006 and 2009. Sever political turmoil in Syria and Libya with associated human disasters from 2011 onwards and the formation of terrorist mercenary groups, which eventually took over important oil fields in Syria, Iraq and Libya, piracy and terrorist and mercenaries threats in new oil fields in Africa, the standoff between Russia and the West over Ukraine in 2014, and several other events which emphasise the energy security vulnerability. Other energy security events result from natural disasters like the Katrina and Rita hurricanes impacts, which affected USA energy prices.

Moreover, nuclear energy as a source of energy appears to be fraught with serious risks. The nuclear energy incidents of the meltdown of the nuclear reactor in the Three Miles Island in the USA (1979), Chernobyl in the Soviet Union (1986), and Fukushima Japan (2011), along with the radioactive material waste disposal problems, prove that nuclear is not the solution to energy security. Costs, safety and technology, are prohibitive for most economies in transition and almost all developing countries.

These events, threats and shocks affect the energy importers in transit and producing countries' economic security and national security. It forces every country on the planet into reconsidering its strategies and policies for energy security risks mitigation.

The severe threat of CO_2 emissions from hydrocarbon fuels to the life, economy and environment is a fundamental issue to consider in energy security risk mitigation. Climate change and environmental degradation in generating energy using fossil fuels is a very serious issue that was recognised increasingly but only in the past two or three decades. Increasing clean Renewable Energy (RE) share in the total energy mix has become an urgent worldwide target to reduce the serious impact of hydrocarbon energy used for growth on environmental degradation and reduce countries reliance on imported hydrocarbons (Nathaniel et al., 2021). Barriers for RET (Kabel & Bassim, 2020) are increasingly re-moved at a growing pace, and as a result, there is an increasing share for RE in the energy mix, International Renewable Energy Agency (IRENA, 2020).

Energy diplomacy to maintain the reliability, availability and affordability of energy supply has been growing due to different energy security events. It is a part of foreign policy and national security. There is no commonly accepted or suggested energy diplomacy definition; however, its objective is to resolve the external energy security risks and issues between sovereign states. Exporting countries also have energy security, economic and national security interests to protect, and they use energy diplomacy to maintain the flow, avoid disruptions and maintain fair trade conditions.

In the early twentieth century, energy issues were predominantly resolved by the powerful corporations and governments that were supporting them; however, after World War II, the changes in political power and the substantial increase in energy security risks in importing, exporting and in transit countries, necessitated the use of energy diplomacy instruments for national security.

Growing energy transition to RE will change the current energy security risks, diplomacy policies, and national security for producers, consumers and transit countries. The recent estimates by specialised international energy and economic organisations show a growing transition to renewable, that will gradually reduce what was almost complete dependence on hydrocarbons. This transition results from the continued reduction in costs, environmental issues, sustainability of supply, improvements in technology, and increased security of supply of locally produced renewables. The result will be a corresponding growing transition in the negotiating power and energy diplomacy policies of the hydrocarbon producers and importers.

2 Concepts and Evolving Definitions of Energy Security

The concept of energy security evolves as the challenges related to energy are growing with the growth in demand, trade competition increase in growth in developing countries, and the pressures of producers for better revenues increase (Jewell & Brutschin, 2019; Kester, 2018; Szulecki, 2018, 2020). The concept of energy security initially emphasised the need for "physical availability" of reliable and adequate supply and "affordability", i.e. at an acceptable price level. Subsequently, in the 2000s "accessibility and acceptability" were added. These were initially proposed for healthcare in the eighties and subsequently used for education and food security. Since the 1990s, "Sustainability" has become an important issue after recognising global warming issues. The United Nations (UN) SDGs, 2015, recognised "Affordable and Clean Energy" in goal seven and combating climate change in goal 13. These are related to energy security while limiting CO_2 emission from hydrocarbons use. Energy poverty issues are increasingly discussed under the concept of energy security, and it is a security issue for hundreds of millions of people in developed and developing countries suffering from difficulties in obtaining energy for heating or cooking.

Several studies for the dimensions of energy security include protection from potential risks that would cause disruption and resilience to withstand these disruptions. The studies with different measures, and assumptions, argued the accuracy of energy security definitions, investigated its indicators and differed on what should be considered energy security and included (Sovacool & Mukherjee, 2011; Vivoda, 2010; Winzer, 2012).

Defining energy security in the more established context of security studies and "securitization" leads to considering the energy security issues as "existential" and hence implement exceptional measures (Szulecki, 2020). Exceptional measures appear to be implemented to mitigate serious energy security threats by breaking norms, not military intervention. The US introduction of the "light tight oil" to mitigate their low energy security, and the EU considered a costly gas supply pipelines through the Caspian Sea to mitigate the Russian gas line supply threat.

Cherp and Jewell (2014), and Leung et al. (2014) suggest that securitization requirement of closer specification of "Security for whom?", "Security for what values?" and "Security from what threats?" should be applied to energy securitization. Though similar questions, including "what" is being protected?" against what" is it being protected? "who" "is doing what" to protect?, and moreover, how to mitigate the risks? have been used (Koyama & Kutani, 2012).

The difference between energy importers seeking the "security of supply" and exporters looking for "security in demand" is important in energy security concepts. A typical definition of supply security by the United Nations in 2000 is "the continuous availability of energy in varied forms, in sufficient quantities, and at reasonable prices". Demand security is the stable trade relationship between the producer and the importer (Customer), where the customer purchases often provide a significant part of the producer's national revenues. Both the exporters and importers are seeking the continuity of the trade flow.

The British Government policy on energy security is principally concerned that consumers must have access to their needs of energy services (physical security) at affordable costs that avoid excessive instability (price security) and also that legally binding targets on carbon emission are achieved (U.K. Department of Energy and Climate Change, 2012).

The European Commission defined EU long-term strategy for energy supply security as ensuring: "the well-being of citizens and the proper functioning of the economy, the uninterrupted physical availability of energy products on the market, at a price which is affordable for all consumers (Private and industrial), while respecting environmental concerns and looking towards sustainable development" (de Sampaio Nunes, 2002). The IEA has a similar definition "Adequate and reliable supplies of energy at affordable prices" (IEA, 2007). The UN SDGs simple short definition of Goal 7 of the "Affordable and Clean Energy" and goal 13 on Climate change appear to address all others. In conclusion, these definitions appear to be different only in wording, but the meanings are substantially the same.

From the oil and gas producer's perspective, energy security would probably more simply mean the continuity of demand at fair prices, with fair extraction conditions and secure delivery. Proceeds are essential for development and welfare in producing countries, as most of these countries rely on these proceeds as the primary country income and use it to reduce taxes and provide for subsidies. The sudden oil price collapse in 2014/2015 badly affected several oil-producing countries, particularly those who did not account for the risks of relying on oil extraction and export as the main economic activity. The sudden reduction in revenues hit hardly the development plans, welfare programs and ongoing projects in several oil-producing countries. Furthermore, several of these countries had to take sudden measures to increase tax revenues and reduce subsidies leading to more pressures on their citizens and foreign labour force working on development projects. The uncertainties in assessing the risks and future expectations for energy and oil prices in the short, medium and long-range are too many. In recent years, the necessity for safe delivery has become more evident with the oil smuggling incidents by ISIS (Bassim, 2015).

3 Policies for Energy Security Risk Management

Setting appropriate energy security strategies and implementation policies must be based on a comprehensive identification and assessment of the country or region energy security threats and opportunities. The identification process is based on the initial categorising of the sources of energy security risks, then identifying the risks in each category. The risk identification process of energy security issues usually is based on rigorous reviews of past events and experts' advice of potential risks in each category. The expert panel assesses each risk severity and probability of occurrence and may be followed by a detailed quantitative analysis.

Table 3 in Sect. 3, for example, shows a list of "metrics" used to evaluate the US energy security index. Vulnerability evaluation of the energy security Index "metrics" is expected to be based on detailed studies to identify the associated risks for each metric and their likelihood and severity. These evaluations of "metrics" form the complete index. The studies made are based on the judgement of panels of experts and form the basis for broader discussions and debates at specialised government circles and possibly hearings for formulating the security strategies. Implementation policies to mitigate the risks, and energy/economic diplomacy policies, when applicable, are based on the agreed strategies. Figure 5 in Sect. 3 shows the successive substantial improvements in the USA energy security and its future forecasts after implementing the US Energy Security Index from 2011 onwards. The Index can be used to test the level of risk resulting from different energy supply shock scenarios. The resulting risk level may point to the necessity for adopting strategies and policies to mitigate the risk. These strategies and policies may include some of the proposed below in this section, for example, diplomacy, diversity or others. The Australian Government, for example, used such scenarios to test supply chain virtual shocks on the energy security resilience, respond economically and use appropriate response strategies and policies (Australian Gov., 2011).

One of the criticisms in the literature is that there is no clear relation between the index results and the policies. The index is used to compare the progress in energy security with reference to a base year when energy security was low, so it is necessary for showing how much success or otherwise have been achieved using a selected strategy or its' policies.

This logical risk management procedure becomes a cumbersome process with some complexities of energy security risks, as it can involve and impact several sovereign countries, economies, markets, and legislation and regulations. An example of this complexity is found for example in the disruptions in the gas supply to the EU from Russia through Ukraine, attempts for more than two decades by EU and US to construct an alternative direct line from Asia through the Caspian Sea, and recent USA diplomacy policy to supply US gas to EU.

Strategies and policies for energy security risk mitigation evolve and are modified or improved depending on external and internal changes that occur due to the strategies and policies level of success or otherwise. For instance, the "light tight oil revolution changed the US energy security risk strategies and policies entirely between 2005 and 2020.

USA strategy for energy moved from 2005 explanation of strategy as "quite dialogue with producing countries", to 2014 driving the world oil prices down, Fig. 3. The Global Energy Institute (GEI), Index of US Energy Security Risk (2020a), announced that the low prices due to the current lower demand, coupled with oversupply, make it difficult for US producers to stay in business.

Policies for energy security risks management include several methods and mitigation measures. Energy Charter Secretariat (2015) suggested some of the following policies for successfully mitigating energy security risks.

3.1 Using Alternative Energy Sources—RET

Risk avoidance is the first risk mitigation measure that should be considered in combating complicated risks with far-reaching economic and strategic effects like energy security risks. The continuation of using hydrocarbons as the primary energy source is fraught with serious political, environmental, transportation, reliability, availability and price volatility risks. It is bound to create more security issues in the future due to the growing demand, trade competition over energy resources, and gradual depletion in the long run.

These risks will be reduced with the increase in RE share in the energy mix, which the International Renewable Energy Agency (IRENA) predicts will constitute 73% of the installed capacity and over 60% of all power generation in the "Transforming Energy Scenario" by 2050 (IRENA, 2020). RE barriers, particularly the high investment costs and technical issues (Kabel & Bassim, 2020), are being successfully alleviated, encouraging the reluctant financial institutions to invest in RE. The continued cost reductions in RE to an economic level and technological advances will prompt the acceleration in the RET (IEA, 2019). The World Economic Fourm built an index for fostering the energy transition (World Economic Forum, 2021) to monitor countries' progress towards energy transition.

The gap between the demand for energy and the growing RE supply from hydropower, solar and wind power is still high. However, there is a continuous improvement to reduce this gap, although it is the long-term solution for the environmental degradation, availability, affordability and security issues. Several countries' Governments have been implementing stimulating policies in financial and tax incentives, loans, feed-in tariffs

Renewable Portfolio Standard (RPS). Meanwhile, financial institutions considered financing RE to be risky, one of the main barriers to RE's spread (Kabel & Bassim, 2019). Studies recently indicated that the cost of RE has become economical and that specific systems are becoming cheaper than fossil fuels. This cost reduction will undoubtedly encourage financial institutions to finance RE projects and encourage governments to enact more incentives policies.

Different scenarios are proposed to explore the energy demand in the period up to 2050, considering the probable reductions in CO_2 levels. A "Business as usual" scenario suggests an increase in energy demand of 25% by 2050, while scenarios for rapid CO_2 reduction by 70% and net-zero suggest an increase of 10% (British Petroleum, 2020). These scenarios explain, with some uncertainty, the range of what may happen in the period up to 2050 and highlight the ongoing efforts for RET.

3.2 Energy Diplomacy

Energy diplomacy grew as a branch of foreign policy understandably to resolve energy security issues between countries through diplomacy, negotiating and facilitating trade exchanges between sovereign states. So far, there is no commonly accepted or even suggested definition (s), likely due to the differences in the country's conditions, market realities and requirements. However, the main diplomacy goal is expected to ensure the country's secure access to affordable, reliable, and sustainable energy. Diplomatic agendas have been used for other political gains from using energy; for example, the USA used it to resolve problems in Iraq and Sudan in 2012, and with a change in administration diplomacy in 2017 announced a new era of "energy dominance" (Boersma & Johnson, 2018). For energy producers, the objective of diplomacy is to promote trade deals and provide technical backing to users where necessary. There are, however, limitations to what diplomacy can achieve within market realities and constraints.

3.3 Strengthening the Legislative and Regulatory Framework

Energy security can be improved, in some cases, by attention to agreements made and to strengthening the legislative and regulatory framework as essential components for energy security. For example, the solid legislative and regulatory framework is one of the strategic pillars used by the European Union to deal with the dominant gas supplies from Russia, as Europe experienced two significant gas disruptions of supplies due to dispute between the Russian gas supplier GAZPROM and the Ukrainian gas company (Boersma & Johnson, 2018).

3.4 Diversification

In risk management, risk reduction and control are some of the main strategies used to reduce risks. Diversification is a widely used energy security risk reductions in both supply and demand. Diversification includes using alternative energy sources and suppliers, using alternative supply routes, using different methods for generating power, whereas diversification for producers (exporters) means different consumers, and alternative supply methods. Diversification of energy generation using RE is covered in 3.1.

An example of diversification of supply and route can be found in the EU, initiative for the 'Southern Gas Corridor' through the Caspian sea to diversify the sources of supply and reduce Europe's dependence on the Russian gas supply. The total length is 3500 km at an estimated cost of $45 billion. Similarly, Russia is developing oil and gas pipelines in Eastern Siberia to diversify its markets to reduce its dependence on the EU. In conclusion, both importers and exporters have been diversifying to reduce their risks. Diversification is a very well-known risk reduction strategy in business operations where supplies are obtained from competing sources, and the products are offered in the open markets to improve reliability and reduce business security risks. However, the size of operations in the energy industry and markets and the energy security risk costs are challenging and also it often occurs across several sovereign countries.

3.5 Supply Expansion (Development of Domestic and Foreign Resources)

To mitigate energy security risks, consumers consider strategies and policies to develop and expand supply in domestic and overseas resources. For example, in the past decade, importers increased the exploration and production of gas from fields in different geographic zones and countries. Security is coupled with the reduction of harmful emissions to the environment.

The USA, the largest importer of oil with limited domestic reserves, has implemented supply expansion policies by developing domestic resources. The development of "light tight oil" and shale gas in the past ten years is a successful example of these policies. As a result, the USA weak energy security in 2011 was turned in 2017 to "energy dominance" and pushed the USA into the highest energy security ranking of the 25 large energy user group (Global Energy Institute, 2020b).

Meanwhile, this was a significant factor in reducing the market price of hydrocarbon energy to a low level in 2014/2015 (Bassim, 2015), which negatively impacted the security of producers and transit countries' budgets and development plans. Figure 1 shows the oil prices severe plunge down during the period from June 2014–December 2015.

The "light tight oil" and gas contributed significantly to this unmatched collapse in oil prices, together with lower demand for oil in Europe and China at the time, in addition to the steady supply of oil from OPEC. The price and demand shocks hit the producers hard, particularly with the political and "diplomacy" difficulties in several oil-exporting countries.

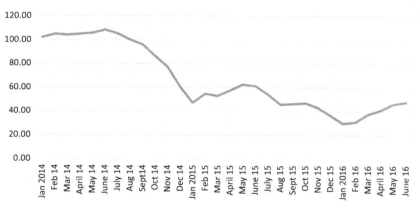

Fig. 1 Crude oil average prices (US$/bbl)—2014–2016 (*Source* World Bank. [2021]. Commodity Price Data. *The Pink Sheet*)

3.6 Security Enhancement

As a foreign policy branch, energy diplomacy is intended to ensure affordable, reliable, sustainable and modern energy by negotiating and facilitating fair trade exchanges between sovereign states. For energy producers, the objective of diplomacy is to maintain demand, promote fair trade deals, and provide technical backing to users where necessary.

However, lately, this has not been the case, and unexpectedly, military actions have been considered a strategic option in the twenty-first century. ISIS took military control of oil extraction facilities in Syria and Iraq. Undoubtedly, ISIS received support from other countries, transportation, marketing, initial financing, arming and maybe others, which have not been confirmed. Other countries also experienced other incidents in the past decade.

Sever energy and human breaches like this, and far less, requires firm international actions by the UN Security Council, International Court of Justice and others, to prevent the recurrence of dark ages practices. Security loss can be extremely harmful and should be dealt with as a serious issue.

Transportation risks have been a cause for concern in the past and present times. Continued incidents in recent years at the straits of Hormuz and the piracy at the Horn of Africa are examples of the transportation risks. The risks and incidents inherent in the transportation of oil and gas can be more serious for the continuity in the supply chain.

These risks and similar need immediate international action based on legal court judgement, perhaps with military backing to enhance the energy security, alleviate and uproot the reasons of insecurity, and maintain peace and security for every human being, Unilateral and collective actions not based on legal court decisions are inappropriate in the twenty-first century, and may have other political and economic motives or objectives.

3.6.1 Stockpiling

Stockpiling of oil reserves is a strategy for the absorption of risks by building up strategic reserves to create a reserve margin to mitigate potential supply disruptions. This risk mitigation measure has been adopted for decades in many OECD countries.

Coordination of oil stockpiling within IEA member countries is used to create a delay of sudden supply events, reduce the impact, and allow adequate time for counteracting the event. IEA emergency response mechanisms were first set up in 1974, and its member countries' governments are required today to hold oil stocks equivalent to at least 90 days of net oil imports. However, there are growing criticisms for the tied up investments in the facilities and large quantities of retained oil.

3.7 Demand Control and Improving Energy Efficiency

The EU considers energy efficiency to be the European energy security immediate element, and the IEA term "first fuel" describes the multiple benefits of improved energy access, energy security, and the reduction of air pollution and energy costs (IEA, 2020). Reducing energy consumption would improve the security, the effectiveness of the risk mitigation measures, and alleviate severe environmental degradation.

Several countries have been working on improving the efficiency of energy systems from energy generation, through transmission, to final energy usage. The energy intensity (amount of energy needed per GDP) is reduced in several countries (IEA, 2018). As shown in Fig. 2, UK energy consumption grew from 1980 up to 2001, and then decreased to the level of 1980 approximately. UK population have increased by approx. 10 million people in the same period.

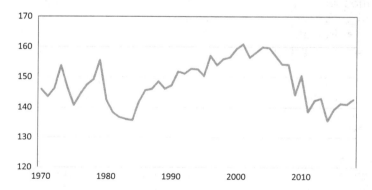

Fig. 2 UK final energy consumption (mtoe) (*Source* UK National Statistics, Department for Business, Energy and Industrial Strategy. [2019]. Energy Consumption in the UK [ECUK] 1970 to 2018, Consumption Tables, Chart C1)

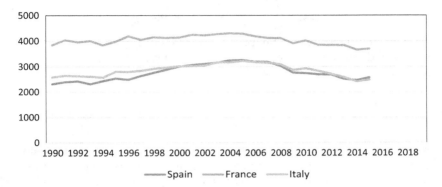

Fig. 3 Energy use (KG of oil equivalent per capita) (*Source* Based on World Bank. [2020]. *World Bank database.* https://data.worldbank.org/indicator/EG.use.pcap.kg.OE?locations)

Similarly, Figure 3 shows a reduction in energy consumption in KG of oil equivalent per capita for three EU countries.

We note based on World Bank Data (2020) that, unlike the trends shown towards reducing energy in Figs. 2 and 3, several developing countries are showing a continued increase in energy consumption.

3.8 Energy Subsidies

Subsidies are used in some countries to reduce energy poverty and improve energy affordability for the needy. In several developing countries, fuels subsidies intended to improve the security of access to energy for their population have been a heavy burden on their ailing budgets (Salman & Bassim, 2019).

These subsidies are discouraged by the IMF and IEA and considered to create market distortions that discourage energy use efficiently. In most countries, subsidies go to the rich, not the poor, causing drastic imbalances in the countries budgets and increase the poverty gap. Developing countries have been encouraged to restructure subsidies to serve the poor and reduce the burden on their budgets.

3.9 Energy Trade and Pricing

Energy consumers secure supplies, and producers gain revenues from energy trade through appropriate contracts that guarantee a fair price level for both supplier and consumer security.

3.10 Vertical Integration, "Asset Swaps", and the Acquisition of Overseas Resources

Asset swaps are used as a policy tool in order to mitigate the supply and demand risks. Vertical integration and mutual exchange of energy business assets could ensure price and volume risks mitigation and promote international energy security. This integration is standard practice in the oil industry, where multi-national corporations invest in exploration, extraction technology and production assets in exchange for a share in the production. This asset swap and integration guarantee the security of supply and demand. In the past two decades, companies from China, India and other countries have done the same.

In conclusion, the above policies for Energy Security Risk Management have been used successfully and are applicable in similar situations. Energy diplomacy is expectedly not very well defined as the country's diplomatic action strategies will be governed by the facts of the security situation.

4 Energy Indexes

There have been several studies of the indicators which determine a country's energy security (Jansen et al., 2004). These indicators are collated to arrive at indexes to show the country's overall energy security level. The studies covered several countries, such as Asia Pacific (Vivoda, 2010), Australia (Australian Gov., 2011), India (Deloitte, 2013), the European Union (Šumskis & Giedraitis, 2015), and Pakistan (Abdullah et al., 2020). Wang and Zhou (2017) provided a detailed comparative study for 162 countries. However, the most important of these Indexes are the IEA model (MOSES) and the USA Global Energy Institute Index for the US Energy Security, together with its similar but separate version, the International Index of Energy Security Risk. The USA Global Energy Institute publishes two yearly reports, one for each of the USA Energy Security Risk and the other in the International Index of Energy Security Risk, to assess energy security risks in the USA and separately for the large energy user countries. The IEA model (MOSES) has also formed the basis of several country studies over the past decade or so, including, for example, India (Pahwa & Chopra, 2013), Georgia (Font, 2020), and Turkey (Kocaslan, 2014). The International Index Energy Security Risk consistently publishes an annual report since 2013, covering the energy security for 25 countries of the large energy user group.

The connection between the index score and the resulting country ranking on the one hand and the strategic planning and policies to mitigate these risks, on the other hand, require explanation. The country index value and ranking indicate the status of country security, in line with any other index, for example, indexes for poverty, human development, inequality and others. However, it alarms the policymakers to reconsider their strategies and policies if the index values are low compared to a base year or other countries. It also provides a basis for countries within similar grouping or conditions to benefit from the experience of one another. The detailed studies and analysis of the individual indicators and metrics highlight the specific risks. Hence, strategy planners and policymakers formulate the response strategies and policies to improve the security level. Based on the agreed strategies, the policymakers initiate energy diplomacy moves where applicable.

For example, the USA used the "opportunity" provided by the abundance of new energy to initiate a new strategic policy and imitate diplomatic moves to persuade the EU to change its strategies and policies used to control the energy security risk "threats" of supply disruptions from the dependence on the single supply of gas fuel line from Russia through Ukraine.

The World Economic Forum (WEF) issued in 2012 the "Global Energy Architecture Performance Index" to provide the policymakers with information on the weaknesses and strengths to improve the energy systems. Energy access and security, sustainability and contribution to economic growth are assessed using 18 indicators for 127 countries (World Economic Forum, 2017). In the development of the Index, WEF introduced the "Global Energy Transition Index-(ETI)". The ETI report is issued annually and compares countries' RET using three dimensions: energy access and security, environmental sustainability, economic development and growth (World Economic Forum, 2021). These three interconnected dimensions represent the energy triangle provide a more inclusive view of energy security, whereas other indices only consider security and environment. The Index measures the current energy system performance and countries readiness for energy transition (World Economic Forum, 2021).

4.1 IEA Model (MOSES) for Short-Term Energy Security

IEA introduced a Model in 2011 for Short-Term Energy Security (MOSES) to evaluate and group the IEA Countries' energy security risks of disruption and their ability to deal with the disruptions, i.e. their resilience (Jewell, 2011). The IEA groups the countries with similar energy systems' profile, but It does not rank the energy security for the IEA countries. The IEA model, MOSES, uses quantitative indicators that measure the risks of energy disruptions and resilience. It analyses risk and resilience connected to "external factors", i.e. imported energy, and "domestic factors" related to domestic production, transformation, and energy distribution for seven primary energy sources and two groups of secondary fuels.

The IEA index, MOSES, can be used to identify national energy policy priorities by analysing the effect of different policies on a country's energy security. It can also be used to track a country's changes over time in energy security disruption and resilience (profiles).

Energy systems analysis examines all parts of the system, i.e. energy supply, transformation and distribution, and end-use energy services. The IEA model analyses the vulnerabilities of primary energy sources.

Risks can be divided into external risks, including risks due to suppliers, such as geopolitical changes or transportation problems, whereas internal risks are, for example, due to disruption in production or transformation. It can be represented in the Table 1 as follow.

"MOSES" uses thirty indicators that characterise primary energy source and secondary fuel to analyse the above four dimensions. Experts assess energy supply security risks and resilience on a low, medium, and high-risk scale for each of the 30 indicators. Thus, a security profile is built, taking into account that the resilience of some elements may mitigate some risks, and some particular risks may aggravate each other (Table 2).

Each of the above energy sources is further analysed, and a grouping of countries is made. Countries are categorised in the following diagram

Table 1 IEA Energy Security Model (MOSES)—Measured dimensions

Risk		Resilience
External Risks	Risks of disruption of energy imports	The capability of responding to disruption in energy imports risks e.g. using alternative suppliers or supply routes
Internalrisks	Risks in the production or transformation of energy	The capability of responding to disruption in domestic energy supply risks due to production or transformation e.g. using fuel stock

from those with low-risk high resilience profile "A" to countries with High Risk—Low Resilience profile at "E" (Fig. 4).

4.2 Discussion of the General Idea of the Global Energy Institute Indexes

4.2.1 US Energy Security Index

US Energy Security Index was introduced in 2011 by the Global Energy Institute, Chamber of commerce, USA, to assess the US vulnerabilities and has been issued annually since, Global Energy Institute (2020a,b). The objective of the index is to assess the level of stability and associated risks and indicate if the energy security level is improving or getting worse over time. The index monitors the energy security risk and quantifies and rationalises the related data in the USA.

The energy security risk was set at 100 for the index score of 1980 to provide a sense of the relative potential hazard, as that year was a high vulnerability year for U.S. energy security.

A separate International Energy Index has also been created and is used for providing a basis for comparison of the levels of energy security between the USA and the "large energy user group". There are differences between the US Index and the International index variables due to data limitations, which require the use of a different, smaller set of metrics for the International Index. In addition, the scores for these countries are reported in relation to an average reference index measuring risks for the Organisation for Economic Co-operation and Development (OECD)

Table 2 Risk and resilience (Res.) indicators used in MOSES

Energy source	Dimension		Indicator	Source(s)
Crude Oil	External	Risk	Net Import Dependence	IEA
			The weighted average of political stability supplies	IEA, OECD
		Res	Entry points (Ports and Pipelines)	IEA
			Diversity of Suppliers	IEA
	Domestic	Risk	The proportion of offshore production	IEA
			The volatility of domestic production	IEA
		Res	Stock level	IEA
Oil Products	External	Risk	Net Import Dependence	IEA
		Res	Diversity of Supplies	IEA
			Entry points (Ports and Pipelines)	IEA
	Domestic	Res	Number of Refineries	IEA
			The flexibility of refining infrastructure	IEA
			Stock Level	IEA
Natural gas	External	Risk	Net Import Dependence	IEA
			The weighted average of political stability of suppliers	IEA, OECD
		Res	Entry point (LNG ports and pipelines)	IEA
			Diversity of suppliers	IEA, World Bank
	Domestic	Risk	The proportion of offshore production	IEA
		Res	Daily send-out capacity from underground and LNG storage	IEA
			Natural gas intensity	IEA

(continued)

Table 2 (continued)

Energy source	Dimension		Indicator	Source(s)
Coal	External	Risk	Net import dependence	IEA
		Res	Entry points (Ports and pipelines)	IEA
			Diversity of suppliers	IEA
	Domestic	Risk	The proportion of mining that is underground	Various National Sources

Source Jewell, J. (2011). *The IEA Model of Short-Term Energy Security (MOSES)*

member countries. The OECD average risk index is calibrated to a 1980 base year value of 1000.

The US Energy Security Index includes four Sub-Indexes that identify the major areas of risk to U.S. energy security. It incorporates 37 different measures of energy security risk. The Index looks back in time to 1970 and forward in time to 2040.

The risk levels can be changing with time as risk-mitigating actions are implemented. For example, the USA had hit the worst energy security level of risk in 2011; an official assessment was made in 2013 for U.S. Energy Security Risk. The assessment raised questions on the "uncomfortably high" level of risk and vulnerability of US welfare, military, and life aspects. The US vulnerability due to energy security risk was projected to remain high. The assessment was followed by comprehensive and continued research for monitoring, evaluation of the risks involved, and undoubtedly, a risk mitigation action plan was implemented.

Only five years later, in 2018, the Chamber of Commerce report claimed a substantial improvement in the U.S. energy security index because of the firm application of the policy of "Supply Expansion (development of domestic)". The "light tight oil" revolution reduced the energy security risk substantially between 2012 and 2017, and on the security index of 37 metrics, the score plunged 24 points from its record high of 77.5. This process shows the importance of identifying the energy security risks, implementing mitigating strategies to combat these risks, and the high importance of having a tool to measure the improvements or worsening of the energy security levels.

Construction of the US Energy Security Index:

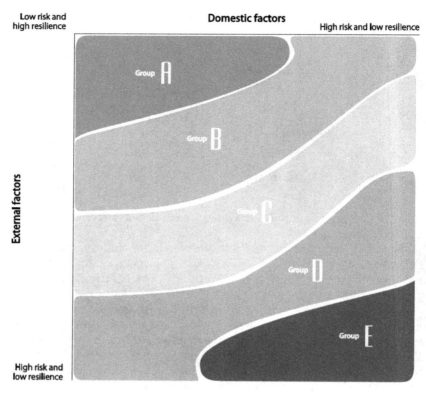

Fig. 4 Schematic diagram for identifying energy profiles in IEA countries (*Source* Jewell, J. [2011]. *The IEA Model of Short-Term Energy Security [MOSES]*)

The construction of the index is shown in the A–D steps below.

A. There are 37 different energy security metrics, which make up the index (Global Energy Institute, 2020a, b). A list of the variables used in the index is shown in the Table 3.
B. These measures are distributed in nine categories:

1. Global fuels.
2. Fuel imports.
3. Energy expenditures.

4. Price and market volatility.
5. Energy use intensity.
6. Electrical power sector.
7. Transportation sector.
8. Environmental.
9. Basic science and energy research and development.

C. Furthermore, each of the 37 metrics is mapped into one or more of the following four sub-indexes:

   a. Energy security
   b. Geopolitical
   c. Economic
   d. Environmental

D. These four sub-indexes are then combined into ONE index, where the weighted average of the four sub-indexes constitutes the overall index of the Energy Security Risk.

Figure 5 indicates the successive reductions in the US energy security risk changes, year after year after the peak year in 2011. This group of curves indicates that the US is adopting proper strategies and policies to improve the energy risks after 2011, when the Index of US Energy Risk Report was first issued.

4.2.2   The International Energy Security Index:
The objective of the International Index of Energy Security Risk is to:

a. Allow comparisons of energy security risks across countries and country groups, and
b. Observe how these risks change over time.

It measures energy security risks in two ways:

1. In absolute terms; and
2. Relative to a baseline average of the OECD countries calibrated to a 1980 base year value of 1000.

The report is issued annually after its first issue in 2011 (Global Energy Institute, 2020a, b). Due to data limitations in the different countries of

Table 3 Variables used in the US energy security index system

Index of U.S. Energy Security	Metrics Summaries 4 Sub-Indexes	9 Categories		
	Geopolitical 30% of Index	1. Global fuel metrics	1.	Security of World Oil Reserves
			2.	Security of World Oil Production
			3.	Security of World Natural Gas Reserves
			4.	Security of World Natural Gas Production
			5.	Security of World Coal Reserves
			6.	Security of World Coal Production
		2. Fuel import metrics	7.	Security of U.S. Petroleum Imports
			8.	Security of U.S. Natural Gas Imports
			9.	Oil and Gas Import Expenditures
			10.	Oil and Gap Import Costs per Dollar of GDP
		3. Energy expenditure metrics	11.	Energy Expenditure per Dollar of GDP
			12.	Energy Expenditure per Household
			13.	Retail Electricity Prices

Economic 30% of Index	4. Price and market volatility metrics	14.	Crude Oil Prices
		15.	Crude Oil Price Volatility
		16.	Energy Expenditure Volatility
		17.	World Oil Refinery Utilisation
		18.	Petroleum Stock Levels
	5. Energy use intensity metrics	19.	Energy Consumption Per Capita
		20.	Energy Intensity
		21.	Petroleum Intensity
		22.	Household Energy Efficiency
		23.	Commercial Energy Efficiency
		24.	Industrial Energy Efficiency
Reliability 20% of Index	6. Electric power sector metrics	25.	Electricity Capacity Diversity
		26.	Electricity Capacity margins
		27.	Electric Power Transmission Line Mileage

(continued)

Table 3 (continued)

7. Transport sector metrics		28.	Motor Vehicle Average MPG
		29.	Vehicle-Miles Travelled Per Dollar of GDP
Environmental 20% of Index		30.	Transportation Non-Petroleum Fuel Use
8. Environmental metrics		31.	Energy-Related CO_2 Emission
		32.	Energy-Related CO_2 Emission Per Capita
		33.	Energy-Related CO_2 Emission Industry
		34.	Electricity Non-CO_2 Generation Share
9. Research and develop. metrics		35.	Industrial Energy R and D Expenditure
		36.	Federal Energy and Science R & D Expenditure
		37.	Science and Engineering Degrees

Source Based on Global Energy Institute. (2020a, b). International Index of Energy Security Risk. US Chamber of commerce, USA

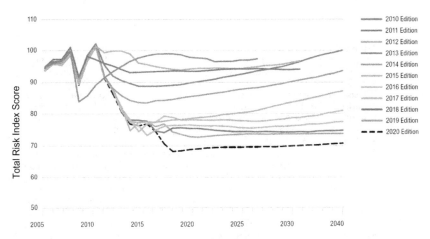

Fig. 5 Changes in forecasts of US energy security index after 2010 (*Source* Global Energy Institute. [2020a, b]. International Index of Assessing Risk in a Global Energy Market, U.S. Chamber of Commerce, USA)

the large energy user group, it was necessary to balance between what is considered theoretically ideal and the realistically possible. As a result, a smaller set of metrics are used in the International Energy Security Index. Only 29 metrics are used in the International Index, which compares to the 37 used for the US Energy Security Index. Twenty of these metrics are "country-specific", and the remaining nine metrics are "universal" metrics that apply equally to every country (e.g., the price of crude oil) (Table 4).

The international index is developed by adapting the U.S. Index metrics and developed methodology, and therefore, there is a substantial similarity between both indexes. The data for some countries lacked historical coverage and a forecasting system extending into the future for adequate time (decades). Furthermore, non-OECD countries data suffered from data gaps. These countries' incomplete databases and the unavailability of reliable data dictated the difference between the U.S. and the international indexes. Nevertheless, less-than-perfect data can be used if its limitations and usefulness are taken into consideration. Data for the index were selected by ensuring that the data were valuable analytically and considered reliable by users of the Index.

Mainly EIA data were used and reliable data from other good sources like the World Bank, IEA, and BP. These sources provide a vast amount of

Table 4 The international energy security index metrics

1.	**Global Fuels Metrics** Measure the reliability and diversity of global reserves and supplies of oil, natural gas, and coal. Higher reliability and diversity mean lower risk to energy security These metrics consist of 11 sub-metrics like Security of World Oil Reserves, Security of World Oil Production, Security of World Natural Gas Reserves, Security of World Natural Gas Production, Security of World Coal Reserves and others as detailed in table A1-3 of the reference below this table
2.	**Fuel Import Metrics** Measure the exposure of the national economies to unreliable and concentrated supplies of oil and natural gas, and coal: higher supply reliability and diversity and lower import levels Petroleum import exposure, natural gas import exposure, coal import Exposure, total energy import exposure, fossil fuel import expenditures per GDP
3.	**Energy Expenditure Metrics** Measure the magnitude of energy costs to national economies and the exposure of consumers to price shocks. Lower costs and exposure mean lower risk to energy security Energy expenditure intensity, energy expenditures per capita, Retail electricity prices and Crude Oil Prices
4.	**Price and Market Volatility Metrics** Measure the susceptibility of national economies to large swings in energy prices. A lower volatility means lower risk to energy security
5.	**Energy Use Intensity Metrics** Energy Use Intensity measures energy use related to population and economic output. Lower use of energy by industry to produce goods and services means lower risk to energy security Energy consumption per capita, energy intensity and petroleum intensity
6.	**Electric Power Sector Metrics** Measure indirectly the reliability of electricity generating capacity. Higher diversity means lower risk to energy security Electricity capacity diversity, Non-CO_2 Emitting Share of Electricity Generation
7.	**Transportation Sector Metrics** Measure the efficiency of energy use in the transport sector per unit of GDP and population. Greater efficiency means lower risk to energy security Transport energy per capita and Transport energy intensity
8..	**Environmental Metrics** Environmental Measure the exposure of national economies to national and international mandates for greenhouse gas emission reduction. Lower emissions of carbon dioxide from energy mean lower risk to energy security CO_2 Emissions Trend, Energy-Related CO_2 Emission Per Capita and CO_2 GDP Intensity

Source Global Energy Institute (2018). International Index of Energy Security Risk. US Chamber of commerce, USA
Tables A1-2, "Classification of Energy Security Metrics Used in the International Index", and A1-3 "Metrics Used to Create International Index of Energy Security Risk" of the International Energy Security Risk, Global Energy Institute, US Chamber of Commerce, 2018

reliable data and country-by-country information on energy production, energy consumption, population, GDP, carbon dioxide emissions, and many other energy-related measures. Time series were developed accordingly, for a wide range of energy security risk metrics, for OECD nations and all individual countries and groups of countries. The International Index incorporates the risk index scores for all of the countries globally.

Interestingly, as a base for evaluating the metric on reliability, an index on freedom has been used. The perception is that more political freedom leads to more consistency and reliability in decisions. Countries demonstrating a significant degree of political and civil rights liberties are expected to be more politically stable and reliable as trading partners. Also, these countries would not use oil supplies to achieve geopolitical aims; though these may not be correct in their entirety, it is likely to be correct in as far as that freedom leads to more reliable and consistent decisions.

The Freedom House, founded in October 1941 and based in the United States, is an independent non-governmental organisation (NGO). It is responsible for researching political freedom, human rights and democracy. The organisation issues a report on freedom in the world annually, which evaluates each country's degree of political civil liberties and political freedom. The report in recent years has become essential for policymakers as well as political scientists.

It has developed composite indexes for political rights and civil liberties to measure freedom for over 190 countries. The Freedom House index measure of freedom is used in several metrics related to global reserves, production and imports and in the diversity of global fuel supplies. Hence, by weighting each country's reserves or production of oil, natural gas, and coal by its respective Freedom House weighting, an aggregate global Freedom-weighted metric is developed that can provide a proxy for reliability. This metric and its reliability can be tracked and assessed over time.

The trends in energy security risks in selected countries can be deduced from the International Index. Understanding market conditions, policies, and other events affecting energy security can be gained by observing a country's progress.

5 Methods

5.1 US Energy Security Index Method

The metrics are based on several measures with different units, and in order to assemble them into the index, it would be necessary to transform them into comparable units or (building Blocks) to build the four sub-indexes and then the Index of the U.S. Energy Security Risk. The value for the year 1980, a high-risk year, is set as a reference at 100. The time series for each metric was normalised, and the values for all other years are then set in proportional relation to the 1980 value.

5.2 International Energy Security Index Method

The metrics have different units and are assembled into the index by transforming the metrics into comparable units. An international benchmark had to be created against which the individual countries could be compared. An average from the OECD provides a good measure of a range of developed countries. Each of the 29 metrics was normalised to the OECD baseline. The value for 1980 equalled 1000. The indexed value for subsequent years for each metric is adjusted proportionally higher or lower relative to this 1980 value.

The country-level metrics were normalised by calibrating their 1980 values with reference to the common OECD 1980 baseline. Importantly, data for the OECD Countries enable an OECD-wide value for all metrics, as the data are generally timely, complete, and wide-ranging.

6 Discussions and Conclusions

This chapter focussed on the energy security risks, risk evaluation metrics, and proposed mitigation strategies and policies. The chapter discussed the indexes and presented two of the indexes used to evaluate countries' overall energy security risks. In this chapter, the energy security risk is described in similar terms to those used in risk management standard practices for other applications, as such standard practices are not addressed clearly in the energy security literature.

The use of the Energy index in the IEA countries, the USA, the large energy user group, and other countries provides a valuable tool for measuring, comparing, tracking and improving the energy security issues in these countries.

The complexity of energy security calls for a collective international effort to reach balanced policies that would help all countries, including the developing countries, with growing needs for energy at affordable costs. This collective effort is necessary to improve energy security for all people. International efforts for mitigating energy security threats through robust energy trade agreements, and diplomatic efforts, are essential for maintaining the basic goals of energy availability, affordability, sustainability and economic growth. This high diplomacy and human role can be promoted and played by the United Nations through its UNDP and the UN Economic and Social Council.

Hence, there is a need to create an extended network of experts who can engage in constructive policy dialogue, with greater collaboration among a broader range of stakeholders (Charles et al., 2019), including scholars, data scientists, regulators and politicians, business leaders, and representatives of civil society.

The Indexes have been used to examine countries' responses and resilience to virtual supply shocks. Countries develop mitigation strategies and policies, including initiating diplomatic actions to resolve actual and forecasted impacts of shocks.

Continued efforts and research are necessary to improve the indexes. The following outlines are proposed:

1. The inclusion of the growing RE in the index. The increase in RE use will reduce the dependence on hydrocarbon, reduce the risk from a single main commodity, and reduce environmental degradation.
2. The Index should be adapted to assess the security of the producing, consuming and transit countries.
3. The Index should be simplified to evaluate energy security risks for vulnerable developing countries, with less comprehensive and weak data.
4. Further methodological improvements for calculating the indexes by taking into account modern megatrends can be made. In particular, the arrival of big data and associated technologies and approaches (Charles & Gherman, 2013, 2015, 2018; Charles et al., 2021, 2022) has opened up new opportunities, enabling greater insight into the complexity of decision-making in energy policy.
5. The severe impacts of conflicts on energy security require that the Indexes' should include metrics for conflicts.

6. Formulate policies to reduce the impact of RE proliferation on the security of demand on producing and transit countries for these countries to continue development.

Acknowledgements The authors are thankful to the reviewers for their valuable comments on the previous version of this work.

References

Abdullah, F. B., Iqbal, R., Hyder, S. I., & Jawaid, M. (2020). Energy security indicators for Pakistan: An integrated approach. *Renewable and Sustainable Energy Reviews, 133*, 110122.

Australian Government, Department of Resources, Energy and Tourism (RET). (2011). National Energy Security Assessment of Australia. http://www.ret.gov.au

Bassim, M. (2015). Future expectations for energy in the Middle East and North Africa (MENA) region. *European Centre for Energy & Resource Security, 47*, 5–8.

Boersma, T., & Johnson, C. (2018). *US energy diplomacy* (Columbia University, SIPA Center on Global Energy Policy Working Paper). https://energypolicy.columbia.edu/sites/default/files/pictures/CGEPUSEnergyDiplomacy218.pdf

British Petroleum. (2020). British petroleum energy outlook 2020. *BP Energy* Economics.

Charles, V., & Gherman, T. (2013). Achieving competitive advantage through big data: Strategic implications. *Middle-East Journal of Scientific Research, 16*(8), 1069–1074.

Charles, V., & Gherman, T. (2018). Big data and ethnography: Together for the greater good. In A. Emrouznejad & V. Charles (Eds.), *Big data for the greater good* (pp. 19–34). Springer.

Charles, V., Emrouznejad, A., & Gherman, T. (2021, Accepted/In press). Strategy formulation and service operations in the big data age: The essentialness of technology, people, and ethics. In A. Emrouznejad & V. Charles (Eds.), *Big data for service operations management* (pp. 1–30). Springer's International Series in Studies in Big Data. Springer-Verlag.

Charles, V., Gherman, T., & Emrouznejad, A. (2022, Accepted/In press - Nov 2021). The role of composite indices in international economic diplomacy. In V. Charles & A. Emrouznejad (Eds.), *Modern indices for international economic diplomacy*. Springer-Palgrave Macmillan.

Charles, V., Gherman, T., & Paliza, J. C. (2019). Stakeholder involvement for public sector productivity enhancement: Strategic considerations. *ICPE Public Enterprise Half-Yearly Journal, 24*(1), 77–86.

Charles, V., Tavana, M., & Gherman, T. (2015). The right to be forgotten—Is privacy sold out in the big data age? *International Journal of Society Systems Science, 7*(4), 283–298.

Cherp, A., & Jewell, J. (2014). The concept of energy security: Beyond the four As. *Energy Policy, 75*, 415–421.

de Sampaio Nunes, P. (2002). Towards a European strategy for the security of energy supply. *VGB Powertech, 82*.

Deloitte. (2013). Securing tomorrow's energy today: Policy and regulation, long term energy security. *IEC*. www.deloitte.com/in

Energy Charter Secretariat. (2015). *International energy security: Common concept for energy producing, consuming and transit countries*. ISBN 978-905948-054-4.

Font, E. (2020). *MOSES energy security ratings for Georgia*. World Experience for Georgia (WEG). http://weg.ge/en/moses-energy-security-ratings-georgia-0

Global Energy Institute. (2018). International Index of Assessing Risk in a Global Energy Market, U.S. Chamber of Commerce, USA.

Global Energy Institute. (2020a). Index of US Energy Security Risk, U.S. Chamber of Commerce, USA.

Global Energy Institute. (2020b). International Index of Assessing Risk in a Global Energy Market, U.S. Chamber of Commerce, USA.

International Energy Agency IEA. (2007). World Energy Outlook.

International Energy Agency IEA. (2018). Energy Efficiency 2018 and World Energy Outlook 2018.

International Energy Agency IEA. (2019). World Energy Outlook 2019. https://www.iea.org/reports/world-energy-outlook-2019

International Energy Agency IEA. (2020). *World Energy Balances: Overview, Statistics Report*. https://www.iea.org/reports/world-energy-balances-overview

IRENA. (2020). *Global renewables outlook: Energy transformation 2050*. International Renewable Energy Agency. ISBN 978-92-9260-238-3. www.irena.org/publications

Jansen, J., van Arkel, W., & Boots, M. (2004). *Designing indicators of long term security*. Netherlands Environmental Assessment Agency.

Jewell, J. (2011). *The IEA model of short-term energy security (MOSES) primary energy sources and secondary fuels* (IEA Working Paper). https://www.iea.org/publications/freepublications/publication/moses_paper.pdf

Jewell, J., & Brutschin, E. (2019). The politics of energy security. In *The Oxford handbook of energy politics*.

Kabel, T. S., & Bassim, M. (2019). Literature review of renewable energy policies and impacts. *European Journal of Marketing and Economics, 2*(2), 28–41.

Kabel, T. S., & Bassim, M. (2020). Reasons for shifting and barriers to renewable energy: A literature review. *International Journal of Energy Economics and Policy, 10*(2), 89–94.

Kester, J. (2018). *The politics of energy security: Critical security studies.* Routledge.

Kocaslan, G. (2014). International energy security indicators and Turkey's energy security risk score. *International Journal of Energy Economics and Policy, 4*(4), 735.

Koyama, K., & Kutani, I. (2012). *Developing an energy security index, study on the development of an energy security index and an assessment of energy security for East Asian countries* (Chapter 2, pp. 7–47). Economic Research Institute for ASEAN and East Asia (ERIA).

Leung, G. C., Cherp, A., Jewell, J., & Wei, Y. M. (2014). Securitization of energy supply chains in China. *Applied Energy, 123*, 316–326.

Nathaniel, S. P., Murshed, M., & Bassim, M. (2021). The nexus between economic growth, energy use, international trade and ecological footprints: The role of environmental regulations in N11 countries. *Energy, Ecology and Environment* (pp. 1–17).

Pahwa, M. S., & Chopra, A. S. (2013). Energy security models—A critical review and applicability in Indian context. *International Journal of Research and Development—A Management Review (IJRDMR), 2*(2), 17–20.

Salman, D., & Bassim, M. (2019). Political stability, austerity measures, external imbalance, and debt impact on the Egyptian economy. In *Impacts of political instability on economics in the MENA Region* (pp. 74–102). IGI Global.

Sovacool, B. K., & Mukherjee, I. (2011). Conceptualizing and measuring energy security: A synthesized approach. *Energy, 36*(8), 5343–5355.

Šumskis, V., & Giedraitis, V. R. (2015). Economic implications of energy security in the short run. *Ekonomika, 94*(3), 119–138.

Szulecki, K. (2018). The multiple faces of energy security: An introduction. In *Energy security in Europe* (pp. 1–29). Palgrave Macmillan.

Szulecki, K. (2020). Securitization and state encroachment on the energy sector: Politics of exception in Poland's energy governance. *Energy Policy, 136*, 111066.

UK Department of Energy and Climate Change. (2012). *Energy security strategy.* Presented to Parliament by the Secretary of State for Energy and Climate Change by Command of Her Majesty.

UK National Statistics, Department for Business, Energy and Industrial Strategy. (2019). Energy consumption in the UK (ECUK) 1970 to 2018, consumption tables, Chart C1.

United Nations Development Programme, Human Development Report. (2020). *The next frontier, Human Development and the Anthropocene.*

United Nations, Economic and Social Council. (2019). Progress towards the Sustainable Development Goals (SDGs). *Report of the Secretary-General.* https://undocs.org/E/2019/68

United Nations Population Division. (2019). *World population prospects.* https://population.un.org/wpp/Graphs/Probabilistic/POP/TOT/900

Vivoda, V. (2010). Evaluating energy security in the Asia-Pacific region: A novel methodological approach. *Energy Policy, 38*(9), 5258–5263.

Wang, Q., & Zhou, K. (2017). A framework for evaluating global national energy security. *Applied Energy, 188,* 19–31.

Winzer, C. (2012). Conceptualizing energy security. *Energy Policy, 46,* 36–48.

World Bank. (2019). *2019 tracking SDG7: The energy progress report.*

World Bank. (2020). *World Bank database.* https://data.worldbank.org/indicator/EG.use.pcap.kg.OE?locations

World Bank. (2021). Commodity price data. *The Pink Sheet.*

World Bank Data. (2021). *Population total.* https://data.worldbank.org/indicator/SP.POP.TOTL. Accessed April 2021.

World Economic Forum. (2017). *Global Energy Architecture Performance Index Report 2017.*

World Economic Forum. (2021). *Fostering effective energy transition.* http://www3.weforum.org/docs/WEF_Fostering_Effective_Energy_Transition_2021.pdf. Accessed May 2021.

Yergin, D. (2006). Ensuring energy security. *Foreign Affairs, 85*(2), 69–82.

CHAPTER 7

On Re-Imagining the Role of Big Mac Index in Promoting International Economic Diplomacy: Some Perspectives

Ullas Rao, Paul J. Hopkinson, and N. R. Parasuraman

1 INTRODUCTION

Economic commentators have long viewed BMI with circumspection for deriving its intuitive appeal primarily from a theoretical standpoint. As tempting as it may sound to accept the underlying narrative, we provide a compelling argument to view BMI as complimentary to the

---

U. Rao (✉) · P. J. Hopkinson
Edinburgh Business School, Heriot-Watt University, Dubai,
United Arab Emirates
e-mail: u.rao@hw.ac.uk

P. J. Hopkinson
e-mail: P.Hopkinson@hw.ac.uk

N. R. Parasuraman
Shri Dharmasthala Manjunatheshwara Institute for Management Development,
Mysore, India
e-mail: nrparasuraman@sdmimd.ac.in

© The Author(s), under exclusive license to Springer Nature Switzerland AG 2022
V. Charles and A. Emrouznejad (eds.), *Modern Indices for International Economic Diplomacy*, https://doi.org/10.1007/978-3-030-84535-3_7

market-determined exchange rate. BMI should be afforded an influential role in guiding policymakers toward framing economic policies aimed at advancing Ricardo's international trade theory premised on comparative advantage with benefits accruing to economies participating in global trade of goods and services.[1]

"The Economist" developed BMI to determine an implied exchange rate as opposed to a market-determined exchange rate by tracing the pricing of a commodity universally available for the same dollar. McDonald's most famous recipe—"hamburgers"—perfectly suited the definition. Given the complete standardization of the product across all the regions, it stood as an easy substitute for a universally available commodity. Exchange rate, then, was simply computed by comparing the price of a hamburger available in two different market economies expressed either on similar currency denomination or employing countries' respective currency denominations. For example, in January 2016, the price of a hamburger in US was $4.93. In India, the equivalent dollar price during the same time was $1.90. Now, the implied exchange rate as per the principles of Purchasing Power Parity (hereafter, PPP) may be computed as shown below.[2]

$$S = \left[\frac{P_1}{P_2}\right]$$

where:

S = Exchange rate
P_1 = cost of good X in currency 1 (Hamburger's price in USD equivalent in India)
P_2 = cost of good X in currency 2 (Hamburger's price in USD in the U.S.)

In the above example after substituting the figures, the implied exchange rate is arrived as 0.385. This implies that if a hamburger costs $1 in US, the equivalent price in India is $0.385. Thus, if the prevailing market

---

[1] The extension of Ricardo's influential work on international trade theory now encompasses the all-important services sector.

[2] The illustration is reproduced from a similar one provided in the "The Economist" (*The Economist*, 2016).

exchange rate in January 2016 was US $1 = INR 66.80, in terms of BMI, it should be US $1 = INR 25.71.[3] This also potentially implies that the Indian rupee or INR was significantly undervalued by as much as 61.44% on that day.

As the above example demonstrates, the BMI essentially incorporates the principle of PPP by measuring the price of a similar commodity available in two different market economies. On hindsight, while this may look appealing, one potential limitation lies in its failure to consider a wider basket of goods, whose inclusion might have a potential implication on the computed figure! Notwithstanding the above, BMI has become an important cornerstone as a policy reference tool for gauging behavior of exchange rates modeled on the PPP principle.

The objective of this chapter is to enable discerning readers to gain an appreciation of the BMI phenomenon, which is accomplished by presenting the theoretical underpinnings in a succinct manner, without compromising the underlying rigor while avoiding complex mathematical derivations.

As "The Economist" puts it: "BMI was invented as a lighthearted guide to ascertain whether currencies are at their 'correct' level. 'Burgernomics' was never intended as a precise gauge of currency misalignment; rather, merely as a tool to make exchange-rate theory more digestible." While not intending to serve as an alternative contribution within the crowded confines of exchange-rate theory, BMI has been accorded an influential space within the realms of discussion surrounding nuanced disciplines on Economics and International Finance. Simply put, it permits a lay person to decipher the reasoning surrounding the valuation of a currency. At this stage, it is pertinent to observe that the exchange rate may be determined using two distinctive approaches: one based on market principles, and another based on the theory of PPP (Inman, 2015).

Alongside, the influence remitted by key macro-economic variables, the former approach primarily relies on the interplay of forces of demand and

---

[3] The process of computing an implied exchange rate is explained further in the paper.

supply for a particular currency in a foreign-exchange market.[4] Exogenous factors including significant political developments also tend to exert enormous pressure in the determination of an exchange rate.[5]

Alternatively, according to PPP, theoretically speaking, the price commanded by a product bearing exactly similar attributes in two different market economies denominated in two different currencies must be similar. The extent to which a product reflects variation in prices—however insignificant—helps in explaining the relative under/overvaluation of a currency vis-à-vis another. Now, a key challenge facing an economist is to identify a product available across different geographies with exactly similar physical and functional attributes. An acceptable way might be identification of a "basket of products and services bearing similar attributes"; however, the practical difficulties associated with implementation might leave such an exercise cumbersome, and importantly, prone to errors (Stylianou, 2014).

It is precisely in keeping with the above practical difficulties that "The Economist" came up with the idea of Burgernomics; at the heart of which, lies the BMI. Perhaps there is no other comprehensible product that comes any way near to McDonald's, Big Mac. With a presence in virtually every other country, Big Mac comes with unrivaled product homogeneity (Citrinot, 2015). As a good approximation, Big Mac serves as an equally meaningful purpose in determining exchange rates by applying the principles of PPP.

As we proceed further by presenting an illustrative methodological treatment, it is useful to note that the observed variations in the prices of Big Mac in two different countries offer a plausible explanation towards deciphering the relative valuation of a currency. Let us take a very simple example to drive the above point. Say, the price of a single Big Mac in Zurich, Switzerland is 4 CHF, while the price in New York, USA is 8 USD. It is evident that by comparing these prices, we arrive at an implied exchange rate viz. 1 CHF = 2 USD. Contrary to the exchange rate implied by the relative pricing of Big Mac, the foreign exchange market might (also, the actual exchange rate) accord a value, say, 1 CHF = 2.5 USD. If so, a preliminary glance will reveal that the Swiss Franc on

---

[4] Foreign-exchange markets typically exist alongside capital markets serving an influential platform for traders to exchange currencies based on the principle of price discovery.

[5] The impending political crises in key countries in West Asia and their impact on foreign exchange is one such example.

market basis is overvalued by 20%. From a business perspective, this would render the Swiss exporters grudging the importers, who in this case, stand to derive a marginal benefit. From a macro-economic perspective, this would also mean that the Swiss Government having parked most of its foreign reserves in the form of investments in US Treasuries would stand to gain as it yields a slightly greater elbow room to trim its import bill. Conversely, if we observe that the price of Big Mac in Mumbai, India, and Los Angeles, USA stands at 120 INR and 4 USD, respectively, according to PPP, this simply implies an exchange rate of 1 USD = 30 INR. On the other hand, if the exchange rate on a foreign exchange market is say, 1 USD = 60 INR, it would imply that the Indian Rupee on market basis is undervalued by 50%. In this instance, it will be the Indian exporters who will be having the last laugh. For the Govt. of India, it would imply that the import expenditures will be strained leaving a strain on its fiscal position.[6]

From the above hypothesized illustrations, we observe that the differences in exchange rates because of the two distinctive approaches—market-determined and PPP—the potential implications on the prevailing business environment (micro level) and governments (macro level) may be significant. Even a cursory glance on the above examples would imply that while the economies witnessing an undervaluation in their respective currencies would prefer to have an exchange rate based on PPP; countries faced with a prospect of overvaluation would prefer an exchange rate determined on the strength of market fundamentals[7] (Jagannathan, 2012).

2 Construction of Big Mac Index

Having looked at the implications of the differences in exchange rates evidenced by two distinctive methodologies, we now proceed toward understanding the construction of Big Mac Index in an elaborate manner. Before understanding the math behind the process, it is useful to identify all the ley variables used in constructing the index.

---

[6] Here, we refer to fiscal position synonymously with fiscal deficit. Fiscal deficit in its simplest sense implies a scenario where a country's expenditures exceed its revenues.

[7] This may hold good in an idealistic scenario if the economic fundamentals remain enormously disciplined evident by a robust fiscal position and manageable levels of inflation.

2.1 The Variables

The variables commonly used for constructing the BMI entail the following.

(a) Price of Big Mac in currency 1
(b) Price of Big Mac in currency 2
(c) Market-determined foreign exchange rate.

With the above variables, we now proceed by detailing a methodological treatment involved in constructing the BMI. Let us take an example in respect of India, where the following details are available.

(a) Price of Big Mac in India = INR 150
(b) Price of Big Mac in USA = USD 3
(c) Market-determined exchange rate: 1 USD = 60 INR.

(i) Method

The exchange rate computed by the BMI simply involves the computation using the PPP framework.
According to PPP,

$$S = \left[\frac{P_1}{P_2}\right]$$

where:

S = Exchange rate as determined by PPP
P_1 = cost of good X in currency 1 (or Big Mac price in USD equivalent in India)
P_2 = cost of good X in currency 2 (Big Mac price in USD in US)

Putting the above inputs in place, the exchange rate on a PPP basis is reflected as: 1 USD = 50 INR. When we compare this to the market-based exchange rate at 1 USD = 60 INR, we find that the Indian Rupee is undervalued by $\left[1 - \left(\frac{50}{60}\right)\right]$ viz. 16.67%. Alternatively, the same results may also be arrived by expressing the price of Big Mac in India in USD.

Price of a Big Mac in USD will be $\left(\frac{150}{60}\right)$ viz. 2.5 USD. Therefore, on a relative basis, the undervaluation is to the extent of $\left[1 - \left(\frac{2.5}{3}\right)\right]$ viz. 16.67%.

As a useful corollary, the exchange rate as determined by Big Mac Index/PPP may also be derived from the market-determined exchange rate by using the following equation.

S = market-determined exchange rate x $\left[1 - \left(\frac{P_1}{P_2}\right)\right]$.

That is, 60 x $\left[1 - \left(\frac{2.5}{3}\right)\right]$ will yield a value of 50.

(ii) Advantages and limitations of the Index

(Clements et al., 2010) emphatically argue the BMI at least in the "short-run" mimics random-walk[8] implying efficiency in discovery of exchange rate. One of the most striking features of the Big Mac for both economists and non-economists alike lies in the computational ease with which it may be constructed. So long as the inputs—big mac prices in two different currencies—are available, it lends construction of the index as a straightforward process. Employing the index stands as the first barometer of performance to gauge the relative under or overvaluation in comparison to exchange rates determined by the demand and supply principles of the foreign exchange market. Valuation of exchange rates has assumed considerable significance in recent times owing to the re-emergence of the "external threats" posed on country's international trade. The latter is best evident in the skirmishes with its concomitant impact on financial markets in the bitter trade war between the two largest economies—U.S. and China—during Trump's presidential era. So, to that extent, the role of the index in contributing to the wider implications on economic diplomacy cannot be undermined. Finally, Big Mac Index also finds some utility in respect of comparison of real wage rates across different economies. (Juradja & Ashenfelter, 2001) use the BMI to compare the real wage rates across different economies—developed and developing—using the standardized wage rates paid by McDonalds

---

[8] Random-walk was developed by Eugene Fama as part of his outstanding thesis on "efficient market hypothesis. In its simplest sense, it implies no trader has ever an opportunity to earn abnormal returns as the markets impute the prices of securities leaving no advantage for arbitrage arising from price discrepancies" (Fama, 1988).

across different countries. Interestingly, they observe, the wage rates, after adjusting for PPP, are higher in magnitude for U.S., Western Europe, and Japan than Eastern Europe, Korea, and Brazil and much higher in magnitude compared to China and India.

(Mazumder, 2016) has been extremely vocal in denouncing the BMI lamenting the non-conformity of the former to PPP as opposed to, say an iPad, which, according to study is in greater conformity and overcomes the inherent weakness evident in two disadvantages—non-tradability and perishability. Similarly (Josic et al., 2018), point out the short-termism attributable to PPP, in turn, contributing to the weakness of the Big Mac model. Besides, there are two significant limitations surrounding the Big Mac. First, it ignores the forces of demand and supply, which remain the key ingredients in determining an exchange rate on foreign exchange markets. In its present "plain-vanilla" form, the index suffers from lack of sophistication. Two, it also ignores one of the most influential factors, which is the inflation. (Portes & Atal, 2014) find the Big Mac supporting the theory of PPP, but lament over its limited utility for lagging inflation with the problem perpetuating particularly in case of EM economies. (Yasser et al., 2019) share their antipathy toward the Big Mac arising from its failure to account inflation—which, has a dominant role to play in influencing exchange rates.

As a result, in the absence of appropriate reflection toward inflation, Big Mac is relegated to theoretical utility. Consider, the case of Turkish Lira, which has witnessed sharp depreciation because of steadily rising inflation; a phenomenon also attributable to weak form of efficiency (Domac & Oskooee, 1997). In the absence of the comfort of war-chest of foreign reserves, Turkish Central Bank has defended the currency by increasing interest rates—often inviting the rebuke of the political leadership given the ramifications on wider economy evident in increasing the borrowing costs. For an EM like Turkey, which does not boast of a strong export-led economy, depreciating Lira lends imports expensive with far-reaching consequences on political economy. No wonder, under these circumstances the job of a central banker becomes extraordinarily complicated with fixed tenure associated with the position no longer remaining the order of the day.

(iii) Common uses of the index

(Andrei, 2014) underscore the significance of BMI in gauging the relative valuation of currencies based on PPP. Interestingly, they forward an argument linking globalization with cultural identities with the former intrinsically linked to BMI. To elucidate further, we need to look no further than "Project EU" in 1993 culminating in "Euro" in 1999. Euro as a single currency binding all the member nations (with notable exceptions like U.K.) was a watershed moment in the annals of international economic diplomacy. Despite significant cultural and linguistic differences among the EU member states, implementation of single currency—Euro (EUR)—representing the EU block was hailed as a monumental success for championing economic sovereignty ahead of petty political differences. The success of EU culminating into common currency, EUR, offers an interesting case in comparative benefits emerging from economic standardization also evident in BMI.

Seen from the prism of economic philosophy, BMI lends an influential role in advocating the "law of one price".[9] In this context, it is crucial to look at the role of the U.K., which continued to maintain currency sovereignty even as it maintained its membership within the EU. Whilst the U.K. economy has navigated economic turbulence with reasonable success, the Sword of Damocles has always been hanging casting a shadow on the export competitiveness of the U.K. businesses vis-à-vis European entities. The inability to remain unscathed from the emergence of the new geopolitical order favoring the advent of neo-nationalism espousing domestic economic prowess over international cooperation ultimately witnessed the U.K. falling prey to the chorus of complete economic sovereignty from the EU; with the historic referendum on June 23, 2016, commencing the long and treacherous path of severing the official relationship with the union. In the immediate aftermath, the GBP (British Pound) went into a spiraling fall only to be rescued, albeit temporarily, with interventions hastened by the Bank of England (BoE). Even as sceptics (the remain advocates) continued to cast apocalyptic scenarios resulting from the depreciation of the GBP—one of the five reserved currencies mandated by the IMF for member countries to withdraw—the

---

[9] According to Lamont and Thaler, "The Law of one price states that identical goods (or securities) should sell for identical prices" (Lamont & Thaler, 2003).

reality was far more benign. With most of the U.K. multinational deriving bulk of their revenue stream from international operations, depreciating GBP translated as a "blessing in disguise" lending firepower to their export credentials. Unsurprisingly, the benchmark index—FTSE 100—registered modest growth in absolute terms increasing from 6954.2 in 2016 to 7542 in 2019 with compounded annual growth rate (CAGR) of 2.74%. From a competitive standpoint, the EU and the U.K. continue to remain in a constant battle for one-upmanship in the ever-shrinking pie of international trade.

Zongze (2012) makes an emphatic case for the BMI by alluding to its utility in comparing the living standard of different countries by estimating the average number of hours needed by a worker to buy a big mac. Translated as a point of reference for comparing the price of big mac denominated in different currencies, BMI retains its allure as a pivotal reference to gauge the relative valuation of currencies sans external factors including inflation. From this perspective, policymakers have an intrinsic opportunity to gauge the relative under/overvaluation of currencies determined by the foreign exchange markets. It is fair to surmise, the index lends an intellectual arsenal in the hands of policymakers—endowed with the responsibility of guiding trade-related policies—to defend the relative valuation of domestic currency against foreign currencies. As a case in point, economic advisors in U.S. have consistently attributed trade-deficit with China resulting out of purported undervaluation of Chinese Renminbi giving the latter considerable leeway in making its exports competitive and attractive in the international trade arena.

A study by (Yang, 2004) disputes the claim asserting the failure by the Big Mac index to incorporate non-tradable components leading to undervaluation of RMB. The paper further argues in favor of RMB being "overvalued" as China's per-capita income is much lower than U.S.—which is again open for interpretation as the latter is treated as benchmark currency.

Over time, several improvements have been incorporated into the "original model," most notably by "The Economist" popularly referred as "the adjusted Big Mac Index," incorporating GDP to estimate both bilateral valuation (versus a specific currency) and currency's overall valuation (versus a basket of currencies). Forex valuation estimated on above bases have found greater in line with actual values as opposed to the one based on the original index (O'Brien & Vargas, 2016).

3 Perspectives on BMI: National and International

From the points delineated above, it may be fair to assert that the utility of the BMI will be relevant from the relative strength of the economy and therefore from the relative value commanded by the economy's currency vi-a-vis other currencies. We now lend discussion on the BMI from two distinct perspectives: National—looking from the prism of the U.S.—and International, involving selected developed economies and emerging market economies represented by BRICS.

(i) National perspective

U.S. has remained one of the most dominant economies in the world with estimates from WTO suggesting the USD or the "greenback" making up for 85% of the international trade in currency transactions. In this backdrop, it is not uncommon to observe economic commentators lamenting on the hegemonic role played by the U.S. transcending economic influence paving the way for tacit, and sometimes, explicit interventions from a societal standpoint in so far as dominating the world stage is concerned. With the BMI having found its genesis on the ubiquitous hamburgers—the staple fast-food for most Americans—U.S. economy stands in a distinctly advantageous position with the line demarcating the market-based and PPP valuation of USD getting blurred. As one of the five currencies to have been endowed with the international reserve currency under the auspices of IMF,[10] U.S. also enjoys unmitigated advantage of keeping a check on inflation on the strength of unlimited fiscal support aided by the Federal Reserve (Fed), which has often taken refuge in its ability to "print currencies" to support fledgling sectors of the economy—as part of the quantitative easing or QE associated as politically more appropriate moniker.

---

[10] IMF or International Monetary Fund is a leading developmental financial institution lending to developing and poor economies in need of financial resources to sustain and grow their economies. It is based in Washington, DC, U.S.A.

Noble Laureate Professor Paul Krugman championing the Keynesian school of thought has been unsparing in criticizing the U.S. government when its policymakers have resorted to contractionary monetary policies characterized by spending cuts and politically unpalatable specter of raising revenues on the back of higher taxes. These measures have invariably been met with resolute opposition across political and economic isles prompting reversal of policies much to the victory of the civil society. Unbridled spending to resuscitate sectors—some of which appear to be in a perennial state of "coma"—has invariably led to significant rise in the debt-to-GDP ratio, which has remained dangerously elevated in the recent past. Overwhelming sovereignty over currency has essentially meant the U.S. economy and its people remain virtually inflated from economic shocks—with or without recession. Despite remaining export competitive, the Fed has officially maintained a stance to see stronger USD. A stronger currency again spells boom at least by making imports—which something U.S. is dependent on—significantly competitive. In his uncharacteristic style, when the former U.S. President Donald Trump ranked up his frustration over "over-valued" USD making U.S. exports look uncompetitive in the face of rising competition from China, it wasn't unusual to find him a lonely voice with the majority backing-off from backing their own President. At least for the U.S. economy and largely to developed economies led by the G7, BMI appears to offer little to no impediment in dictating national and international economic policies.

Domestic sovereignty, however, lends tacit support to international economic hegemony pursued by U.S. often clandestinely through international development financial institutions like the IMF. Counting U.S. as one of its dominant founding member countries, IMF has been criticized by the recipient nations—which are invariably poor developing economies—of stoking political differences by mandating tough economic reforms as a necessary precursor for borrowing. A case in point was Egypt, which under extreme economic duress was compelled to initiate tough economic measures including de-pegging the Egyptian Pound against USD leading to free-fall of the former, which in turn translated into soaring inflation provoking interest rate hikes by the central bank. Naturally, these measures met stringent resistance from the public, whose economic woes only exacerbated. This naturally begs the question—how currency valuation on the back of BMI compares developed economies vis-à-vis developing economies.

(ii) International perspective

It is not uncommon to find that developing and emerging market economies tend to benefit marginally to a greater degree when the exchange-rates are converted on a PPP basis. This is evident from the fact that—ceteris paribus—such economies would normally be seen as operating in the zone of "undervaluation." In contrast, developed economies might normally operate under the continuum of overvaluation[11] (International Monetary Fund, 2007). More precisely, the state of under or overvaluation will be influenced by a range of key macro-economic variables including the relative fiscal strength of the economy, levels of inflation, and percentage of unemployment, etc. Consider the Exhibits below.

We clearly observe that for developed economies, GDP on per-capita looks much more favorable when exchange rate is determined by market forces as opposed to PPP. This trend is more evident for the two years from 2012 to 2013. However, in 2014, the degree of difference looks much more subdued in 2014, which might explain the possibility of the currencies bracing the prospect of an imminent pressure on their valuation. The extraordinary volatility gripping the markets of developed economies—in the aftermath of global financial crisis—is exacerbated by challenges posed by emerging market economies particularly led by China, which partly helps in explaining the above phenomenon. It comes as no surprise that in the wake of any uncertainty governing economic environment, the asset markets led by equity and forex bear the maximum brunt. With a downward pressure on currency valuation, inflationary scenario too tends to get distorted eventually casting its shadow on the exchange rate.

(iii) The BRICS angle

We now turn our attention to the BRICS market club, which is also reflective of the larger trend exhibited by the world's two largest economies: China and India.

---

[11] This observation is rather generalized and we might expect to see instances of occasional departure should the macro-economic fundamentals be subjected to significant variations.

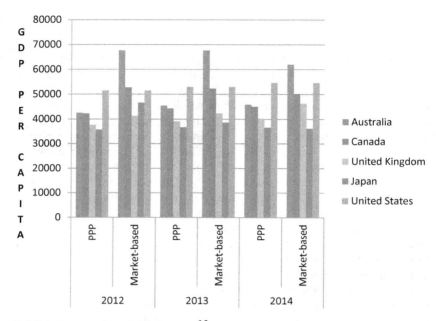

Exhibit 1 Developed Economies'[12] GDP Per Capita: PPP vs. Market-based exchange rate (*Source* World Bank Open Data[13])

Even a casual sight on the above Exhibit reveals that the GDP on a per-capita for the emerging market economies comprising the BRICS block tends to get significantly inflated on a PPP basis as against a market-determined exchange rate regime. From a theoretical standpoint, it therefore implies that expression of key macro variables in USD on PPP basis tends to portray a more benign picture on economic performance of the economy. Perhaps, such a consideration might entail interesting implications from the perspective of Multi-Lateral Financial Institutions including the World Bank and the IMF. As an example, upon conversion of GDP on per-capita from market-determined to PPP, the extant levels of

---

[12] The selected countries in this category are only representative in nature. Even though euro is a single currency, but given the vast differences in the GDP on per-capital in respect of individual economies, it has not been included.

[13] Retrieved from http://www.databank.worldbank.org/data/home.aspx.

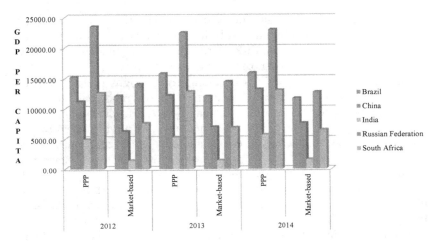

Exhibit 2 BRICS Economies' GDP Per Capita: PPP vs. Market-based exchange rate (*Source* World Bank Open Data[14])

poverty observed in respect of developing economies may appear dramatically diminished. Yet another point that must be brought to fruition pertains to the influence exercised by the inflationary trends in determining market-determined exchange rates. With majority of the emerging market economies reeling under high levels of inflation, the impact tends to be negative with resultant effects seen on foreign exchange market. High levels of inflation tend to favor higher interest rates, which in turn squeezes liquidity and shores up borrowing costs. These cascading effects eventually result in exerting downward pressure on equity markets and encourage "flight of foreign capital" ultimately lending pressure on economy's currency valuation.

(iv) Implications for policymakers—The case for international economic diplomacy

---

[14] Retrieved from http://www.databank.worldbank.org/data/home.aspx.

Undoubtedly, despite all the shortcomings, the Big Mac index continues to play an influential role in determining the intrinsic valuation of currency based on PPP in relation to the market-determined currency valuation factoring the demand-supply scenario prevalent in foreign exchange markets. It is pertinent to highlight the role exerted by the state of the economy in impacting the currency valuation with difference between PPP and market-based systems getting blurred for developed economies (including high-income countries measured on per-capita income) as opposed to emerging and developing economies, where the difference between the two systems remain particularly stark with significant implications on overall economic status. And finally on the other side of the aisle are handful nations with pegged currencies—particularly the six Arab nations making up the GCC—endowed with sufficient foreign reserves built on petrodollars to defend their currencies.

Even as the implications of the difference between the two systems remain less significant for developed economies and nations with pegged currencies, the situation is only exacerbated for monetary authorities led by Central Banks in emerging economies. An inflated per-capita income evident for emerging markets on PPP is essentially misleading as almost all the economies are completely integrated with the international trade order. And with majority of the international trade being transacted in USD (85% by some estimates), it is incongruous to debate the merits and demerits of an exchange rate regime based on PPP.

If BRICS were to be taken as a representative block, it is clear that Russia (as net energy export member of OPEC+ institution) and China (built on cost-competitive manufacturing economy with significant export exposure) stand to gain from increasing trade with an international order rested upon market-based exchange-rate regimen. It is unsurprising to observe both countries wielding significant firepower evident in war-chest foreign reserves accumulated over the years on back of booming export-led growth. China, particularly, stands in an enviable position with an estimated foreign reserve more than $3 trillion. Consequently, both Russia and China have active sovereign wealth funds akin to state-sponsored institutionalized transnational corporations picking stakes across different geographies, markets, sectors, and corporations lending strategic geopolitical advantage alongside economic power.

If we look at India as a standalone example, the picture gets only somber with a per-capita income close to $2000 (determined on market exchange rate) ranked in the low-income category. One might be tempted to forward the argument of PPP for net-importer economy like India. However, it is useful to remind, the inflated per-capita on PPP doesn't necessarily translate into higher economic well-being. This is because real incomes get eroded in the wake of high inflation. To make matters worse, central bankers appointed at the behest of their political masters exhibit extreme stubbornness to raise interest rates to rein-in inflation, lest they invite the rebuke of political bosses, who are ultimately held accountable by the electorate. As Professor Raghuram Rajan (Former Governor of the RBI) succinctly surmised: "the job of a central banker demands lot more political skills than economic." So, for all its fondness and follies, the Big Mac should continue to serve as a useful barometer to measure an intrinsic value of a currency to guide policymakers while dealing with the actual exchange rates determined by market forces.

4 Improvements to Lend BMI More Effective

Several substitutes have been offered to veer the BMI away from a single standardized product, which is the "hamburger." Alternative products equally meeting the criteria are Coca-Cola, Starbucks Coffee, and more recently iPad. Indices constructed on the above have proven to be no more efficient than the traditional index originally developed in 1986. It requires only a cursory glance to release the underpinning weaknesses even with the substitution. Almost all the substitutes without exception have their core presence in the U.S., and with it, follows similar limitations associated with the traditional index.

As already delineated above, the ability of the U.S. to effectively wean inflation away—at least, to a large extent—BMI or indices based on substitutes may not be necessarily representative in reflecting an accurate valuation of currencies. It therefore becomes imperative to impose some form of stochastic function to reflect inflation based on changing scenarios. Of course, such improvements tend to make the unostentatious BMI complicated to discern with the added risk of estimation errors based on the principle of "GIGO."

Another plausible way to lend BMI more realistic might involve computing price of "hamburger" (or any other standardized product for that matter) weighted by the relative market share of currencies in dominating international trade—one that might also give representation to EMs. These improvements would certainly lend greater credibility toward enhancing the appeal of BMI beyond the theoretical confines capable of attracting economic policymakers' serious attention.

5 Summary and Conclusions

Despite the criticisms, BMI is to be viewed as a useful tool in the hands of economic policymakers to gauge the relative valuation of currencies from an intrinsic perspective to lend meaningful comparison with the exchange rates determined on market principles guided by the forces of equilibrium in a foreign-exchange market. The simplicity and discernibility associated with the original model makes it equally appealing to wide range of audiences.

From the discussions above, another interesting fact that emerges is the advantage (at least from a theoretical standpoint) accruing to EMs is the strength in valuation derived by the currencies estimated on the principles of PPP. In such a scenario, previous arguments pointing toward economic hegemony unleashed by nations with dominant currencies falls flat obscuring the concerns leveled by developing economies, which often end-up bearing the brunt in both economic and social terms. Reality, is however, somber. The fact remains that even by the standards of "The Economist"; the index was developed merely with an eye toward making the discussions surrounding the exchange-rate theory more palatable. Beyond the confines of nuanced academic discussions and potential opportunities from an academic perspective, Big Mac Index suffers from severe flaws.

Yet another deficiency attributable to the original index lies in its inability to take into cognizance the factors relating to costs of production. One reason for observing an anomaly between the PPP and market-determined exchange rate—when viewed from a GDP on a per-capita basis—stems from the differences observed in costs of production. That is, given the cheaper source of labor, one would expect the cost of production in China to be much lower as compared to US. In the absence of making an adjustment for such an anomaly, inferences drawn because of the vast differences in figures of GDP on a per-capita under the two approaches are rendered spurious.[15] Toward the end, it is fair to summarize that the merits in utilizing the Big Mac Index may not go much beyond eliciting distinctive views from eclectic audiences of economics.

REFERENCES

Andrei, L. S. (2014). *Globalisation and cultural identity dilemmas*. Econstar.

Citrinot, L. (2015, September). *Big Mac Index: Most ASEAN currencies undervalued...and this is not over*. Retrieved from Asean Travel Web site. http://asean.travel/2015/09/13/big-mac-index-most-asean-currencies-undervalued-and-this-is-not-over/

Clements, K. W., Lan, Y., & Seah, S. P. (2010). The Big Mac Index two decades on: An evaluation of burgernomics. *International Journal of Finance & Economics*, 31–60.

Domac, I., & Oskooee, M. B. (1997). Turkish stock prices and the value of Turkish Lira. *Canadian Journal of Development Studies*, 139–150.

Fama, E. F. (1988). Efficient capital markets: II. *Journal of Finance*, 1575–1617.

Inman, P. (2015, May). *Big Mac Index inflames debate over Chinese yuan's value*. Retrieved from The Guardian Web site: https://www.theguardian.com/business/2015/jul/16/big-mac-index-chinese-yuan-value

International Monetary Fund. (2007, March). PPP versus the market: Which weight matters? *Finance & Development, 44*(1).

Jagannathan, R. (2012, January). *A dollar at 32? Big Mac says so, but don't count on it*. Retrieved from Firstpost.com Web site: http://www.firstpost.com/business/economy/a-dollar-at-rs-32-big-mac-says-so-but-dont-count-on-it-184991.html

Josic, H., Wittne, Z., & Barisic, A. (2018). *Investigating the determinants of Big Mac Index: A panel data analysis*. Faculty of Economics & Business, University of Zagreb.

Juradja, S., & Ashenfelter, O. (2001). *Cross-country comparison of wage rates: The Big Mac Index*. Princeton University.

Lamont, O. A., & Thaler, R. H. (2003). Anomalies: The law of one price in financial markets. *Journal of Economic Perspectives*, 191–202.

Mazumder, S. (2016). iPad purchasing parity: Farewell to the Big Mac Index. *Economic Bulletin*, 2128–2136.

---

[15] The Economist has overcome this anomaly by constructing an adjusted index as opposed to the raw index by constructing a 'line of best fit' involving the variables relating to market-based exchange rate and the country's GDP per-capita. The methodological treatment involving the same is beyond the scope of discussion of this paper. Interested readers are invited to look at some useful academic papers including (Ong, 1997) for a better appreciation of the methodological treatment.

O'Brien, T. J., & Vargas, S. R. (2016). The adjusted Big Mac methodology: A clarification. *Journal of International Financial Management and Accounting*, 70–85.

Ong, L. L. (1997). Burgernomics: The economics of the Big Mac standard. *Journal of International Money and Finance, 16*(6), 865–878.

Portes, L. S., & Atal, V. (2014). The Big Mac Index: A shortcut to inflation and exchange rate dyamics? Price tracking and predictive properties. *International Business and Economics Research Journal*, 751–756.

Stylianou, N. (2014, January). *Food for thought on foreign exchange rates: The Big Mac Index 2014*. Retrieved from The Telegraph Web site: http://www.telegraph.co.uk/news/interactive-graphics/10595724/Food-for-thought-on-foreign-exchange-rates-The-Big-Mac-index-2014.html

The Economist. (2016, January 7). *The Big Mac Index*. Retrieved from The Economist Web site: http://www.economist.com/content/big-mac-index

Yang, J. (2004). Nontradables and the valuation of RMB—An evaluation of the Big Mac Index. *China Economic Review*, 353–359.

Yasser, M., Mussad, M., & Sanad, N. (2019). Does BIGMAC Index consider as a substitute for inflation rate. *Global Journal of Management and Business*, 17–21.

Zongze, R. (2012). A. In A. Dirlik & Y. Keping (Eds.), *Chinese perspectives on globalisation and autonomy: Issues in contemporary Chinese thought & culture* (pp. 329–346). Brill.

CHAPTER 8

Country Risk Analysis: Theory, Methodology, and Applications

Nitin Arora and Sunil Kumar

1 POLITICAL ECONOMY OF MEASURING COUNTRY RISK

The topographical,[1] cultural,[2] and ignorance[3] hypotheses are unable to clarify the rationale of social arrangements prompting relative poverty and

---

[1] A hypothesis which claims that the great divide between rich and poor countries is created by geographical differences.

[2] A hypothesis that relates prosperity to culture; the culture hypothesis, just like the geography hypothesis, has a distinguished lineage, going back at least to the great German sociologist Max Weber, who argued that the Protestant Reformation and the Protestant ethic it spurred played a key role in facilitating the rise of modern industrial society in Western Europe. The culture hypothesis no longer relies solely on religion, but stresses other types of beliefs, values, and ethics as well.

[3] A hypothesis which asserts that world inequality exists because we or our rulers do not know how to make poor countries rich.

N. Arora
Department of Economics, Panjab University, Chandigarh, India
e-mail: nitineco@pu.ac.in

S. Kumar (✉)
Faculty of Economics, South Asian University, New Delhi, India
e-mail: skumar@econ.sau.ac.in

© The Author(s), under exclusive license to Springer Nature Switzerland AG 2022
V. Charles and A. Emrouznejad (eds.), *Modern Indices for International Economic Diplomacy*, https://doi.org/10.1007/978-3-030-84535-3_8

inequality, while the central role of institutions broadly defines the rules that govern the economic and political behavior of a nation (Acemoglu & Robinson, 2012). Undoubtedly, the extractive[4] idea of economic and political institutions causes a nation's failure, while inclusive[5] institutions create powerful forces toward economic growth. Consequently, it turns into a relevant issue to check whether the institutional arrangement in a nation is of an extractive or inclusive nature. The predominance of extractive institutions in a country will clearly influence the nation's ability to transfer payments unfavorably, thus enhancing the risk of defaulting on major financial, political, and social liabilities. The recent experiences show that a financial crisis inside a country resembles an infection that spreads to other countries. It not only obliterates wealth as well as prompts political instability, mass protests, and increased joblessness. This brings conflict inside a nation and also hampers international diplomacy. A troubled state loses its credibility in international forums and in an extreme case may also lose its sovereignty. In the most recent past, we have seen that the exposure of the world to the U.S. subprime mortgage crisis set off a worldwide downturn, whose after-effects have not fully disappeared till now. Hence to maintain international economic order and to serve the economic interest and policies of the state, the policymakers must have access to early warning systems that could anticipate any disorder and thus insulate a nation from any economic and political turmoil. The set of indicators involved in the construction of a system should help policymakers to recognize early signs of bond defaults or foreign currency crises that could be catastrophic and incite international crises. These early warning signals ought not exclusively to have the option to foresee but should likewise anticipate when a country could fall into crises.

Currently, prominent credit rating agencies like Fitch Ratings, Moody's, S&P Global Ratings, and so on provide all the necessary information to investors on the economic and political climate (imperative for gauging the risk of default) of the multitude of nations. These rating agencies are independent third parties that assist the interested parties

---

[4] Extractive because such institutions are designed to extract incomes and wealth from one subset of society to benefit a different subset.

[5] Inclusive economic institutions create inclusive markets, which not only give people freedom to pursue the vocations in life that best suit their talents but also provide a level playing field that gives them the opportunity to do so.

to overcome asymmetric information by utilizing standard procedures. These agencies measure the country risk index based on various dimensions and guide the investors before they take their investment decision. While validating the credibility of the global financial system, these agencies provide a forward guidance indicator (FGI) to the investors and thus channelize the capital flows from the countries of plenty to countries of need. Therefore, their work has led to being described as pre-eminent since they give the correct image of the state of financial affairs inside a country to keep up international harmony. Indeed, the prime role of the rating agencies is to check the dominance of extractive institutions and provide sufficient inputs to firms, particularly multinational corporations (MNCs), in making investments. The assessment of country risk by these agencies is essential for MNCs to discount their future return and attain net present value (NPV) of investment in a country. In case the discounting factor is sufficiently high so much that the NPV is ending up being negative, the MNCs shall avoid investment.

The country risk analysis involves several dimensions of risk associated with economy, polity, sovereignty, exchange, transfer, neighborhood, subjectivity. The economic risk is related to the currency crisis and default possibility at external debt. Numerous factors cause debt and currency crises for a nation. In this context, fragile GDP growth, high joblessness, lack of demand, technological dualism, and so on are a couple to name among numerous others. Many times the excessive government intercession in markets may cause such negative externalities that prompt failure and incoherence of markets and the persistence of extractive institutions.

One may capture the political risk through an array of indicators of political stability. The internal and external political stabilities are generally a matter of great concern. It normally concurs that only a stable government may guarantee a consistent and stable policy environment that is a must for forecasting the behavior of economic agents. In case the government is unstable, the forecasting of investment returns will be a tedious job. A U-turn in the policy environment because of an abrupt change in the political atmosphere (e.g., from liberal to protectionist) will certainly hamper the expected profits of investors. The outburst of civil war, a surge in terrorism, rampant corruption, and so forth are numerous factors that may cause a political crisis in a country and encourage extractive institutions. Among external political stability factors, tweaking with the international political order is vital as well. The international sanctions on a country (for instance, economic sanctions on Iran by international economic order) primarily because of following a nuclear testing policy by it, is a fine example of external political instability. A situation is undesirable for investors if it is marked by conflicts in the goals of the internal political setup and that of the international political order.

The sovereignty risk is related to the factors representing the freedom of a country to make economic and political decisions. The primary measuring stick to quantify such risk is the quantity of debt raised by the government from both internal and external sources. An individual or a country prefers to go for purchasing debt instruments based on some expected return. However, insolvent governments are generally at a high risk of default on discounting such debt instruments. Many times the external debt is provided on the basis of strict terms and conditions of lending institutions, which adversely affect the country's sovereignty to frame policies.

Under the floating exchange rate regime, the price of one unit of currency (say U.S. $) in terms of the number of units of other currency is controlled by market forces and, hence, is volatile enough. High volatility in the exchange rate of a currency makes a venture riskier since the depreciation in the exchange rate will give a lesser return in foreign currency when contrasted to a situation of autarky. In contrast, stability in the exchange rate assists in forecasting returns in a better manner. The exchange rate depreciates due to many economic and political forces. For example, a deterioration in the balance of payments may cause depreciation in the exchange rate. An unstable political environment too causes a loss in the confidence of country's currency and subsequently enhances the exchange risk. Further, the country may confront transfer risk when it doesn't allow foreign currency transfers out of the nation. A classic example of such a situation is Malaysian credit controls after the Asian currency crisis of 1997–1998. Such type of capital controls prevents foreign traders or investors from retrieving profits or dividends from the host country.

The geographic location of a country matters too in the assessment of country risk. If the neighboring country is posing a threat of war, political disturbance, and so on, the investment becomes a risky venture. However, location in the vicinity of peace-loving nations is an additional source of motivation to investors. Sharing neighborhood matters even if the economic factors are investment appealing; sharing borders with a disturbed terrorist country causes threat of human and non-human capital loss that an investor always wants to avoid.

The last is the subjectivity risk. The choices, tastes, and habits of various countries are unique, and so the product inclinations change altogether across nations. An item that remains in high demand in one country may totally fall flat in other countries because of the indifferent attitude of the customers in other markets. In this context, one can take the case of the market for a beef burger in India. The demand for a beef burger always stays low in India because of the tastes and preferences of the majority of Indians. Any investor who sells the beef burger elsewhere keeps away from the Indian market because of the high subjectivity risk associated with this item.

In sum, there are different sorts of risks related to investment planning. The dominance of any of the aforementioned risks associated with an investment in a nation may distort the confidence and preference of the investors. In such case, the investment may be diverted to another country having a lower risk. In a competitive world, countries are creating opportunities to allure investors. So an increased country risk may offer a disadvantage to the relatively weaker nation and can distract the investor's preference. Thus, a robust composite index of country risk serves as an essential tool to evaluate the degree of risk associated with an investment in a given nation. Based on the numerical value of the country risk index, investors can decide whether a country is a paradise or hellfire for their investments. Against this brief background, this chapter offers a survey of methodological frameworks available in the extant literature to construct an index of country risk.

2 Methodologies for Constructing a Country Risk Assessment Index and Prominent Indices

Levy and Yoon (1996) provide a detailed overview of the methods to assess country risk (see Table 1 for details). The most commonly used methodological frameworks are: consensus risk index based on perceptions and evaluations of experts (Backhaus & Meyer, 1984; Miller, 1992); scoring models that aggregate index data on different risk variables (Dahringer & Miihlbacher, 1991; Hake, 1982; Miiller-Berghoff, 1984); the analytic hierarchy process which gages relative importance of relevant variables from judgmental data (Saaty, 1972, 1980; Sauber et al., 1991); simulation surveys which develop scenario-based risk-perception data (Karakaya & Stahl, 1991; Punnett, 1994); other statistical methods

Table 1 Methods of country risk assessment

Risk assessment method	Input measures	Output measures	Advantages	Disadvantages	Selected references
Panel of experts	Perception of country risk	Consensus risk index	Combines experts' knowledge and practice; amenable to group-decision process	Time-consuming; nonobjective; experts' bias; difficulty identifying qualified experts	Backhaus and Meyer (1984), Miller (1992)
Discrete scoring model	Interval index for each risk attribute	Average risk index or average factor-score risk	Easy application of quantitative techniques; ease of comprehension, computation, and interpretation	Arbitrariness in estimating weights of attributes for qualitative information	Blank et al. (1982), Hake (1982), Miiller-Berghoff (1984), Backhaus et al. (1985), Backhaus and Meyer (1986)
Analytic hierarchy process	Judgemental assessment for each risk attribute	Relative weights of risk attributes	Combines management judgment and intuition; amenable to group-decision process	Possible inconsistency or bias in determining information categories	Jensen (1986), Saaty and Vargas (1994)
Simulation survey	Intention of early/late entry for different risk scenarios	Probability estimates for entry decision	Flexible for scenario design; combines regression or discriminant analysis	Time-consuming and costly for survey design, data collection, and analysis and evaluation	Karakaya and Stahl (1991), Punnett (1994)
Full fuzzy scoring model	Categorical assessment of each risk variable	Fuzzy envelope for country risk	Performs linguistic analysis; propagates complete information from stage to stage	User interprets fuzzy envelope subjectively; interpretation may vary among users	Levy and Yoon (1995)

(continued)

Table 1 (continued)

Risk assessment method	Input measures	Output measures	Advantages	Disadvantages	Selected references
Reduced fuzzy scoring model	Categorical assessment of each risk variable	Point estimate of Fuzzy envelope for country risk	Performs linguistic analysis; propagates easy-to-interpret scalar from stage to stage	Loss of full information; potentially restrictive single-category summary; subjective interpretation of fuzzy envelope that may vary among users	Levy and Yoon (1993)

Source Levy and Yoon (1996)

such as regression and factor analyses (Backhaus & Meyer, 1984, 1986; Erramilli, 1991). The fuzzy logic-based technique developed by Levy and Yoon (1995) has also been incorporated among many other methods to assess country risk.

In his extensive survey, Nath (2008) highlighted the popular quantitative methods and listed out indicators needed to analyze country risk. The major techniques discussed by Nath (2008) are discriminant analysis, principal component analysis, logit model, generalized logit model, tobit analysis, classification and regression tree (CART) method, artificial neural network (ANN), and hybrid neural network (HNN). Basu et al. (2011) evaluated country risk in India using the country beta model of Erb et al. (1996).

Mate (2017) followed a basic risk assessment methodology where experts assigned subjective scores for each risk factor. The scoring was based on economic modeling results, open sources country information, and market data. The overall country risk score was determined as a weighted average of the different risk indicators. Several institutions calculate country risk ratings. One of the first indices to measure country risk was the Institutional Investor Index, also known as the Country Credit Survey, which ceased publication in 2016. This index gages sovereign credit risk, encompassing political risk, exchange rate risk, economic risk, sovereign risk, and transfer risk. For arriving at an index figure in the range between zero and 100 for each country, the survey used strict confidential information provided by senior economists and sovereign-risk analysts at global banks and money management and securities firms. The country with an index value of 100 was viewed as the most credit-worthy country with minimal probability of default.

S&P Global Ratings, the largest credit rating agency, issues short-term and long-term credit ratings. This agency assesses the country risk on an alphabetic scale from AAA to D, with AAA as the highest rating. This rating depends on the scores given to five factors on a six-point numerical scale from 1 (strongest) to 6 (weakest). The five factors are Institutional effectiveness and political risks (Political score), Economic structure (Economic score), External liquidity and international investment position (External score), Fiscal flexibility and fiscal performance combined with debt burden (Fiscal Score), and Monetary flexibility (Monetary score). The political and economic scores are combined to make a political and economic profile of a nation, and the external, fiscal, and monetary scores form the flexibility and performance profile of a country. The two profiles provide an 'indicative rating level' used to determine the foreign currency sovereign rating and local currency sovereign rating.

Fitch Investor Service developed a regression-based model involving 18 economic and financial variables that help in assessing the country risk. These underlined variables are broadly recorded under four categories: (i) Macroeconomic Policies and performance, (ii) Public finance, (iii) External finance, (iv) and structural characteristics of the economy. The first category incorporates key macroeconomic variables of the consumer price index, real GDP growth, and the volatility of real GDP growth. The budget balance, gross debt, interest payments, and public foreign currency debt are included in the second category. The commodity dependence, current account balance plus net foreign direct investment, gross sovereign debt, external interest services, and official international reserves fall under the third category. The final category contains financial market depth, GDP per capita, composite governance indicator, reserve currency status, and the number of years since the default. The credit ratings range between AAA and D, with AAA being the best rating.

The Business Environment Risk Intelligence is a US-based company that provides a rating system that permits comparisons between countries for the past, the present, and three-to-five-year forecast horizon. This rating system helps in gaging the business climate, political stability, and currency risk and facilitates the international executives to implement the investment decisions successfully. The underlined rating system is in the form of the Profit Opportunity Recommendation (POR) index for a country. The POR index is the weighted average of three sub-indices: (i) Operations Risk Index (ORI), (ii) the Political Risk Index (PRI), and (iii) the Remittance and Repatriation Factor (R-Factor). Euromoney country risk (ECR) is an online platform that provides real-time risk scores for more than 175 individual countries based on the experts' assessment of country risk experts. The expert panel, comprising economists and political scientists, contributes real-time scores in 15 categories relating to economic, political, and structural risk. The composite country risk score is then obtained by combining the consensus scores of experts with data from the IMF/World Bank on debt indicators and survey data on sovereign access to international capital markets. ECR's composite score for a country is the weighted sum of six distinct dimensional indices with the unique weighting scheme: (i) political risk (30%), (ii) economic performance (30%), (iii) structural assessment (10%), (iv) debt service, (v) credit ratings based on Moody's or S&P's or Fitch's rating (10%),[6] and (vi) access to bank finance/capital markets (10%). The weighting scheme clearly features that relatively high weights are given to the first three dimensions, which are primarily qualitative, and relatively small weights are assigned to the last three dimensions, which are fundamentally quantitative. Based on ECR's scores, countries are placed in the range of Tier 1 = AAA(80–100) to Tier 5 = C(0–35.9).

The Economist Intelligence Unit (EIU) of The Economist has developed a country risk model to quantify country risk at aggregate and disaggregate levels for 131 countries. The country risk model spotlights major risks emanating in key areas of sovereign debt, currency, banking sector, political and economic structure. The risk rating model system gives a composite country risk score as well as computes the individual scores for sovereign risk, currency risk, banking sector risk, political risk,

---

[6] Moody's established in 1900, issued its first sovereign rating just before World War I. By 1929, Poor's Publishing rated Yankee bonds issued by 21 national governments. The Standard Statistics, another rating agency rated various countries' sovereign default by 1935. Poor's Publishing and Standard Statistics merged to form S&P in 1941. After World War-II, S&P and Moody's again began to rate Yankee bonds and so they jointly dominated at the turn of twenty-first century, with a combined market share of about 80 percent of all ratings revenue (see Bhatia [2002, p. 6], for a brief history of Sovereign Rating by S&P and Moody's and Fitch).

and economic structure risk. The model produces short- and medium-term economic and political forecasts for the country, which can be utilized by financial institutions and companies in decision-making. In addition, EIU computes the overall business environment score for over 80 countries and generates a unique set of forward-looking business environment rankings. To estimate the overall scores, the methodological framework employed needs in the first stage to score 91 indicators on a scale from 1 (very bad for business) to 5 (very good for business). These indicators are then used to compute ten category scores, which are in the final stage aggregated using the unweighted average method to calculate an overall business environment score. The EIU additionally publishes ViewsWire and Democracy Index alongside the Country Risk Service.

The IHS Markit has its scoring system to measure country risk. The HIS Markit gives forward-looking risk ratings for six aggregate and twenty-two sub-aggregate risk categories for 211 countries and places each country in the system of 7 risk banks. According to IHS methodology, the country risk is divided into the following categories: political, economic, legal, tax, operational, and security risk. As shown in Table 2 these categories are divided into further sub-categories. The IHS strategic risk methodology gives equal weight to each category and sub-category. The overall country risk scores are calculated as the equally-weighted

Table 2 Risk categories and their sub-categories in the country risk analysis of IHS Markit

Political	*Economic*	*Legal*	*Tax*	*Operational*	*Security*
Government instability	Capital transfer	Enforcement Contract	Inconsistency Tax	Corruption	Civil war
Policy instability	Currency depreciation	Expropriation	Tax increase	Infrastructure disruption	Interstate war
State failure	Inflation	State contract alteration	Labor strikes	Protests and riots	
Recession	Regulatory burden	Terrorism			
Sovereign default					
Under development					

Source IHS Strategic Risk Methodology

Table 3 HIS country risk bands

Low	Moderated	Elevated	High	Very High	Severe	Extreme
0.1–0.7	0.8–1.5	1.6–2.3	2.4–3.1	3.2–4.3	4.4–6.4	6.5–10

Source IHS Strategic Risk Methodology

average of the categories, and the categories scores are computed as the equally-weighted average of their sub-categories (IHS, 2017).

In the methodological framework of IHS Markit, political risk measures the government and policy instability. Elements of economic risk include macroeconomic indicators, growth prospects, currency strength, and sovereign default risk. Operational risk mirrors the level of corruption, employee representation, and the rate of the regulatory burden. Security risk includes the risk of ongoing or expected armed conflicts and acts of terrorism. Tax risk focuses on the risk of changes in the tax environment, while legal indicators measure the risk that the government will expropriate or nationalize assets. Risk is scored on a 0.1–10 scale for each sub-category, with intervals of 0.1 magnitudes. The IHS Global Insight (*GI*) scores split the country risks into seven bands.

Table 3 shows the risk bands ranging from low to extreme risk. The scale is logarithmic, which means that the ranges of risk bands are different. Consequently, it implies more effective differentiation between countries at both lower and higher ends of the scale.

The US-based think-tank the Heritage Foundation, with the collaboration of the Wall Street Journal, publishes the Index of Economic Freedom, which ranks 184 countries based on 12 aspects of economic freedom ranging from property rights to financial freedom under four major categories: the rule of law, size of government, regulatory efficiency, and open markets. The index values range between 0 and 100, with 0 meaning "no economic freedom" and 100 meaning "total economic freedom".

Another well-known index is the International Country Risk Guide (ICRG) published by the Political Risk Services (PRS) Group. The ICRG rating framework includes 22 indicators encompassing political, financial, and economic risk dimensions to compute individual country risk ratings for a sample of 146 countries. In addition to a composite index of country risk, ICRG provides three indices for underlined sub-categories. The political risk index, which estimates the country's political stability position, depends on a set of 12 indicators. These indicators are government stability, socioeconomic conditions, investment profile, external conflict, corruption, military in politics, religion in politics, law and order, ethnic tensions, democratic accountability, and bureaucracy quality. The financial risk component assesses a country's ability to finance its official, commercial, and trade debt obligations. This component is based on 5 indicators: total foreign debt as a percentage of GDP, debt service as a percentage of exports of goods and services, current account as a percentage of exports of goods and services, international liquidity as months of import cover, and exchange rate stability as a percentage change. The main intent of the economic risk component is to measure the country's economic strengths and weaknesses. To compute this component, the ICRG uses a set of five key economic indicators. These indicators are GDP per capita, real annual GDP growth, annual inflation rate, budget balance as a percentage of GDP, current accounts as a percentage of GDP.

In constructing the composite index, the political risk rating contributes 50 percent of the combined rating, while the financial and economic risk ratings contribute equally with weights of 25 percentage points. The following formula is used to calculate the composite country risk rating for a country, say X:

$$CPFER_X = 0.5PR_X + 0.25FR_X + 0.25ER_X$$

where $CPFER$ = Composite country risk rating, PR = political risk rating, FR = financial risk rating, ER = economic risk rating indicators. The highest overall rating (theoretically 100) indicates the lowest risk, and the lowest rating (theoretically zero) indicates the highest risk. As a general guide to grouping countries, one may use the following categorization given in Table 4.

3 WEIGHTING METHODS

It is a widely agreed fact that the subjective weights are many times illogical. Therefore, it has been emphasized that one should use the objective weights of each indicator/dimension/category/component/subcategory based on a scientific method out of the many available methods. The commonly used methods for obtaining objective weights are either parametric or non-parametric. Among parametric methods, the

Table 4 Comparable risk categories for an individual country

Category	CPFER
Very high risk	00.0 to 49.9 points
High risk	50.00 to 59.9 points
Moderate risk	60.00 to 69.9 points
Low risk	70.00 to 79.9 points
Very low risk	80.00 to 100 points

Source The Handbook of Country and Political Risk Analysis, PRS Textbook

regression-based techniques of generating weights are prominent ones. In this category, the Principal Component Analysis and Factor analysis are of great use for analysts to estimate weights needed for country risk index by grouping collinear indicators, representing economic, financial, and political risks. In this regard, the underlined indicators can be used to construct such dimensional indices, which can act as a proxy of all the indicators. For example, let ER_1, ER_2, ..., ER_m are m indicators of economic risk. These m indicators may be classified into a few factors which represent all these indicators. Let us assume that ER_F1, ER_F2, ..., ER_F_k are k factors extracted out of m indicators, representing economic risk. Now the dimensional index of Economic Risk (ER) can be constructed as a weighted average of all these factors, i.e.,

$$ER_i = \frac{w_{ER_1} \times ER_{1,i} + w_{ER_2} \times ER_{2,i} + \cdots\cdots + w_{ER_m} \times ER_{m,i}}{\sum_{m=1}^{M} w_{ER_m}};$$

$$i = 1, 2, \ldots, n \text{ countries}$$

The $w_{ER\_F_k}$ is the weight assigned to kth factor and can be determined using the following formula.

$$w_{ER_m} = \left|\max\left(\lambda_j^m\right)\right| \times \left[\text{variance explained by } j\text{th factor with } \max\left(\lambda_j^m\right)\right];$$

$$j = 1, 2, \ldots, k \text{ factors.}$$

In the above formula, λ_j^m is factor loading of mth component variable in jth factor. After the construction of each dimensional/component index (e.g., Political Risk (PR_i), Sovereignty Risk (SR_i), etc.) using the aforementioned methodology, the country risk index can be measured as a simple average of all indices with the assumption of equal weights of all indices in explaining country risk.

However, in the above methodology, though the indicator-specific weights have been determined in an endogenous and objective manner yet the weights of each dimensional/component index have been assumed to be the same in constructing the composite index of country risk for sample countries. Another possible solution under the Exploratory Factor Analysis is to use all indicators of country risk (classified under different dimensions/components) to run a factor analysis. Through this method, the factors will include a mixture of variables based on the degree of correlation among different indicators, and consequently, a vague variable mix may appear in each factor. For example, some political indicators that are highly correlated with an economic indicator may appear into the economic factor with high factor loading. Thus, the structural equations modeling (SEM) based confirmatory factor analysis (CFA) must be preferred over the EFA to construct a composite index of country risk. The CFA model may look like Fig. 1.

In the above model, a latent of country risk has been constructed using latent variables (i.e., dimensions) such as Economic Risk, Political Risk, and Sovereignty Risk, etc. All these latent variables are determined by the component deterministic variables. For example, the latent *Economic_Risk* has been constructed using the *m* deterministic variables *ER1*, *ER2*, ..., *ERm*. Here, it is assumed that *ER1*, *ER2*, ..., *ERm* satisfy the content validity for the latent *Economic_Risk*. The circles contain the error terms in the model, and arrows represent the direction of the relationship. The model parameters can be estimated using techniques like the maximum

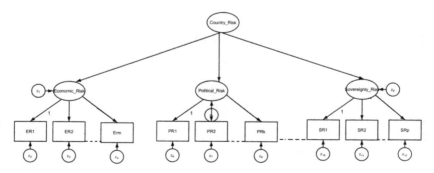

Fig. 1 A CFA-based model to measure country risk (*Source* Authors' Elaborations)

likelihood estimation (MLE) technique etc. The model outlined above is a basic one that is expected to satisfy the construct validity criteria. In case the validity criteria are not satisfied, the model can be modified as per modification indices. The covariance structures may be drawn in case the latent variables of the model are correlated significantly.

Xu and Chung (2018) used the non-parametric Data Envelopment Analysis (DEA) technique to assess the risk of China's belt and road initiative's sustainable investing. The DEA model used is as follows:

$$\left. \begin{array}{l} \theta_i = \max_{w_{ij}} \sum_j^J w_{ij} y_{ij} \\ s.t. \sum_j^J w_{ij} y_{kj} \leq 1 \, \forall k \\ w_{ij} \geq 0 \, \forall j \end{array} \right\} (DEA - CRI)$$

One of the key features of this model is that the composite index of country risk for the i-th country, which is represented by θ_i is constructed by treating all the indicators (y_j, $j = 1, ..., J$) as outputs, thereby considering no inputs in the model. DEA models of this type are called the "benefit-of-the-doubt (BoD)" models in the literature. A value of θ_i closer to unity represents lesser risk and *vice-versa*. The optimization model used is based on an optimistic perspective and generates the weights (ws) that are the highest possible. Given this basic measure of *DEA-CRI*, all advancements of DEA methodology can be incorporated in the modeling framework while constructing a measure of country risk. Note that the θ_i representing country risk score is deterministic in nature, and the usual random error can be separated out from θ_i by using the bootstrapping technique. The θ_i score then obtained after splitting bias will be called the bias-corrected composite index of country risk.

4 Key Indicators for Constructing Country Risk Assessment Index

After a detailed discussion on various methods to construct a country risk index, it turns out to be evident that multiple dimensions of country risk, i.e., economic, political, sovereignty, exchange, transfer risk, etc., can be ascertained based on well-defined indicators. The literature highlights that the significant variables used to explain economic stability are GDP per capita, inflation rate, domestic and foreign savings, export product concentration, merchandised exports and imports, imports of food and fuel, and so forth. The level of unemployment frequently becomes an important determinant of economic risk as high unemployment is associated with low output levels. The capital and money market fluctuations reflected in long and short-term interest rates are likewise used as key indicators of economic stability.

Note here that researchers use either the values of these indicators as such or the detrended values after applying a filtering procedure. The filtering techniques such as The Hodrick-Prescott (H-P) filter or Christiano and Fitzgerald's (2003) band-pass filter are generally used by the researchers to detrend data. An instability index such as $\left[\left(Y_{jt}^{cyclical}/Y_{jt}^{trend}\right) - 1\right] \times 100$ can be constructed for each component variable Y_j at time period t to see the percentage deviation of cyclical value from trend value; higher deviation more instability and *vice-versa*.

Not only actual but expected interest rate also matters in determining economic stability. A low expected interest rate is considered as a measure of expected capital flight or increase in liquidity preference by both domestic and foreign investors. Liquidity preference indicates lesser investment and the possibility of a recession and vice-versa. Likewise, expected GDP per capita may fundamentally affect the current economic activity. In a similar line, many variables in an ex-ante form significantly affect economic activity at present. These expectations so can help to formulate an accurate indicator of economic risk. The expectations or ex-ante variables can be taken into account under the dynamic stochastic general equilibrium (DSGE) framework, and their desired values to grow along a steady-state path can also be computed.

Under a floating exchange rate system, the exchange rate is flexible enough. The balance of payment situation, for the most part, determines the value of a currency in the foreign market and thus indicates the exchange rate risk. A surplus balance of payment may cause currency appreciation, while a deficit may prompt exchange rate depreciation. Currency depreciation up to a certain limit is gainful for a country as it helps to generate international trade in its favor. Notwithstanding, continuous currency depreciation is perilous for a nation as it reduces the confidence of international investors in the falling currency. Along these lines, the current account and capital account deficit (i.e., the balance of payment situation), the exchange rate volatility, and so forth, might be the possible indicators to construct exchange rate risk. Indeed, even different exchange rate indicators are available for researchers to evaluate the exchange rate volatility; the simple and real effective exchange rates are accessible for the consideration of policy planners. In the literature, the researchers have focused on the utilization of real effective exchange rate as the suitable measure of exchange rate fluctuations. High volatility in the exchange rate reflects high exchange rate risk and vice-versa.

The debt situation determines the sovereignty risk, and the external debt servicing index as constructed by Wilson (1979) can be used as an index of sovereignty. Four economic and financial ratios/indicators are often used in building the External Debt Servicing Index. The external debt servicing capacity ratio is the first ratio and measures a country's net external earnings and transfers in a given year relative to the current portion of its total external public debt. Months of imports covered is the second indicator in the list and estimates the adequacy of a country's internationally accepted liquid foreign reserve assets. The third ratio is the ratio of total external debt to GDP. The fourth ratio is the compressibility ratio, which measures how much of current earnings from exports and net private transfers have to be spent on vital imports such as food and fuel, and current payments for external debt.

Now we discuss the key indicators for constructing an index of political risk. The International Country Risk Guide (ICRG) published by the PRS Group offers a detailed methodology to build the political risk index. In addition, categorical variables might be utilized to assess the political risk. Various dimensions of political instability can be defined, and the underlined indicators can be coded as binary variables derived from the responses in the form of "Yes" or "No". At long last, the number of affirmative responses is counted, and a ratio of the number of affirmative responses to total responses might be considered as an index of political instability; the higher the ratio more will be the political instability. Different sorts of risk, viz. location and subjectivity risk, so on, can likewise be computed using the categorical variables; either dichotomous or polychotomous variables can be used to represent such variates. In the polychotomous category, ordered response variables can be used to rank the preference of scale value for a given situation.

5 Conclusions and Some Future Concerns

In sum, the country risk analysis is vital for any investor in the international market. Even the governments of different countries find some merit in constructing such an index because the international lending and its strength to service and repay the debt vigorously rely on the relative positioning of the country on such index. Many international aids are, therefore, related to the evaluation of the status of risk of investment in a country. The major types of risks are economic, political, sovereignty, exchange, location, transfer risk, and so forth. Among all, the economic and political risks are the key risks that explain the maximum amount of variation in any index of country risk.

The economic risk assessment is a technical issue that depends upon an assortment of indicators. Most of these indicators are accessible in the databases of the World Bank, IMF, OECD. The leading data sets are World Development Indicators by the World Bank, International Financial Statistics by IMF, Direction of Trade database by IMF, Government Financial Statistics by IMF, World Integrated Trade Solution (WITS) database, Transparency in Trade (TNT) database, and so on.

Major methods to construct country risk are based on either expert evaluation/judgment or quantitative methods such as principal component analysis, discriminant analysis, logit and probit model estimations, exploratory and confirmatory factor analysis, artificial neural network, and data envelopment analysis. The key errand is to generate a set of weights that can be assigned to each underlined dimension that may act as a proxy for a specific type of instability. The arbitrary weight assignment is subject to severe criticism, while the construction of scientific weights is recommended for getting an accurate estimate of the country's risk index. Notwithstanding, each method is subject to some merits and demerits. Therefore, for a precise inference about country risk, one ought to never rely on a single index. Alternative indices of country risk should be constructed, and rank distribution of countries should be built based on each measure of country risk.

References

Acemoglu, D., & Robinson, J. (2012). *Why nations fail: The origins of power, prosperity and poverty*. Profile Books Ltd.

Backhaus, K., & Meyer, M. (1984). Intemationale Risiko-Baromater. *Absatzwirtschaft, 27*(10), 64–74.
Backhaus, K., & Meyer, M. (1986). Country risk assessment in international industrial marketing. In K. Backbaus & D. T. Wilson (Eds.), *Industrial marketing* (pp. 245–273). Springer-Verlag.
Backhaus, K., Meyer, M., & Weiber, R. (1985). A lisxel model for country risk assessment. In N.K. Malhotra (Ed.), *Developments in Marketing Science*, Vol. 8, Atlanta, GA: Academy of Marketing Science, 437–441.
Basu, S., Deepthi, D., & Reddy, J. (2011). *Country risk analysis in emerging markets: The Indian example* (Working Paper No. 326, Indian Institute of Management).
Bhatia, A. V. (2002). *Sovereign credit ratings methodology: An evaluation* (IMF Working Paper No. WP/02/170). Treasurer's Department, International Monetary Fund. Available at https://www.imf.org/external/pubs/ft/wp/2002/wp02170.pdf
Blank, S., La Palombara, J., & Sacks, P. M. (1982). Political analysis and forecasting in the private sector: An overview of the new firm-centric analytical formats. In W. Veit (Ed.), Political risk analysis: A new approach to old problems?, Bonn, Bad Godesberg, FRG: Vierteljahresberichte - Probleme der Entwicklungslander, 90 (December), 357–384.
Christiano, L. J., & Fitzgerald, T. J. (2003). The band pass filter. *International Economic Review, 44*, 435–465. https://doi.org/10.1111/1468-2354.t01-1-00076
Dahringer, L. D., & Miihlbacher, H. (1991). *International marketing: A global perspective*. Addison-Wesley Publishing Company.
Erb, C. B., Harvey, C. R., & Viskanta, T. E. (1996). Expected returns and volatility in 135 countries. *Journal of Portfolio Management Spring, 22*(3), 46–58.
Erramilli, M. K. (1991). The experience factor in foreign market entry behavior of service firms. *Journal of International Business Studies, 22* (3), 479–501.
Hake, B. (1982). Der BERI-Index, ein Hilfsmittel zur Beurteilung des Wirtschaftspolitischen Risikos von Auslandsinvestitionen. In W. Liick & V. Trommsdorf (Eds.), *Internationalisierung der Unternehmung* (pp. 463–473). Duncker u. Humblot.
IHS. (2017, January 17). *IHS country risk ratings—Strategic risk methodology*. http://connect.ihs.com
Jensen, R. E. (1986). Comparison of consensus methods for priority ranking problems. *Decision Sciences, 17*(2), 195–211.
Karakaya, F., & Stahl, M. J. (1991). *Entry barriers & market entry decisions*. Quorum Books.
Levy, J., & Yoon, E. (1993). On global market entry decision: A comparison of different methodologies. presented to the Session on Global Issues in

Operations Management at the Fourth Annual Meeting of the Production and Operations Management Society (POM-93), Boston, MA, October 3-5, 1993. Abstracted in the POM-93 Bulletin, No. 4, p. 18.

Levy, J., & Yoon, E. (1995). Modeling global market entry decision by Fuzzy Logic with an application to country risk assessment. *European Journal of Operational Research, 82*, 53–78.

Levy, J. B., & Yoon, E. (1996). *Methods of country risk assessment for international market-entry decisions*. Report No. 11-1996, The Pennsylvania State University, Institute for the Study of Business Markets.

Mate, P. (2017, April 20–21). How to measure country risk: Market indicators versus country risk ratings. MultiScience-XXXI.microCAD International Multidisciplinary Scientific Conference, University of Miskolc, Hungary. ISBN 978-963-358-132-2.

Miller, K. D. (1992). A framework for integrated risk management in international business. *Journal of International Business Studies, 23*(2), 311–331.

Miiller-Berghoff, B. (1984). *Die Eigene Exportindustxie Stiker Forden*. Blick durch die Wirtschaft (February 3), 3–4.

Nath, H. K. (2008). *Country risk analysis: A survey of the quantitative methods* (SHSU Economics & Intl. Business Working Paper No. SHSU_ECO_WP08-04).

Punnett, B. J. (1994). *Experiencing international business and management* (2nd ed.). Wadsworth Publishing Company.

Saaty, T. L. (1972). *An eigenvalue allocation model for prioritization and planning*. University of Pennsylvania.

Saaty, T. L. (1980). *The analytic hierarchy process*. McGraw Hill Company.

Saaty, T. L., & Vargas, L. G. (1994). Nonnegative solutions of linear algebraic systems with ratio scale coefficients. *Proceedings of the Third International Symposium on AHP*, 61–66.

Sauber, M. H., Sanchez, P., & Tummala, V. M. R. (1991). Launching new products for LDC's: The AHP approach. *Journal of Global Business, 2*(2), 31–37.

Wilson, O. J. (1979). Measuring country risk in a global context. *Business Economics, 14*(1), 23–27.

Xu, Q., & Chung, W. (2018). Risk assessment of China's Belt and Road Initiative's sustainable investing: A data envelopment analysis approach. *Economic and Political Studies*. https://doi.org/10.1080/20954816.2018.1498991

CHAPTER 9

Understanding the Corruption Perceptions Index

Emigdio Alfaro

1 Introduction

This section contains a general discussion of the concept of corruption and the CPI and their effects in national and international economics, business, and corporate diplomacy. First, some definitions of corruption, its types, manners in which the corruption appears, and its consequences are explained. Next, the CPI, its origins, and its implications are detailed. After that, the consequences of corruption and their measures through the CPI in diverse national and international contexts are explained.

1.1 The Corruption Perceptions Index: A General Idea

Corruption and the general idea of the CPI have been explained by diverse authors. Corruption affects policies and practices (Maxwell et al., 2011), damages global sectors, such as global health (Mackey et al., 2016)

E. Alfaro (✉)
Universidad César Vallejo, Lima, Peru

and humanitarian assistance (Maxwell et al., 2011), and reduces development and economic growth (Sari, 2017; Wilhelm, 2002); however, corruption could also reduce bureaucracy (Horsewood, 2012). It can also be differentiated between "petty corruption" and "grand corruption" (Atkinson, 2011). It is important to indicate that Transparency International's Corruption Perceptions Index measures corruption in 180 countries (Transparency International, 2019a) and has been published since 1995 (Lin & Yu, 2014), annually (Steger & Burgmans, 2003).

Referring to corruption, Chimdi (2019a) explained: "This involves primordial attachments in the award of contracts and appointments, embezzlement and misappropriation of public funds, inflation of contract sums" (p. 198). Chimdi (2019a) also indicated that "corruption involves the diversion of the people's common good for ones' selfish aggrandisement" (p. 198) and that "it also manifests itself through nepotism, tribalism, favouritism and many more dubious forms" (p. 198). As it can be appreciated, corruption appears in diverse ways and demonstrates a crisis of values of the people who realized corrupted actions.

Maxwell et al. (2011) indicated: "The definition of corruption is critical, because it is at the heart of a framework on what is and is not addressed in the implications of corruption for policy and practice" (p. 142) and that "Despite its importance, finding one universal definition of this concept that can be used to frame all responses has challenged scholars and practitioners alike for almost 50 years" (p. 142). A common definition of corruption around the world could be very difficult to be obtained due to the diverse values, habits, and beliefs of the people; however, it could be necessary for elaborating international and national policies for reducing corrupted actions around the world.

Corruption has been damaging diverse global sectors including global health. In this respect, Mackey et al. (2016) explained: "When corruption infiltrates global health, it can be particularly devastating, threatening hard gained improvements in human and economic development, international security, and population health" (p. 1). Mackey et al. (2016) also indicated: "Yet, the multifaceted and complex nature of global health corruption makes it extremely difficult to tackle, despite its enormous costs, which have been estimated in the billions of dollars" (p. 1). Additionally, Sari (2017) commented: "Corruption demoralizes the ethical and social justice as well as economic development which leads to a variety of problems for living standards and negatively affects overall development of the country" (p. 1675). Wilhelm (2002) also pointed out that "corruption is increasingly argued to be a barrier to development and economic growth" (p. 177). Then, a multifaceted and integrative solution for combating corruption in diverse global sectors including global health, social justice, etc., could be necessary for the short, medium, and long term.

Corruption could reduce bureaucracy. In this respect, Horsewood (2012) commented: "An opposing view is that if the administrative arrangements in a country are particularly burdensome then corruption might facilitate trade by cutting through the red tape" (p. 2). Horsewood (2012) also explained: "There is the possibility that entry into the EU might lead to a tightening up of rules and regulations in the CEECs, which might create a barrier to international transactions" (p. 2) and that "As a consequence EU membership might not result in the forecast economic gains due to the increased bureaucracy and the inability to use certain practices to 'oil the wheels of trade'" (p. 2). Although the idea of reducing bureaucracy through corruption could appear as a good consequence, it is not correct due to the benefit in the reduction of bureaucracy, which will benefit only a reduced group of organizations, leaving aside the rest of the organizations which are competing in the global and local arena.

Corruption has also been present in humanitarian assistance and this fact has been studied rarely. In this respect, Maxwell et al. (2011) explained: "Corruption in humanitarian assistance only occasionally makes headlines in the media, usually when a major scandal is unearthed" (p. 140). Maxwell et al. (2011) also indicated: "Yet corruption—whether or not it is exposed by the media—can cause harm and prevent humanitarian assistance from reaching the people who need it" (p. 140). Additionally, Maxwell et al. (2011) explained: "Corruption rarely has been the topic of research, and while there is significant accumulated good practice on corruption generally, there is relatively little that is specifically on humanitarian assistance, despite the obviously challenging nature of the context of humanitarian emergencies" (p. 140).

Corruption has implications for aid agencies and is related to local power relationships (Maxwell et al., 2011). Maxwell et al. (2011) indicated: "Corruption is strongly related to local power relationships and it thrives on bad governance and chronic exploitation" (p. 157). Maxwell et al. (2011) also explained:

The implications for aid agencies are two-fold. First, to truly understand and address corruption requires deep and nuanced local knowledge. It is all about programming with regard to context, but with standards that are more universal in nature. Second, corruption is driven by the very same forces that development, justice and human rights programmes seek to address. Thus, local humanitarian interventions need to be informed by the ongoing work of local development and human rights programmes and humanitarian action. (p. 157)

It is necessary to differentiate "petty corruption"—for small and discrete transactions of minor officials—from "grand corruption"—transactions of officials who occupy key positions (Atkinson, 2011). The term "petty corruption" was defined by Atkinson (2011), who indicated that the term is used "to describe relatively small, discrete transactions involving minor officials, typically bureaucrats (using the term broadly) entrusted with distributive or regulatory authority (Scott, 1972)" (p. 451). Atkinson (2011) also indicated that: "These officials occupy positions at key points in the approval process, which they use to seek bribes or kickbacks from citizens who are endeavoring to obtain political authorization" (p. 451) and that "The authorization sought typically involves either relief from a burden imposed by the state, or access to a privilege or opportunity controlled by the state" (p. 451).

The specialists of Transparency International (2019a) explained that the Corruption Perceptions Index (CPI) "measures the perceived levels of public sector corruption in 180 countries and territories" (p. 2) and that "Drawing on 13 surveys of business people and expert assessments, the index scores on a scale of zero (highly corrupt) to 100 (very clean)" (p. 2). About CPI, Ogwang and Cho (2014) indicated: "The corruption perception index (CPI), which measures the degree of corruption perception in the public sector in a particular country/territory, is one of the most popular measures of corruption" (p. 2).

Lin and Yu (2014) mentioned: "Since Transparency International first released its annual Corruption Perceptions Index (CPI) in 1995, the CPI has quickly become the best known corruption indicator worldwide" (p. 140) and that "The CPI has been widely credited with making comparative and large-N studies of corruption possible, as well as putting the issue of corruption squarely in the international policy agenda" (p. 140). Additionally, Wilhelm (2002) indicated that "Publication of the CPI has had a major political impact in several countries such a Pakistan,

Malaysia, and Argentina as governmental leaders reacted to the results" (p. 182) and that "These leaders know about the connection between perceived corruption and direct foreign investment" (p. 182). As can be appreciated, CPI has become the most used corruption perceptions index in diverse countries.

CPI also includes the list of countries which are rogue states (Steger & Burgmans, 2003). In respect, Steger and Burgmans (2003) explained: "Something which will benefit from the 'Grey War' will be the fight against corruption" (p. 67) and that "those countries in which corruption is endemic are also those that harbour terrorists or offer a fertile ground for terrorist movements" (p. 67). Steger and Burgmans (2003) also indicated:

> Transparency International (TI), the global anti-corruption NGO, publishes an annual "Corruption Perception Index", which lists the same nations as those on the US list of rogue states. TI praises companies with a strong anti-corruption policy, who "walk the talk": Unilever, for example, recently withdrew from Myanmar (Burma) and Bulgaria, because in these countries no business could be conducted without bribery. (p. 67)

1.2 Effects of Corruption and Corruption Perceptions Index in National and International Economics, Business, and Corporate Diplomacy

This section contains the effects of corruption and CPI in national and international economics, business, and corporate diplomacy. Corruption affects organizations at both national and international levels, considering their cultural contexts (Kagotho et al., 2016). Governments must combat corruption to avoid its negative effects on development and the economic growth of the countries (Sari, 2017). Combating corruption continues to represent a tenacious challenge (Hause, 2019) and requires the participation of the corporate, economic, and commercial diplomacy (Ali & Adeli, 2018).

1.2.1 Effects of Corruption and Corruption Perceptions Index in National and International Economics and Business

The combat of corruption is a challenge that can be realized with anti-corruption standards and via the commitment and training of the employees of international firms (Hause, 2019). Corruption affects access to medical care (Hsiao et al., 2019), institutional confidence (Pellegata & Memoli, 2016), and is related to deforestation directly (Koyuncu & Yilmaz, 2008); however, the distrust of the consumers in multinational firms in diverse countries is not affected by the CPI (Cénophat, 2017) and corruption is influenced by organizational, institutional, and cultural contexts (Kagotho et al., 2016). Less corrupt nations have a virtuous cycle of economic growth (Wilhelm, 2002).

About the challenge of combating corruption, Hause (2019) explained: "Corruption continues to represent a tenacious challenge to internationally active companies" (p. 281). Hause (2019) also indicated: "According to prevailing international anti-corruption standards, a company can be held criminally liable if it does not put all necessary and reasonable organizational measures in place to prevent corruption" (p. 281) and that "The regular training of employees is considered one of the most effective ways to prevent corruption" (p. 281).

Hsiao et al. (2019) constructed a multilevel model for evaluating the relationship between paying bribes and reported difficulties of obtaining medical care, with a survey data in adults from 32 Sub-Saharan African countries in the period 2014–2015. The results of the study of Hsiao et al. (2019) revealed:

> Having paid bribes for medical care significantly increased the odds of reporting difficulties in obtaining care by 4.11 (CI: 3.70–4.57) compared to those who never paid bribes, and more than doubled for those who paid bribes often (OR = 9.52; 95% CI: 7.77–11.67). Respondents with higher levels of education and more lived poverty also had increased odds. Those who lived in rural areas or within walking distance to a health clinic had reduced odds of reporting difficulties. Sex, age, living in a capital region, healthcare expenditures per capita, and country Corruption Perception Index were not significant predictors. (p. 1)

Cénophat (2017) studied the impact of consumers' concerns about corruption on their distrust of multinational firms, using data from 12 countries (p. 19) and found that "concerns about corruption were no longer significantly related to distrust of multinationals" (p. 19); however "corruption perception index has a positive relationship with consumers' distrust" (p. 19). Cénophat (2017) also indicated: "the data did not reveal any significant relationship between consumers' concerns about corruption and corruption perception index of the focal country" (p. 19).

If the country of origin is appreciated as more corrupt, then this fact will increase the distrust of the consumers of multinational firms.

Kagotho et al. (2016) explained: "Although corruption among public officials is often driven by individual factors, their behavior is also heavily influenced by organizational, institutional, and cultural contexts (De Graaf & Huberts, 2008; Vian, 2008)" (p. 469). Kagotho et al. (2016) also indicated: "Fighting corruption often requires multiple complementary measures that target internal governance, improve transparency, and engage the public in promoting accountability" (p. 470). Additionally, Kagotho et al. (2016) pointed out: "Internal accountability mechanisms that tighten personnel management, procurement, and oversight processes can reduce the opportunity to misallocate resources" (p. 470). Considering all the mentioned factors, the implementation of quality systems could avoid the realization and the effects of corruption in organizations.

Pellegata and Memoli (2016) analyzed the effects of corruption on institutional confidences through CPI and concluded the presence of reverse causality between corruption and institutional confidence (p. 391). Additionally, Alsherfawi Aljazaerly et al. (2016) studied the impact of corruption (measured by CPI) on "stock market development focusing exclusively on Gulf Cooperation Council (GCC) countries with its special characteristics of combining richness with relatively high level of corruption" (p. 117). Alsherfawi Aljazaerly et al. (2016) evaluated a model which considered Market Capitalization as dependent variable with the following independent variables: (a) Corruption (measured with Corruption Perceptions Index), (b) Foreign Direct Investment, (c) Oil Price, (d) Domestic Credit to Private Sector, and (e) Gross Domestic Product's Growth (p. 122). The results of the study of Alsherfawi Aljazaerly et al. (2016) revealed:

> Results from an estimation of alternative regression models on a panel of six GCC countries over the period 2003–2011, through which CPI is legitimately comparable, confirms a positive impact of corruption on stock market development, where the latter is measured by market capitalization. This is consistent with the view that corruption greases the wheels of economy by expediting transactions and allowing private firms to overcome governmentally imposed inefficiencies. (p. 117)

Although some groups of investors were involved in corruption scandals in the USA, the CPI of USA had been declining from 1995 until 2011. In this respect, Stevens (2013) explained: "The Enron, Worldcom, and Tyco scandals caused harm to American investors and loss of confidence in American businesses, but the harm was limited to certain groups of investors and employees" (p. 368). Stevens (2013) also remarked: "the steady decline in the U.S. CPI score over 16 years, ranging from the highest score of 7.79 in 1995 to the lowest score of 7.1 in 2011, which represents a 9% drop" (p. 367). Additionally, Stevens (2013) indicated:

> Clearly, this measure shows an increased perception of governmental corruption in the United States. As government and business are closely linked in the United States, this index also provides an interesting reflection of the American business climate. The U.S. decline is consistent with the Gallup Poll decline for business executives and supports the notion that the world may have a lower perception of the U.S. business climate than in previous years. (p. 367)

Corruption affected global environment through the deforestation and the reduction of cropland. In this respect, Koyuncu and Yilmaz (2008) evaluated the impact of corruption (measured via the CPI), the rural population growth, the percentage of permanent cropland, and the gross domestic product growth on deforestation. Kouyncu and Yilmaz (2008) identified "a positive correlation between corruption and deforestation" (p. 220) and that "This finding is statistically significant and valid in both univariate and multivariate analyses for all periods and corruption indices" (p. 220). Finally, Kouyncu and Yilmaz (2008) explained:

> The Results indicate that corruption, except one model, has more explanatory power than rural population growth variable, which is the most prominent determinant of deforestation in the literature. Hence, its adverse effect should be taken into consideration as serious as the other major causal factors in combating against depletion of forests.
>
> Food and Agriculture Organization (FAO) sees the corruption as one of the major threats to world's forest resources. Policies and measures taken towards reducing corruption, therefore, will help to decrease illegal forest activities (e.g. illegal logging and timbering, smuggling of forest products etc.) and in turn depletion of forests. (p. 220)

The reduction in corruption is necessary for increasing economic growth. After the completion of a study which used international data from 85 countries, Wilhelm (2002) concluded that "in less corrupt nations, a virtuous cycle is apparently operating, with economic growth, corruption fighting, building trust, and innovation all reinforcing each other" (p. 185). About the corruption in global businesses, Beets (2005) indicated: "In global business, business organizations and their representatives frequently encounter corruption and may be the perpetrators, victims, or simply participants in such acts" (p. 65). Beets (2005) also explained:

> While international corruption has existed in multiple forms for several years, many individuals, companies, nations, and international organizations are currently attempting to reduce or eliminate corrupt acts because of their harmful effects on local economies and the quality of life of citizens. (p. 65)

1.2.2 Effects of Corruption and Corruption Perceptions Index in Corporate Diplomacy

In this section, some concepts in relation to corporate diplomacy, and the effects of corruption and the CPI in the corporate diplomacy are presented.

The Corruption and the Corporate Diplomacy

Corporate diplomacy is perceived as being related to corporations and their country's national image. In this respect, Ali and Adeli (2018) defined Corporate Diplomacy as follows: "Corporate Diplomacy is an independent topic, related to corporates that make/present their country of origin's national image" (p. 679). Ali and Adeli (2018) also defined National Image as follows: "a topic in public diplomacy, which is traditionally managed by official government authorities" (p. 679) and explained that "in new public diplomacy, it is mostly dominated by private actors such as NGOs and private companies" (p. 679). As it can be appreciated, corporate diplomacy involves both non-governmental organizations and firms, considering their country's national image.

Ordeix-Rigo and Duarte (2009) defined Corporate Diplomacy as: "a process by which corporations intend to be recognized as representatives of something that might be a concept or a country or its related values" (p. 549). About Corporate Diplomacy, Ordeix-Rigo and Duarte (2009) also indicated that: "becomes a complex process of commitment towards society, and in particular with its public institutions, whose main added value to the corporation is a greater degree of legitimacy or 'license-to-operate', which in turn improves its power within a given social system" (p. 549). As it can be appreciated, corporate diplomacy is related to the values of a society and its public institutions and corporations, and gives its power to the society into a social system.

It is important to understand the differences between corporate diplomacy, economic diplomacy, and commercial diplomacy; also, it is important to view the differences between business diplomacy and corporate diplomacy. In this respect, Ali and Adeli (2018) explained that White (2015) indicated that "corporate diplomacy is different from commercial or economic diplomacy" (p. 684). Based on White (2015), Ali and Adeli (2018) also explained: "Economic diplomacy is the negotiations for the government's economic policy" (p. 684) and "Commercial diplomacy is used to pursue interests of businesses and for commercial development" (p. 684), and that "Both economic and commercial diplomacies are led by the government while corporate diplomacy is conducted by private corporations" (p. 684). Additionally, Ali and Adeli (2018) said that White (2015) differentiated between business diplomacy and corporate diplomacy as follows:

> Business diplomacy only seeks profit-making purposes, while corporate diplomacy pursues both profitable goals and the interests of the nation. In order to meet these expectations, corporate diplomacy uses various tools such as Corporate Social Responsibility (CSR) and cultural diplomacy.
>
> Moreover, corporate diplomacy sometimes needs to cooperate with government officials in order to achieve its goals. However, it is probable that companies are not interested in engaging in politics. (p. 684)

Additionally, Westermann-Behaylo et al. (2015) defined Corporate Diplomacy as follows: "an umbrella concept that encompasses the international relations literature, the PCSR literature, the corporate political activity literature, and the peace through commerce literature" (p. 391). Westermann-Behaylo et al. (2015) named PCSR to Political Corporate Social Responsibility.

Another important and related concept is public diplomacy. In this respect, Ordeix-Rigo and Duarte (2009) explained: "Public diplomacy is an increasing popular preoccupation of governments worldwide, especially aimed at achieving acceptance of their foreign policies abroad, in which corporations have traditionally played a secondary role" (p. 549). Ordeix-Rigo and Duarte (2009) also indicated: "However, as it happens with governments, corporations have understood long ago the challenges of being accepted abroad" (p. 549).

Corporate diplomacy includes the decision-making of organizations about international, organized crime, and the corruption of firms. In respect, Steger and Burgmans (2003) indicated: "Terrorism and organized crime have used the same infrastructure for globalization as have companies: easy travel, telecommunications, open financial markets, etc. It is no small wonder that they have prospered" (p. 11). Steger and Burgmans (2003) also indicated: "Up to a couple of years ago, organized crime as terrorism was only a local issue, occurring in the less developed spots of the world, where multinational companies had to routinely deal with kidnappings for ransom, blackmail and widespread corruption" (p. 11). Additionally, Steger and Burgmans (2003) explained: "Most nations made new commitments and established restrictions designed to eight corruption, money-laundering and illegal trade with new vigour, as an indispensable precondition for fighting global terrorism" (p. 11).

The Corruption Perceptions Index and the Corporate Diplomacy

CPI has been impacting to the corporate diplomacy and the related decision-making of policies for reducing the corruption. In respect, Badawi and AlQudah (2019) studied the impact of anti-corruption policies on the profitability and growth of 392 firms listed in the Singapore Stock Exchange for the period 1995–2014 with a panel data regression using two models: (a) a model for measuring the relation between corruption and profitability measured with net profit margin and (b) a model for measuring the relation between corruption and company growth measured with the total asset growth. In both models, two sub-models which added micro-variables to corruption and micro-variables and macro-variables together were evaluated, considering economic data from DataStream and the CPI (Badawi & AlQudah, 2019).

Badawi and AlQudah (2019) concluded: "anti-corruption policies that was conducted in Singapore over the period from 1995 to 2014 resulted in better firm performance measured by net profit margin (1-point index improvement increases net profit margin by about 12.8%) and asset growth (1-point index improvement increases total asset growth by about 11.7%)" (p. 179). Badawi and AlQudah (2019) also commented: "Since this result might not be generalized in all countries with different level of growth, further research is suggested to investigate the factors that differentiate the anti-corruption policy effect among different countries including national culture that may impacts the fanatical system" (p. 179).

Considering the reality of Nigeria due to the reduction of the CPI since 2016 until 2017, Chimdi (2019b) recommended the bid for a permanent seat in the United Nations Security Council (UNSC) to improve the situation of Nigeria. Additionally, Tang et al. (2018) studied the good or bad barrels in the environmental context as a proxy of high or low probability of found dishonesty, respectively (p. 920), with a sample of 6382 managers in 31 geopolitical entities across six continents, and theorizing that:

> The magnitude and intensity of the relationship between love of money and dishonest prospect (dishonesty) may reveal how individuals frame dishonesty in the context of two levels of subjective norm—perceived corporate ethical values at the micro-level (CEV, Level 1) and Corruption Perceptions Index at the macro-level (CPI, Level 2), collected from multiple sources. (p. 920)

As was expected, the results of the study of Tang et al. (2018) revealed: "managers in good barrels (high CEV/high CPI), mixed barrels (low CEV/high CPI or high CEV/low CPI), and bad barrels (low CEV/low CPI) display low, medium, and high magnitude of dishonesty, respectively" (p. 920) and that

> With high CEV, the intensity is the same across cultures. With low CEV, the intensity of dishonesty is the highest in high CPI entities (risk seeking of high probability)—the Enron Effect, but the lowest in low CPI entities (risk aversion of low probability). CPI has a strong impact on the magnitude of dishonesty, whereas CEV has a strong impact on the intensity of dishonesty. We demonstrate dishonesty in light of monetary values and two frames of social norm, revealing critical implications to the field of behavioral economics and business ethics. (p. 920)

A bad position in the CPI of the country do not reduce the corporate relationships among the organizations of countries which have mutual businesses, necessarily. As an example, in 2016, Cambodia appeared as the most corrupt country in Southeast Asia in the position 156th in the CPI (Hu et al., 2019, p. 189). Hu et al. (2019) indicated: "China and Cambodia have a long history of formal bilateral relations" (p. 180), "The two countries established diplomatic ties in 1958" (p. 180), "The two countries share many views and positions on major international and regional issues, as well as enjoying mutual diplomatic cooperation" (p. 180), and that "Chinese enterprises investing in Cambodian infrastructure construction not only are engaging in economic cooperation but also can have an impact on political relations between the two countries" (p. 196). Hu et al. (2019) also explained:

> In 2007, the World Bank International Finance Corporation conducted a survey of more than 500 companies in Cambodia. Of the companies, 60 percent noted that they must offer government officials "unofficial expenses or gifts" simply to have things move smoothly in affairs such as customers, tax, licenses, and so forth. When companies bid on government contracts, 70 percent of the money is spent on bribes. (O'Neill, 2014)

> Government corruption represents a political risk, which severely tests transnational investors, particularly in two respects. On the one hand, foreign companies are required to pay illegal "fees" if they want to enter the Cambodian market; otherwise, they will not be accepted. However, this fact does not improve the efficiency of local government officials and only directly increases the operating costs. (p. 189)

Radu et al. (2015) evaluated "the impact of coercive instruments of foreign policy (in the form of economic sanctions) on the level of corruption in the target countries" (p. 53). The factors which were used for the analysis of the corruption level were the following: (a) factor 1: the level of civic and fiscal education, (b) factor 2: collecting and owning of operations by foreign capital, (c) factor 3: taxation versus poor taxes collecting, (d) factor 4: national entrepreneurship, and (e) factor 5: strongly bureaucratic economic openness (Radu et al., 2015, p. 62). The results of the study of Radu et al. (2015) revealed:

> The economic sanctions, especially the sanctions extended throughout the economy, often hit the target with no or very few discriminatory measures to reduce their potential impact on ordinary citizens. Therefore, the sanctions "targeted", such as the freezing of financial assets, reduction or suspension of sales of military weapons and travel bans for officials, could

be better strategies for decision makers, in order to put a direct pressure on the management target and reduce costs by constraining the target subjects.

In order to avoid the negative consequences of the coercive economic diplomacy, the policy makers should consider alternative ways of action in relation to a hostile regime, such as the commitment through diplomatic communications and providing economic incentives (external aid and low-interest loans). These strategies are less likely to determine an isolation of the target country and at the same time to lead to an infusion of capital. A financially stable company is less likely to commit acts of corruption, rather than another one at subsistence. Such policies may also have a success rate higher than the sanctions, meaning that they could induce a change of behavior / mentality in the countries concerned, by creating incentives to target leaders which would make them take positive actions towards the requirements of foreign powers. (p. 65)

Seelke (2014) indicated that El Salvador was in the position 112 of 180 countries in the CPI (p. 147). Seelke (2014) also indicated: "Many also have had serious concerns about corruption in the police, prisons, and judicial system, although the attorney general's office and the Supreme Court have taken steps to address these issues" (p. 147). About the gangs in El Salvador and the relationships with US government, Seelke (2014) explained:

U.S. agencies have engaged with El Salvador and other Central American governments on gang issues for more than a decade, with some regional efforts housed in the U.S. Embassy in San Salvador. In July 2007, an interagency committee announced the U.S. Strategy to Combat Criminal Gangs from Central America and Mexico, which emphasized diplomacy, repatriation, law enforcement, capacity enhancement, and prevention. Between FY2008 and FY2016 (the most recent year available), Congress provided nearly $50 million to support a variety of anti-gang efforts in the northern triangle countries.

On the law enforcement side, U.S. funds support vetted police units working on transnational gang cases with U.S. law enforcement. In cooperation with vetted law enforcement units in El Salvador, U.S. law enforcement has brought criminal charges against thousands of MS-13 members in both countries. Since 2012, anti-gang cases have been bolstered by the establishment of an electronic monitoring center in San

Salvador and efforts to target the financing of MS-13, designated by the Treasury Department as a Transnational Criminal Organization subject to U.S. sanctions pursuant to E.O. 13581. (p. 167)

2 Construction of the Index

The diverse data sources and the methods which were used in the index system are presented in this section. The 13 data sources which were used in the index system are detailed joined to the corruption questions for the evaluation. The methods for the calculation of the index also are detailed.

2.1 Data Sources of the Index

The specialists of Transparency International (2019c) indicated the 13 data sources for elaborating the Corruption Perceptions Index 2018, which were the following:

1. African Development Bank Country Policy and Institutional Assessment 2016
2. Bertelsmann Stiftung Sustainable Governance Indicators 2018
3. Bertelsmann Stiftung Transformation Index 2017–2018
4. Economist Intelligence Unit Country Risk Service 2018
5. Freedom House Nations in Transit 2018
6. Global Insight Business Conditions and Risk Indicators 2017
7. IMD World Competitiveness Center World Competitiveness Yearbook Executive Opinion Survey 2018
8. Political and Economic Risk Consultancy Asian Intelligence 2018
9. The PRS Group International Country Risk Guide 2018
10. World Bank Country Policy and Institutional Assessment 2017
11. World Economic Forum Executive Opinion Survey 2018
12. World Justice Project Rule of Law Index Expert Survey 2017–2018
13. Varieties of Democracy (V-Dem) 2018. (p. 1)

About each one of the 13 data sources, the specialists of Transparency International (2019c) indicated the evaluated aspects with corruption questions as appear in the following paragraphs.

2.1.1 African Development Bank Country Policy and Institutional Assessment 2016

About The African Development Bank (AfDB), the specialists of Transparency International (2019c) commented: "is a regional multilateral development bank, engaged in promoting the economic development and social progress of countries on the continent" (p. 2). In the study "African Development Bank Country Policy and Institutional Assessment 2016," the corruption questions for the evaluation were the following:

Corruption question(s)

Experts are asked to assess:

Transparency, accountability and corruption in the public sector.

"This criterion assesses the extent to which the executive can be held accountable for its use of funds and the results of its actions by the electorate and by the legislature and judiciary, and the extent to which public employees within the executive are required to account for the use of resources, administrative decisions, and results obtained. Both levels of accountability are enhanced by transparency in decision-making, public audit institutions, access to relevant and timely information, and public and media scrutiny. National and sub-national governments should be appropriately weighted."

Each of three dimensions are rated separately:

(a) the accountability of the executive to oversight institutions and of public employees for their performance
(b) access of civil society to information on public affairs
(c) state capture by narrow vested interests

For the overall rating, these three dimensions receive equal weighting. (p. 2)

2.1.2 Bertelsmann Stiftung Sustainable Governance Indicators 2018

About the Bertelsmann Stiftung, the specialists of Transparency International (2019c) indicated that "was founded in 1977 as a private foundation" (p. 3) and that "As a think tank they work toward improved education, a just and efficient economic system, a preventative healthcare system, a vibrant civil society and greater international understanding" (p. 3). In the study "Bertelsmann Stiftung Sustainable Governance Indicators 2018," the corruption questions for the evaluation were the following:

Corruption question(s)

Experts are asked to assess:

Corruption prevention

"D4.4 To what extent are public officeholders prevented from abusing their position for private interests?"

This question addresses how the state and society prevent public servants and politicians from accepting bribes by applying mechanisms to guarantee the integrity of officeholders: auditing of state spending; regulation of party financing; citizen and media access to information; accountability of officeholders (asset declarations, conflict of interest rules, codes of conduct); transparent public procurement systems; effective prosecution of corruption." (p. 3)

2.1.3 Bertelsmann Stiftung Transformation Index 2017–2018

In the study "Bertelsmann Stiftung Transformation Index 2017–2018," the corruption questions for the evaluation were the following:

Corruption question(s)

Experts are asked to assess:

"Q3.3 To what extent are public officeholders who abuse their positions prosecuted or penalized?" Assessments range from:
- a low of 1, where "Officeholders who break the law and engage in corruption can do so without fear of legal consequences or adverse publicity."
- to a high of 10, where "Officeholders who break the law and engage in corruption are prosecuted rigorously under established laws and always attract adverse publicity."

"Q15.3 To what extent does the government successfully contain corruption?" Assessments range from:

- from a low of 1, where "The government fails to contain corruption, and there are no integrity mechanisms in place."
- to a high of 10, where "The government is successful in containing corruption, and all integrity mechanisms are in place and effective." (p. 4)

2.1.4 *Economist Intelligence Unit Country Risk Service 2018*

About the Economist Intelligence Unit (EIU), the specialists of Transparency International (2019c) explained that "was established in 1946 as the research body for The Economist newspaper" (p. 6), "Since then, it has grown into a global research and advisory firm that produces business intelligence for policy makers worldwide" (p. 6), and that "650 full-time and contributing analysts work in and on over 200 countries/territories" (p. 6). In the study "Economist Intelligence Unit Country Risk Service 2018," the corruption questions for the evaluation were the following:

Corruption question(s)

Specific guiding questions include:

- Are there clear procedures and accountability governing the allocation and use of public funds?
- Are public funds misappropriated by ministers/public officials for private or party political purposes?
- Are there special funds for which there is no accountability?
- Are there general abuses of public resources?
- Is there a professional civil service or are large numbers of officials directly appointed by the government?
- Is there an independent body auditing the management of public finances?
- Is there an independent judiciary with the power to try ministers/public officials for abuses?
- Is there a tradition of a payment of bribes to secure contracts and gain favours? (p. 6)

2.1.5 *Freedom House Nations in Transit 2018*

About the Freedom House, the specialists of Transparency International (2019c) indicated: "Founded in 1941, Freedom House is an independent watchdog organisation that supports the expansion of freedom around the world" (p. 7) and that "Freedom House supports democratic change, monitors freedom and advocates for democracy and human rights" (p. 7). In the study "Freedom House Nations in Transit 2018," the corruption questions for the evaluation were the following:

Corruption question(s)

The Freedom House experts are asked to explore a range of indicative questions, including:

- Has the government implemented effective anti-corruption initiatives?
- Is the country's economy free of excessive state involvement?
- Is the government free from excessive bureaucratic regulations, registration requirements, and other controls that increase opportunities for corruption?
- Are there significant limitations on the participation of government officials in economic life?
- Are there adequate laws requiring financial disclosure and disallowing conflict of interest?
- Does the government advertise jobs and contracts?
- Does the state enforce an effective legislative or administrative process—particularly one that is free of prejudice against one's political opponents—to prevent, investigate, and prosecute the corruption of government officials and civil servants?
- Do whistleblowers, anti-corruption activists, investigators, and journalists enjoy legal protections that make them feel secure about reporting cases of bribery and corruption?
- Are allegations of corruption given wide and extensive airing in the media?
- Does the public display a high intolerance for official corruption? (p. 7)

2.1.6 Global Insight Business Conditions and Risk Indicators 2017

About IHS Global Insight, the specialists of Transparency International (2019c) indicated: "Founded in 1959, IHS Global Insight is a global information company employing more than 5,100 people in more than 30 countries around the world" (p. 9) and that "It provides a wide range of online services covering macroeconomics, country risk and individual sector analysis" (p. 9). In the study "Global Insight Business Conditions and Risk Indicators 2017," the corruption question for the evaluation were the following:

Corruption question(s)

Experts are asked to assess:

The risk that individuals/companies will face bribery or other corrupt practices to carry out business, from securing major contracts to being allowed to import/export a small product or obtain everyday paperwork. This threatens a company's ability to operate in a country, or opens it up to legal or regulatory penalties and reputational damage. (p. 9)

2.1.7 IMD World Competitiveness Center World Competitiveness Yearbook Executive Opinion Survey 2018

About IMD, the specialists of Transparency International (2019c) indicated: "IMD is a top-ranked business school with expertise in developing global leaders through high-impact executive education" (p. 10) and that "100 per cent focused on real-world executive development, offering Swiss excellence with a global perspective, IMD has a flexible, customized and effective approach" (p. 10). In the study "IMD World Competitiveness Center World Competitiveness Yearbook Executive Opinion Survey 2018," the corruption question for the evaluation were the following:

Corruption question

Survey respondents were asked:

"Bribery and corruption: Exist or do not exist". (p. 10)

2.1.8 Political and Economic Risk Consultancy Asian Intelligence 2018

About the Political and Economic Risk Consultancy (PERC), the specialists of Transparency International (2019c) indicated: "is a consulting firm specialising in strategic business information and analysis for companies doing business in the countries of East and Southeast Asia" (p. 11) and that "As part of its services, PERC produces a range of risk reports on Asian countries, paying special attention to critical socio-political variables like corruption, intellectual property rights and risks, labour quality, and other systemic strengths and weakness of individual Asian countries/territories" (p. 11). In the study "Political and Economic Risk Consultancy Asian Intelligence 2018," the corruption question for the evaluation were the following:

Corruption question(s)

"How do you grade the problem of corruption in the country in which you are working?". (p. 11)

2.1.9 The PRS Group International Country Risk Guide 2018

About PRS Group, the specialists of Transparency International (2019c) indicated: "Based in the vicinity of Syracuse, New York, since its founding in 1979, the PRS Group has consistently focused on political risk analysis" (p. 12). In the study "The PRS Group International Country Risk Guide 2018," the corruption question for the evaluation were the following:

Corruption question(s)

This is an assessment of corruption within the political system. The most common form of corruption met directly by businesses is financial corruption in the form of demands for special payments and bribes connected with import and export licenses, exchange controls, tax assessments, police protection, or loans. The measure is most concerned with actual or potential corruption in the form of excessive patronage, nepotism, job reservations, exchange of favours, secret party funding and suspiciously close ties between politics and business. (p. 12)

2.1.10 World Bank Country Policy and Institutional Assessment 2017

About World Bank, the specialists of Transparency International (2019c) explained: "The World Bank was established in 1944, is headquartered in Washington, D.C. and has more than 10,000 employees in more than 100 offices worldwide" (p. 13), "The World Bank is made up of two development institutions: the International Bank for Reconstruction and Development (IBRD) and the International Development Association (IDA)" (p. 13), and that "The IBRD aims to reduce poverty in middle-income and creditworthy poorer countries, while IDA focuses on the world's poorest countries" (p. 13). In the study "World Bank Country

Policy and Institutional Assessment 2017," the corruption questions for the evaluation were the following:

Corruption question(s)

Experts are asked to assess:

Transparency, accountability and corruption in the public sector.

"This criterion assesses the extent to which the executive can be held accountable for its use of funds and the results of its actions by the electorate and by the legislature and judiciary, and the extent to which public employees within the executive are required to account for the use of resources, administrative decisions, and results obtained. Both levels of accountability are enhanced by transparency in decision making, public audit institutions, access to relevant and timely information, and public and media scrutiny. A high degree of accountability and transparency discourages corruption, or the abuse of public office for private gain. National and sub-national governments should be appropriately weighted."

Each of three dimensions is rated separately:

(a) accountability of the executive to oversight institutions and of public employees for their performance;
(b) access of civil society to information on public affairs; and
(c) state capture by narrow vested interests. (p. 13)

2.1.11   World Economic Forum Executive Opinion Survey 2018

About the World Economic Forum, the specialists of Transparency International (2019c) indicated: "is an independent international organisation committed to improving the state of the world by engaging business, political, academic and other leaders of society to shape global, regional and industry agendas" (p. 15) and that "Incorporated as a not-for-profit foundation in 1971, and headquartered in Geneva, Switzerland, the Forum is not tied to political, partisan or national interests" (p. 15). In the study "World Economic Forum Executive Opinion Survey 2018," the corruption questions for the evaluation were the following:

Corruption question(s)

Survey respondents were asked:

(On a scale of 1 - 7 where 1 means very common and 7 means never) "In your country, how common is it for firms to make undocumented extra payments or bribes connected with the following:

   a) Imports and exports
   b) Public utilities
   c) Annual tax payments
   d) Awarding of public contracts and licenses
   e) Obtaining favourable judicial decisions". (p. 15)

2.1.12 *World Justice Project Rule of Law Index Expert Survey 2017–2018*

About the World Justice Project (WJP), the specialists of Transparency International (2019c) indicated: "is an independent, not-for-profit organisation working to advance the rule of law for the development of communities of opportunity and equity" (p. 16) and that "The WJP's multi-national, multi-disciplinary efforts are dedicated to developing practical programmes in support of the rule of law around the world" (p. 16). In the study "World Justice Project Rule of Law Index Expert Survey 2017–2018," the corruption questions for the evaluation were the following:

Corruption question(s)

Index 2: Absence of corruption

A total of 53 questions are asked of experts on the extent to which government officials use public office for private gain. These questions touch on a variety of sectors within government including the public health system, regulatory agencies, the police, and the courts.

Individual questions are aggregated into four sub-indices:

   2.1 Government officials in the executive branch do not use public office for private gain
   2.2 Government officials in the judicial branch do not use public office for private gain

2.3 Government officials in the police and the military do not use public office for private gain
2.4 Government officials in the legislature do not use public office for private gain

Only the scores provided by the experts were considered for the CPI calculations. The four sub-indicators are then averaged to create a single score. (p. 16)

2.1.13 Varieties of Democracy Project 2018
About Varieties of Democracy (V-Dem) Project, the specialists of Transparency International (2019c) indicated: "provides a multidimensional and disaggregated dataset that reflects the complexity of the concept of democracy as a system of rule that goes beyond the simple presence of elections" (p. 17). In the study "Varieties of Democracy Project 2018," the corruption questions for the evaluation were the following:

Corruption question(s)

Question: How pervasive is political corruption? (v2x_corr)

The directionality of the V-Dem corruption index runs from less corrupt to more corrupt (unlike the other V-Dem variables that generally run from less democratic to more democratic situation). The corruption index includes measures of six distinct types of corruption that cover both different areas and levels of the political realm, distinguishing between executive, legislative and judicial corruption. Within the executive realm, the measures also distinguish between corruption mostly pertaining to bribery, and corruption due to embezzlement. Finally, they differentiate between corruption in the highest echelons of the executive (at the level of the rulers/cabinet) and in the public sector at large. The measures thus tap into several distinguishable types of corruption: both petty and grand; both bribery and theft; both corruption aimed at influencing law making and that affects implementation.

Aggregation: The index is arrived at by taking the average of (a) public sector corruption index (b) executive corruption index (c) the indicator for legislative corruption and (d) the indicator for judicial corruption. In other words, these four different government spheres are weighted equally in the resulting index. (p. 17)

2.2 Methods

For calculating the CPI, the specialists of Transparency International (2019b) described the following steps:

1. Select data sources: Each data source that is used to construct the CPI must fulfil the following criteria to qualify as a valid source:
   - Quantify perceptions of corruption in the public sector
   - Be based on a reliable and valid methodology, which scores and ranks multiple countries on the same scale
   - Be performed by a credible institution
   - Allow for sufficient variation of scores to distinguish between countries
   - Give ratings to a substantial number of countries
   - The rating is given by a country expert or business person
   - The institution repeats their assessment at least every two years

   The CPI 2018 is calculated using 13 different data sources from 12 different institutions that capture perceptions of corruption within the past two years. These sources are described in detail in the accompanying source description document.

2. Standardise data sources to a scale of 0-100 where a 0 equals the highest level of perceived corruption and 100 equals the lowest level of perceived corruption. This standardisation is done by subtracting the mean of each source in the baseline year from each country score and then dividing by the standard deviation of that source in the baseline year. This subtraction and division using the baseline year parameters ensures that the CPI scores are comparable year on year since 2012. After this procedure, the standardised scores are transformed to the CPI scale by multiplying with the value of the CPI standard deviation in 2012 (20) and adding the mean of CPI in 2012 (45), so that the data set fits the CPI's 0-100 scale.

3. Calculate the average: For a country or territory to be included in the CPI, a minimum of three sources must assess that country. A country's CPI score is then calculated as the average of all standardised scores available for that country. Scores are rounded to whole numbers.

4. Report a measure of uncertainty: The CPI is accompanied by a standard error and confidence interval associated with the score, which captures the variation in scores of the data sources available for that country/territory. (p. 1)

3 Views and Applications

This section contains views and applications of the CPI at the national and the international levels. Some studies that included applications of the CPI inside diverse countries and some studies with the applications of CPI jointly with other social problems are detailed in this section.

3.1 At the National Level

Some applications of the CPI to studies in Pakistan, Bulgaria, Canada, Finland, Denmark, Korea, Russia, Czech Republic, Ukraine, Singapore, and Nigeria are presented in this section. Saeed et al. (2018) studied the relationship among the corruption and governance in post 9/11 Pakistan considering the CPI indexes since 2005 until 2010 (decreasing trend) comparing with the CPI indexes since 2011 until 2014 (increased corruption perceptions) (p. 108). In respect, Saeed et al. (2018) concluded:

> Evidence from different government regimes during post 9/11 Pakistan suggests that, governance has an inverse relationship with corruption incidence. Moreover, a multitude of factors affected governance and corruption including conflict, politics, security, and the role of elites and power structures. It is clear, however, that bad governance contributes significantly towards increased corruption in Pakistan. Evidence in this paper suggests that, during peak conflict periods of 2007 through 2010, corruption perceptions in Pakistan remained highly unfavorable. This study supports the notion that improved governance in Pakistan, in the form of greater transparency and rule of law can play an enabling role in curbing the incidence of corruption as well as improving good governance. (p. 111)

Traikova et al. (2017) augmented the Ajzen's Theory of Planned Behavior evaluating "a mediated model of the effects of perceived corruption on attitudes, social norms and perceived behavioral control, which in turn determine entrepreneurial intentions" (p. 1750018-1). With a sample of 231 aspiring entrepreneurs seeking to start a non-farm business in three rural regions of Bulgaria, Traikova et al. (2017) found: "corruption perceptions are partially mediated by entrepreneurial attitudes and perceived control, but not by social norms" (p. 1750018-1) and that "Corruption perceptions are positively associated with entrepreneurial intentions, indicative of the deeply rooted social acceptance of corruption in many transition economies" (p. 1750018-1).

After the analysis of the application of the CPI in some countries, Atkinson (2011) explained: "The citizen surveys carried out on behalf of TI and the World Bank show Canadians to be quite suspicious of the corruption tendencies within key political institutions and not at all confident in the government's ability to overcome corruption problems" (p. 448) and that:

> Even in the countries that sit at the apex of the corruption indices, like Finland and Denmark, not everyone is prepared to give political institutions the benefit of the doubt. In Manion's analysis, there are two blocs of countries that represent two equilibria—"clean government" and "pervasive corruption"—with countries such as Korea, Russia, and the Czech Republic scattered in between. (p. 449)

Berit (2010) studied the elite perceptions of anti-corruption efforts in Ukraine and concluded that "Not surprisingly, Ukrainian elites are familiar with, and fairly negative in their assessment of, national anti-corruption reform" (p. 237). Additionally, Li et al. (2006) studied the relationship between deception and cultural orientation in a Singaporean sample and their results indicated: "despite the fact that Singapore is very low in corruption on the Transparency International Corruption Perceptions Index, vertical collectivism was still able to account for the variance in deception" (p. 199).

Some critics to CPI appeared in the literature review. About that, Madichie (2005) explained: "CPI is not a sufficient indicator of the level of corruption in developing countries such as Nigeria" (p. 320) and that "It adopts a more holistic approach to unmask the entrenched nature of corruption against the background that more often than not only one perspective is reflected in the CPI" (p. 320). Madichie (2005) also indicated:

> Bribery is argued to be another dimension to take into account when designing the CPI, therefore, making it imperative to incorporate the Bribe

Payers Index into the CPI calculus in order to present a more holistic and hence more credible measure of corruption levels in countries – especially Nigeria. (p. 320)

3.2 At the International Level

CPI was evaluated in the relationships of the corruption with other social problems and the human development, in the relationships with the implementation of the e-government and motivated the creation of other indexes. Some related studies are presented in this section.

The corruption affects the development of the basic competences which must be developed by the educational systems. In respect, Báez and Jongitud (2014) studied the relationships among the CPI and the results of Reading, Maths, and Sciences of the Programme for International Student Assessment (PISA) of the Organization for Economic Co-operation and Development (OECD). Báez and Jongitud (2014) concluded that "In general terms, countries where there is a low perception of corruption in their public spheres, and private, also tend to develop educational systems that are better evaluated in quality, specifically in terms of the development of basic skills in their students" (p. 141) and "This gives a glimpse of how corruption can impact the right to quality education" (p. 141).

The gender inequality is related to the fertility and the corruption. In respect, Yoon and Klasen (2018) built composite indices for social institutions related to gender inequality (SIGI) using Partial Least Squares (PLS), Principal Component Analysis (PCA), Partial Least Squares Regression (PLSR), and Principal Components Regression (PCR), and evaluated their relationships with "female education, fertility, child morality and corruption, consistent with economic theory" (p. 78). Yoon and Klasen (2018) also explained:

> A model selection is performed to select the treatment of non-metric variables and also non-linear terms of control variables. Our empirical model shows that gender inequality has positive conditional correlation with fertility and corruption. On the other hand, for female education and child mortality, we have different results depending on whether we use PCA or PLS.

For the female education and child mortality regressions, PLS brings benefits in terms of prediction compared to PCA. We could see which variables are particularly relevant for the prediction of those outcome variables by comparing the PLSR and PCR coefficients and weights.

We have also created new CPIs with PCA and PLS weights instead of using an average as Transparency International (2013), because it is arguable whether all variables in the CPI are equally important. Additionally, variables are prepared differently to drop variables with large errors and not to emphasize certain data sources without clear reasons. We have found a significant association of the SIGI on the new CPI based on PCA conditional on control variables. In other words, more gender inequality associates with more corruption.

On the other hand, the association is only marginally significant for the new CPI based on PLS. We conclude from this analysis that PCA is a superior procedure for generating weights for corruption and social institutions related to gender inequality as it avoids some of the problems associated with the equal weights currently used and it does not suffer from overfitting as PLS. (p. 78)

Linhartová (2017) evaluated the impact of the use of the e-government in the reduction of the level of corruption in 117 countries, "regardless of their geographic location, political regime, or economic development between years 2003 and 2014" (p. 120). Linhartová (2017) concluded: "the use of information technology and the development of e-government contribute to reducing the level of corruption in the country" (p. 120).

After the development of their study which used the Corruption Perceptions Index as indicator of corruption and the E-Government Development Index as indicator of the willingness and capacity of national administrations to use information and communication technologies for delivering public services, Linhartová (2017) concluded: "Used correlation and regression analysis confirmed the possible reduction of corruption both for the most economically developed countries by 0,12% for one percent increase of the use of e-government, as well as by 0,14% of the least economically developed countries" (p. 120). Similar results were obtained by Garcia-Murillo (2013) who concluded: "Using data from a six-year panel (2002–2005 and 2008) for 208 countries, our analysis finds that governments' web presence has reduced perceptions of corruption around the world" (p. 151). Therefore, the use of e-government technologies can contribute to the reductions of the corruption perceptions indexes of the countries.

Ortega et al. (2016) studied how the corruption affects the convergence processes in human development with a sample of 69 countries in the period 1990–2012 and "using the Human Development Index, raw data on life expectancy at birth, mean years of schooling, GNI per capita, and the Corruption Perceptions Index (CPI) published by Transparency International" (p. 691). Ortega et al. (2016) found that "the convergence process across clusters of countries is not homogeneous and that human development follows different patterns of growth" (p. 691) and that "if corruption damages growth in human development across countries, it is mainly caused by its negative impact on growth in income and health achievements" (p. 691).

Mungiu-Pippidi and Dadašov (2016) presented the Index of Public Integrity (IPI) as an alternative approach to capture and measure the national level of control of corruption. Mungiu-Pippidi and Dadašov (2016) also indicated: "The main contribution of the IPI is its use of mostly objective and actionable data to measure control of corruption" (p. 432) and that "Accordingly, the components of the IPI are more sensitive to change over time than the popular aggregated perception-based indicators and enable thus to trace developments in the specific areas relevant for corruption control" (p. 432).

The CPI has motivated additional studies such as the research of Lavena (2013), who studied the Citizen Corruption Permissiveness using 2005–2007 World Values Survey data from Six Latin American countries and constructed an index (p. 345). Another study was realized by Calderón et al. (2009) who evaluated the relationships among the Bribe Payers Index (BPI), the Corruption Perception Index (CPI), and the Doing-Business with the propensity of multinational companies "to pay bribes when operating abroad and the pro-bribery IC conditions in host countries" (p. 320). Calderón et al. (2009) concluded: "Our results suggest a low significance of IC factors in bribe-taking behavior at the country level. Therefore, we conclude that the improvement of IC is not enough to reduce bribery" (p. 320). Calderón et al. (2009) named IC to investment climate.

De Maria (2010) indicated: "CPI was nestled comfortably within the hard neo-liberal logic of transnational capital from where it epitomised a construction of African 'corruption' that was Western, empirical, culture blind, business-centred and monolithic" (p. 157). About CPI, De Maria (2010) also concluded: "is falsely represented as a valid inter-country index of 'corruption', when it is in fact offering highly prized business environment intelligence (of doubtful validity) to support strategic decision-making for capital migration ventures into Africa of (mainly) multi-national corporations" (p. 157).

With a sample of 114 countries, Gheorghe and Gheorghe (2008) evaluated the relationships between corruption (measured by CPI), economic freedom (measured by Index of Economic Freedom), globalization (measured by Index of Globalization), and macroeconomic development through GDP (p. 946). Gheorghe and Gheorghe (2008) concluded: "Macroeconomic results decrease always with certain levels by economic dysfunction such as less of liberty in all economic activities, refusal of globalization and higher corruption perception" (p. 946).

A study about the corruption (using the CPI) and the culture was realized by Li et al. (2006) who explained: "Previous studies have shown that individuals in collectivist cultures may be more corrupt than those in individualist cultures when they are interacting with outgroup members" (p. 199). Li et al. (2006) also indicated: "The countries that are least corrupt, according to the Transparency International Corruption Perceptions Index, tend to have horizontal individualist cultures" (p. 199).

Using a sample of 90 countries of the CPI 2000, Beets (2005) studied "the demand-side of corruption and several related factors in the categories of government, economy and poverty, education, geography, and culture" (p. 65). Beets (2005) also indicated: "Analysis of these factors employed the Corruption Perceptions Index (CPI), formulated annually by Transparency International (TI), and other sources" (p. 65). Additionally, Beets (2005) explained: "Several factors in each of the five categories were found to correlate significantly with perceived corruption" (p. 65).

4 Discussion

In this section, a discussion about the results of studies related to the appropriateness of the indicators of the CPI is presented. The conclusions of previous studies were diverse, considering that conclusions in agree and against the appropriateness of the CPI indicators appeared in the literature review. The indicators of the CPI 2018 were related to the following aspects: (a) the transparency, accountability, and the corruption of the public sector (including the police and the military); (b) the prevention of the abuse of the public officeholders due to the private interests; (c) the prosecution and the penalization of the public officeholders who abuse; (d) clear procedures about the previous aspects; (e) law against corruption; (f) legal protections to whistleblowers, anti-corruption activists, investigators, and journalists, who reported cases of bribery and corruption; (g) the risk that individuals/companies will face bribery or other corrupt practices to carry out business, from securing major contracts; and (h) pervasiveness of the political corruption. However, Gilman (2018) criticized the CPI after the evaluation of diverse articles, indicating that the data sources (named sub-indicators) have important elements in common, and remarking the following:

- Most of the sub-indicators do not focus on corruption. Rather, they emphasize the business environment in the country, its economic development, or the risks of doing business there. More closely related topics include public trust; government transparency; accountability; and state capture. When surveys do address corruption, they typically use only one or two corruption-related questions.
- Corruption itself can mean different things to different people. Most of these sub-indicator surveys are prepared for clients in business, banking, or international trade who pay a substantial fee every year for using their analyses. Several are subscription services sold to companies and international organizations. For that reason, indicators include issues that most in public administration would not view as corruption. These include the lack of open markets, the lack of effective labor rules, difficulty in customs or transportation, or abuse of contract rights. The overall tone of questions and the focus of sub-indicators emphasize the performance of governments as they pertain to businesses.
- The sub-indicators at times solicit perceptions concealed as aggregate information. They ask questions about which those surveyed could have no accurate information, such as how many judges are corrupt, how many parliamentarians are corrupt, and the percentage of annual sales all businesses pay in corrupt payments.
- The presentation of the CPI emphasizes the ranking of countries, but the rankings displayed on the TI website are not the same as a country's score. In practice, this means that a change in score of 0.2 on a 10-point scale can have an impact on the rank of as much as 10

positions. A country score can remain the same in successive years while the ranking can change substantially.
- Although they usually use the same sub-indicators every year, the surveys do not review every country every year. TI requires a minimum of three surveys to rank countries. One country might have 11 sub-indicators, while another country could have only three, so the annual score could reflect information from different years. (p. S77)

The CPI did not consider the opinion or perception of common people about the corruption of the public sector related to the common activities which are realized periodically, in a technical and statistical manner. The lack of consideration of the opinion or perception of common people about the corruption could avoid to view the real dimension of the corruption of the public sector, due to that many people could consider as correct facts to many incorrect things according to their cultures (including their values, habits, and believes) in diverse contexts. However, after the collection of 85,000 European respondents in 24 countries and the comparison of the expert perception indicators and citizen perceptions and experiences, Charron (2016) explained: "the consistency between actual reported corruption, as well as citizen and expert perceptions of corruption, is remarkably high and such perceptions are swayed little by 'outside noise'" (p. 147) and finally concluded: "although existing corruption measures certainly have their share of problems, concerns regarding the validity and bias of perceptions have, perhaps, been overstated" (p. 147).

Similar results were obtained by Tverdova (2011) who studied how people form perceptions about corruption with survey data of system-level indicators in 30 countries, evaluating the relationship between the perceptions of elite and mass evaluations of corruption considering the influence of political allegiances, personal economic conditions, and education. The results of the study of Tverdova (2011) revealed:

> The findings reveal that mass assessments of corruption track closely those of the elites. In addition, more economically fortunate individuals and those who supported the government in the previous election tend to be less critical of corruption. The effect of education is contingent on a country's level of corruption. Specifically, more educated citizens in

"cleaner" countries do not see as much corruption as their less educated counterparts. However, this difference is substantively modest. (p. 3)

Saha et al. (2012) also evaluated whether CPI converges toward consensus over time. In respect, Saha et al. (2012) indicated:

Transparency International's corruption perception index converges towards consensus over time? Furthermore, we estimate the speed of adjustment towards general agreement. The results indicate differences in the degree of concordance, i.e. high level of agreement for the mostly clean and most-corrupt countries but disagreement remains high for the medium corrupt countries. The speed of converge is high for the most-corrupt and mostly clean countries and a decline for the medium corrupt countries. (p. 1)

About the World Bank Institute's Control of Corruption Index and Transparency International's Corruption Perceptions Index, Atkinson (2011) indicated: "These indices show some slight sensitivity to scandalous revelations, but the overall message is one of year-over-year consistency" (p. 445). Atkinson (2011) also indicated: "Very few countries manage to avoid corruption scandals for extended periods" (p. 445). Therefore, it is possible that the scandals have affected the scores of the CPI of diverse countries and these CPI scores could not be representing the level of corruption of the public sector appropriately.

The CPI is a very useful measure that although could be criticable, is a nice measure for guiding decision-making for governmental authorities and for managers and directors of the organizations in the national and international contexts. The CPI must evolve along the time considering the diverse values, habits, and believes of the people in the national and international contexts. Also, the CPI must be analyzed jointly to other social problems for evaluating the corresponding impact and for contributing to decision-making, Future researches about corruption must focus on more objective indicators considering the perceptions and the experiences of the common people in their periodic common activities related to the processes in which the public corruption is present. Additionally, future researches must evaluate simplified ways for measuring the corruption considering the indicators for other human problems, considering: education, health, environment, economics, etc., with the corresponding validity and reliability of the instruments for data collection.

References

Ali, M., & Adeli, I. (2018). Exploring the role of brands in public diplomacy. *Journal of World Sociopolitical Studies, 2*(4), 675–698.

Alsherfawi Aljazaerly, M., Sirop, R., & Mouselli, S. (2016). Corruption and stock market development: New evidence from GCC countries. *Business: Theory and Practice, 17*(2), 117–127.

Atkinson, M. M. (2011). Discrepancies in perceptions of corruption, or why is Canada so corrupt? *Political Science Quarterly, 126*(3), 445–453.

Badawi, A., & AlQudah, A. (2019). The impact of anti-corruption policies on the profitability and growth of firms listed in the stock market: Application on Singapore with a panel data analysis. *The Journal of Developing Areas, 53*(1), 179–204.

Báez, J. F., & Jongitud, J. C. (2014). La influencia de la corrupción sobre el derecho a una educación de calidad: Un estudio de correlación [The influence of corruption on the right to a quality education: A correlation study]. *Revista Prolegómenos – Derechos y Valores, 17*(33), 123–142.

Beets, S. D. (2005). Understanding the demand-side issues of international corruption. *Journal of Business Ethics, 57*(1), 65–81.

Berit, A. (2010). Elite perceptions of anti-corruption efforts in Ukraine. *Global Crime, 11*(2), 217–260.

Calderón, R., Álvarez-Arce, J. L., & Mayoral, S. (2009). Corporation as a crucial ally against corruption. *Journal of Business Ethics, 87*(1), 319–332.

Cénophat, S. (2017). Consumers' concerns about corruption and trust: A multilevel analysis. In *Marketing and Public Policy Conference Proceedings*.

Charron, N. (2016). Do corruption measures have a perception problem? Assessing the relationship between experiences and perceptions of corruption among citizens and experts. *European Political Science Review, 8*(1), 147–171.

Chimdi, G. (2019a). Corruption and good governance in Nigeria: Zooming the lens on the Buhari anti-corruption crusade. *Journal of Gender, Information and Development in Africa, 8*(1), 195–219.

Chimdi, G. (2019b). Through the eye of a needle: An examination of Nigeria's quest for a permanent UNSC chair. *Journal of African Foreign Affairs, 6*(1), 139–164.

De Graaf, G., & Huberts, L. W. (2008). Portraying the nature of corruption using an explorative case study design. *Public Administration Review, 68*(1), 640–653.

De Maria, W. (2010). Why is the president of Malawi angry? Towards and ethnography of corruption. *Culture and Organization, 16*(2), 145–162.

Garcia-Murillo, M. (2013). Does a government web presence reduce perceptions of corruption? *Information Technology for Development, 19*(2), 151–175.

Gheorghe, S., & Gheorghe, C. (2008). Economic freedom, globalization, corruption and macroeconomic results. *Annals of the University of Oradea, Economic Science Series, 17*(2), 946–957.

Gilman, S. C. (2018). To understand and to misunderstand how corruption is measured: Academic research and the corruption perception index. *Public Integrity, 20*(1), S74–S88.

Hause, C. (2019). Fighting against corruption: Does anti-corruption training make any difference? *Journal of Business Ethics, 159*(1), 281–299.

Horsewood, N. (2012). Does corruption hinder trade for the new EU members? *Economics, 6*(1), 2012–2048.

Hsiao, A., Vogt, V., & Quentin, W. (2019). Effect of corruption on perceived difficulties in healthcare access in sub-Saharan Africa. *PLoS ONE, 14*(8), 1–12.

Hu, F., Zhang, X., Hu, M., & Lee, D. (2019). Chinese enterprises' investment in infrastructure construction in Cambodia. *Asian Perspective, 43*(1), 177–207.

Kagotho, N., Bunger, A., & Wagner, K. (2016). "They make money off of us": A phenomenological analysis of consumer perceptions of corruption in Kenya's HIV response system. *BMC Health Services Research, 16*(1), 468–478.

Koyuncu, C., & Yilmaz, R. (2008). The impact of corruption on deforestation: A cross-country evidence. *The Journal of Developing Areas, 42*(2), 213–222.

Lavena, C. F. (2013). What determines permissiveness toward corruption? *Public Integrity, 15*(4), 345–365.

Li, S., Triandis, H. C., & Yu, Y. (2006). Cultural Orientation and Corruption. *Ethics & Behavior, 16*(3), 199–215.

Lin, M., & Yu, C. (2014). Can corruption be measured? Comparing global versus local perceptions of corruption in East and Southeast Asia. *Journal of Comparative Policy Analysis: Research and Practice, 16*(2), 140–157.

Linhartová, V. (2017). *The role of e-government in mitigating corruption.* Retrieved from https://dk.upce.cz//handle/10195/67932

Mackey, T. K., Clare, J., Savedoff, W. D., Vogl, F., Lewis, M., Sale, J., Michaud, J., & Vian, T. (2016). The disease of corruption: Views on how to fight corruption to advance 21st century global health goals. *BMC Medicine, 14*(149), 1–12.

Madichie, N. O. (2005). Corruption in Nigeria: How effective is the corruption perception index in highlighting the economic malaise? *World Review of Science, Technology, and Sustainable Development, 2*(3), 320–335.

Maxwell, D., Bailey, S., Harvey, P., Walker, P., Sharbatke-Church, C., & Savage, K. (2011). Preventing corruption in humanitarian assistance: Perceptions, gaps, and challenges. *Disasters, 36*(1), 140–160.

Mungiu-Pippidi, A., & Dadašov, R. (2016). Measuring control of corruption by a new index of public integrity. *European Journal of Crime Policy and Resolution, 22*(1), 415–438.

Ogwang, T., & Cho, D. I. (2014). A conceptual framework for constructing a corruption diffusion index. *Journal of Business Ethics, 125*(1), 1–9.

O'Neill, D. (2014). Playing risk: Chinese foreign direct investment in Cambodia. *Contemporary Southeast Asia, 36*(2), 173–205.

Ordeix-Rigo, E., & Duarte, J. (2009). From public diplomacy to corporate diplomacy: Increasing corporation's legitimacy and influence. *American Behavioral Scientist, 53*(4), 549–564.

Ortega, B., Casquero, A., & Sanjuán, J. (2016). Corruption and convergence in human development: Evidence from 69 countries during 1990–2012. *Social Indicators Research, 127*(1), 691–719.

Pellegata, A., & Memoli, V. (2016). Can corruption erode confidence in political institutions among European Countries? Comparing the effects of different measures of perceived corruption. *Social Indicators Research, 128*(1), 391–412.

Radu, I., Sabau, M., Şendroiu, C., & Pete, S. (2015). Coercive economic diplomacy—Corruption trigger or deterrent. *Economic Computation & Economic Cybernetics Studies & Research, 49*(1), 53–71.

Saeed, K., Ahmad, S., & Munir, S. (2018). Corruption and governance: Evidence from post-9/11 conflict affected Pakistan. *FWU Journal of Social Sciences, 12*(1), 105–113.

Saha, S., Gounder, R., & Su, J. (2012). Is there a "consensus" towards transparency international's corruption perceptions index? *International Journal of Business Studies, 20*(1), 1–10.

Sari, A. (2017). E-government attempts in small island developing states: The rate of corruption with virtualization. *Science and Engineering Ethics, 23*(1), 1673–1688.

Scott, J. (1972). *Comparative political corruption*. Prentice-Hall.

Seelke, C. R. (2014). El Salvador: Background and U.S. relations. *Current Politics and Economics of South and Central America, 7*(4), 537–570.

Steger, U., & Burgmans, A. (2003). *Corporate diplomacy: The strategy for a volatile, fragmented business environment*. Wiley.

Stevens, B. (2013). How ethical are U.S. business executives? A study of perceptions. *Journal of Business Ethics, 117*(1), 361–369.

Tang, T. L., Sutarso, T., Ansari, M. A., et al. (2018). Monetary intelligence and behavioral economics: The Enron Effect—Love of money, corporate ethical values, Corruption Perception Index (CPI), and dishonesty across 31 geopolitical entities. *Journal of Business Ethics, 148*(1), 919–937.

Traikova, D., Manolova, T. S., Möllers, J., & Buchenrieder, G. (2017). Corruption perceptions and entrepreneurial intentions in a transitional context—The case of rural Bulgaria. *Journal of Developmental Entrepreneurship, 22*(3), 1750018-1–1750018-21.

Transparency International. (2013). *Corruption Perception Index*. Retrieved from http://www.transparency.org/
Transparency International. (2019a). *Corruption Perceptions Index 2018: Executive summary*. Transparency International.
Transparency International. (2019b). *Corruption Perceptions Index 2018: Short methodology note*. Retrieved from http://www.2018_CPI_ShortMethodologyNote_EN
Transparency International. (2019c). *Corruption Perceptions Index 2018: Full source description*. Retrieved from https://www.transparency.org/files/content/pages/2018_CPI_SourceDescription_EN.pdf
Tverdova, Y. V. (2011). See no evil: Heterogeneity in public perceptions of corruption. *Canadian Journal of Political Science, 44*(1), 1–25.
Vian, T. (2008). Review of corruption in the health sector: Theory, methods and interventions. *Health Policy and Planning, 23*(1), 83–94.
Westermann-Behaylo, M. K., Rehbein, K., & Fort, T. (2015). Enhancing the concept of corporate diplomacy: Encompassing political corporate social responsibility, international relations, and peace through commerce. *The Academy of Management Perspectives, 29*(4), 387–404.
White, C. L. (2015). Exploring the role of private-sector corporations in public diplomacy. *Public Relations Inquiry, 4*(3), 305–321.
Wilhelm, P. G. (2002). Corruption Perceptions Index: Implications for business ethics and entrepreneurship education. *Journal of Business Ethics, 35*(1), 177–189.
Yoon, J., & Klasen, S. (2018). An application of partial least squares to the construction of the Social Institutions and Gender Index (SIGI) and the Corruption Perception Index (CPI). *Social Indicators Research, 138*(1), 61–88.

CHAPTER 10

Understanding the Global Terrorism Index

Emigdio Alfaro

1 Introduction

The most obvious threat for global security in the twenty-first century is the terrorism and the massive emergence of terrorist groups is still widely considered as formed by religious fundamentalism; however, the main factors that originated the terrorism were the struggle against poverty and economic inequality as a result of global capitalism, and the vulnerability of the poor people to the influence of outsiders with diverse interests (Anshori et al., 2020, p. 17). Meanwhile, the economic impact of terrorism was estimated around US$ 33 billion in 2018, and since 2000 until 2018, the terrorism cost for the world economy was estimated around US$ 855 billions (Bardwell & Iqbal, 2020, p. 1). Therefore, "terrorism is acknowledged as a global phenomenon and is not confined to any particular region, geographical area or state" (Khan et al., 2020, p. 68) and "The War on Terror (WoT) dramatically altered international, domestic and human security the world over" (Murray & Blannin, 2017, p. 1).

E. Alfaro (✉)
Universidad César Vallejo, Lima, Peru

Sjödin (2019) indicated: "The aim of terrorism is to take command over our feelings and our imagination to compel us to change our ways of life and release a clash between civilizations" (p. 25). Terrorism affected geo-economic and political processes around the world (Stankova et al., 2019, p. 220). The terrorist groups are influenced by their own ideologies and motivations (Neagu, 2017, p. 3). In respect to focus of the strategic purposes of the terrorist groups, Neagu (2017, p. 3) indicated:

> The strategic objectives focuses on obtaining recognition of the terrorist organization locally, regionally and internationally, raising fears of large-scale, destruction of communication infrastructure in order to create uncertainty among the population that authorities can protect them, influencing government decisions, discourage foreign investments, humanitarian assistance programs and tourism. (p. 3)

Some states are sponsors of terrorist groups linked to vital interests (Byman, 2020, p. 12). In respect, Byman (2020) indicated: "the sponsor is often isolated, and ties to terrorist groups are one of its few means of projecting power, imposing costs on an adversary, or otherwise fighting back" (p. 13). Byman (2020) also explained: "At times sponsorship is linked to important domestic constituencies or concerns, further raising the cost of ending support" (p. 13). Moreover, Ikenberry (2005, p. 135) argued that Byman (2005) commented that states back terrorist groups for the following reasons: (a) to influence neighbors, (b) topple regimes, (c) counter U.S. hegemony, or (d) advance ideology objectives. Additionally, many government agencies use the global internet network for cyber-terrorism activities, converting them in a more serious and complicated threat (Alguliyev et al., 2018, p. 35).

A general idea of the terrorism and the GTI of the Institute for Economics & Peace were explained in this section, jointly with the COVID-19 Pandemic's impact on terrorism and the relationships of the socio-economic indicators which are related with terrorism. Additionally, the effects of terrorism and the GTI on the national and international economics and the diplomacy were commented.

1.1 The Global Terrorism Index: A General Idea

The definitions of terror and the terrorism, and the general idea of the GTI are explained in this section. Çetin et al. (2019) explained that the terror expresses: "violence, intimidation, fear, and horror in the human mind" (p. 96) and that "Terrorism involves activities that affect large masses and carried out with a specific purpose" (p. 96). Due to the existence of diverse debatable definitions of terrorism (Institute for Economics & Peace, 2020, p. 6; Upadhyay, 2020, p. 37;), the specialists of the Institute for Economics & Peace accepted the terminology and definitions of the Global Terrorism Database (GTD) and the National Consortium for the Study of Terrorism and Responses to Terrorism (START), and proposed the following definition of terrorism: "the threatened or actual use of illegal force and violence by a non-state actor to attain a political, economic, religious, or social goal through fear, coercion, or intimidation" (Institute for Economics & Peace, 2020, p. 6).

About the Global Terrorism Index, the specialists of the Institute for Economics & Peace (2020) indicated: "The Global Terrorism Index (GTI) is a comprehensive study analysing the impact of terrorism for 163 countries covering 99.7 percent of the world's population" (p. 6). Additionally, the specialists of the Institute for Economics & Peace (2020) sustained that "the index score accounts for terrorist attacks over the prior five years" (p. 6). Newman (2007) also explained: "weak or failed states provide an environment which enables the emergence—or infiltration—and operation of terrorist organizations which launch attacks within these countries or elsewhere" (p. 463).

1.2 The COVID-19 Pandemic's Impact on Terrorism

The COVID-19 pandemic has been contributing to evidence the lack of presence of the governments in diverse sectors and regions in the diverse countries and has been presenting opportunities for terrorist groups for supporting to some populations to improve their life conditions and to provide humanitary support (Anshori et al., 2020; Institute for Economics & Peace, 2020; Upadhyay, 2020). In respect, Upadhyay (2020) explained that "As the Covid-19 spreads globally, there are wide-ranging responses from governments and several communities" (p. 57) and that "In this scenario, terrorism and extremism are also evolving, posing challenges for governments and civil societies alike" (p. 57).

The specialists of the Institute for Economics & Peace (2020) also indicated that COVID-19 pandemic would increase the impact of terrorism in certain regions, and would present complex challenges for counter-terrorism responses in the national and the international levels. Additionally, the specialists of the Institute for Economics & Peace (2020) precised:

> The COVID-19 pandemic could present opportunities for terrorist organisations to consolidate and expand their operations and territory, as governments turn their focus from counter-terrorism operations to addressing the public health crisis. Where a state's presence is already weak, or contested, there could be an opportunity for terrorist organisations to become alternate service providers, gaining favour with local populations through the delivery of essential services or social care. (p. 29)

Anshori et al. (2020) indicated that the word economic growth in 2020 would have a recession as a result of the COVID-19 pandemic, and that is a threat to the global security stability due to the flourish of the terrorism. Anshori et al. (2020) also sustained that the international leaders and organizations (including United Nations) should increase international cooperation including public and private sector for preventing and reducing future terrorism (p. 18). Finally, Upadhyay (2020) pointed out:

> The presence of a pandemic has pushed terrorism out of the news cycle. However, this will prompt them to carry out more pronounced attacks to remain in public memory. It, therefore, becomes pertinent for national governments to identity this imminent threat while tackling the social and economic consequences of the pandemic. Nation-states need to create new means of information sharing and policy coordination for intraand intergovernmental cooperation and honing of counterterrorism capabilities. (p. 58)

1.3 *Socio-Economic Indicators Which Are Related to Terrorism*

There are 15 socio-economic indicators of diverse sources, which are correlated with terrorism, such as: (a) corruption (source: World Bank), (b) equality before the law (source: Varieties of Democracy), (c) extreme poverty (source: International Labour Organization), (d) factionalized elites (source: Fragile States Index), (e) group grievance (source: Fragile

States Index), (f) human rights protection (source: Global State of Democracy), (g) iliteracy (source: UNESCO), (h) internal conflict (source: Global State of Democracy), (i) military expenditure (source: Stockholm International Peace Research Institute), (j) organised crime (source: World Economic Forum), (k) physical violence (source: Varieties of Democracy), (l) prosperity (source: Heritage Foundation), (m) religious / ethnic tensions (source: Global State of Democracy), (n) rule of law (source: World Bank), and (o) share of youth NEET—Not in Education, Employment, or Training- (source: International Labour Organization) (Institute for Economics & Peace, 2020, p. 99). These are only some indicators and it is possible to find many more indicators depending on the culture and the country.

The previous indicators which are related with the GTI according to the GTI 2020 report could generate ideas jointly with other global indicators for forecasting how to reduce the global problem of terrorism. Terrorism is also a risk that affects the decision-making of tourists in the selection of a tourist destination (Stankova et al., 2019, p. 220).

1.4 Effects of Terrorism and Global Terrorism Index on the Economics and the Diplomacy

The effects of terrorism and GTI on the economics and the diplomacy are presented in this section. The GTI reflected a serious global problem for the economics, which must be treated at the national and the international level jointly. The GTI also reflected a serious problem for the diplomacy inside and outside the countries, and must be treated as a whole by multinational institutions.

1.5 Effects of Terrorism and Global Terrorism Index on the Economics.

Diverse studies treated about the effects of terrorism on the economics (Butnaru et al., 2018; Khan et al., 2020; Kovalchuk & Shynkaryk, 2020; Neagu, 2017; Stankova et al., 2019; Varaine, 2020) and the effects of GTI on the national and international economics (Desai, 2017; Sabattini, 2018). Some of those studies are detailed in this section.

Varaine (2020) studied the relationship among the economic deprivation and terrorist activities in the USA since 1948 until 2016 with the Profiles of Individual Radicalization in the United States (PIRUS) database about 1295 domestic terrorists. The results of the study of Varaine (2020) revealed: (a) "far-right terrorism mobilizes more under periods of long-term economic deprivation, while far-left terrorism mobilizes more under improving economic conditions" (p. 667), (b) "the effect of collective deprivation appears to be of socio-tropic nature: it is especially determinant at the national level, rather than at the state or individual level" (p. 667), and (c) "results do not support the view that Islamist terrorism is affected by collective deprivation" (p. 667). Finally, the conclusions of the study of Varaine (2020) were the following:

> The study challenges the view that economic conditions have no role in triggering terrorist mobilization. The differential effect of collective deprivation on farright and far-left terrorism is compatible with system-justification and backlash theories. Besides, the findings suggest that collective deprivation affects radicalization at an early phase rather than the offending phase. (p. 667)

Terrorist attacks affected the mental health of people mainly in three major psychological reactions: (a) trauma and post-traumatic stress disorder symptoms, (b) depressive symptoms, and (c) experiences of anxiety and fear (Khan et al., 2020). Besides, Kovalchuk and Shynkaryk (2020) explained:

> Violence caused by terrorism and fear of terrorism change world economy. It is a change of investments and pattern of consumption, well-being, labour-market and labour, redirecting of state and private financial flows, reduction of profits and price increase, additional charges on safety precautions and other. (p. 657)

Butnaru et al. (2018) explained: "Tourism is an extremely complex phenomenon marked by major factors like the terrorist attacks and the refugees' invasion (the recent waves of migrants)" (p. 885). For contributing to the comprehension of this complex phenomenon, Stankova et al. (2019) studied the effects of terrorism on tourism, considering the international tourism in Europe and the USA and the assumption about that tourism influences by itself to the conditions for terrorist acts.

The results of the study of Stankova et al. (2019) revealed a specific creative-destructive effect of terrorism on tourism revenues; however, increased financial revenues from international tourism is several times greater than an increase in the risk of terrorism, due to the geopolitical factors that lead to diversification mechanisms of tourist regions for distributing the insecurity with political and military control, resulting on the increase of tourism revenues in Europe, Russia, and the USA (p. 232). However, Stankova et al. (2019) indicated that the results would be different in other territorial areas (p. 233). Contrary to the results of the study of Stankova et al. (2019) for the tourism revenues in Europe, Russia, and the USA, the results of the study of North African tourism realized by Neagu (2017) revealed:

> From the onset of the Arab Spring in December 2010 in Tunisia, and then expanded to other African countries, there has been numerous victims among whom tourists, military, police, politicians, journalists, business people, educators, women and children.
>
> Intensification of terrorist attacks led to a decrease a number of tourists visiting these countries. For Egypt, Morocco and Tunisia tourism is one of the most important sources of income and the main reason for why tourists choose to visit these countries. If in the next years the terrorist attacks will continue not only the tourism will be affected, but also air and road transport industry. The hotel industry will also be affected, and this can lead to higher unemployment. (p. 7)

Sabattini (2018) studied the effect of the GTI on foreign direct investment and macroeconomics in Indonesia, Philippines, Thailand, India, and Afghanistan, since 2007 until 2016, with data of terrorism acts from START and Uppsala Conflict Data Program (UCDP), and macroeconomics and foreign direct investment data from World Bank and Bank of Indonesia. The results of the study of Sabattini (2018) revealed: (a) an effect of global terrorism index on foreign direct investment in Thailand and Afghanistan; (b) an effect of global terrorism index on macroeconomic in Indonesia, Thailand, India, and Afghanistan; and (c) there is no effect of foreign direct investment on macroeconomic in Indonesia, Philippines, Thailand, India, and Afghanistan (p. 198).

Desai (2017) explained: "The local dimension of terrorism is important not only because it is where the physical damage is most obvious but also because subjective everyday experiences in a place have been found to influence how people process risk in that place" (p. 2). Desai (2017) also indicated: "These perceptions are tied strongly to the specific place which was attacked, and not simply its representativeness as any other place which might be attacked" (p. 2). Therefore, resilience capacity would minimize or mitigate the impact or the damage of a possible attack in the short, medium, and long term (Desai, 2017). Additionally, Desai (2017) pointed out:

> The urban or rural nature of attack location is important for several reasons. The nature of cities as large agglomerations for production creates both advantages and disadvantages related to terrorism—arguably, many of the same underlying reasons for the existence of cities not only makes them attractive targets for terrorists (Savitch & Ardashev, 2001) but also contributes to their resilience. (see Rose, Avetisyan, & Chatterjee, 2014; Harrigan & Martin, 2002)

Desai (2017) commented: "The local nature of terrorism is especially important when it comes to labor market effects of terrorism" (p. 5). In respect, Desai (2017) explained:

> This is because local labor markets may adjust within one country, or even within a region where mobility is relatively easy, and there could be significant movement of labor across cities. In smaller countries, the costs of moving across localities or cities could factor in to how much local labor markets are affected. In a country level study on labor market effects of terrorism across 165 countries, Berrebi and Ostwald (2016) found that terrorist attacks discourage female labor force participation and increase the gender gap in labor participation. Based on their robust findings at the country level, there could be similar or more nuanced effects in local economies. On the other hand, almost no effect of a 2006 large rocket attack by Hezbollah (and continued threat of future rocket attack) was found on labor market conditions and on migration flows and sorting in badly hit localities (versus other localities) in northern Israel. (see Elster et al., 2017)

2 Effects of Terrorism and Global Terrorism Index on the Diplomacy

Diverse studies explained about the effects of the terrorism or the GTI on the diplomacy at the national and international levels (Chandra, 2020; Helbling & Meierrieks, 2020; Murray & Blannin, 2017; Omenma & Hendricks, 2018). Some of those studies are presented in this section.

Chandra (2020) studied the India's counter-terrorism diplomacy at the United Nations and identified the following type of implementation pillars: (a) normative implementation (de-legitimization of terrorism as the root cause approach and sectoral with a comprehensive approach), (b) coercive implementation (counter-terrorism sanctions and the use of force), (c) legal implementation (contribution to the development of international legal framework against terrorism through its sponsoring, cosponsoring, draft proposal, and consensus-building initiatives), (d) compliance and domestic implementation, and (e) promotion of international cooperation (p. 40).

Helbling and Meierrieks (2020) studied the relationship among transnational terrorism and the restrictiveness of immigration policies, with a sample of 30 OECD countries since 1980 until 2010. About the sample of OECD countries, Helbling and Meierrieks (2020) stated:

> The countries in our sample are: Australia, Austria, Belgium, Canada, Chile, Denmark, Finland, France, Germany, Greece, Hungary, Icel the collective application of pacific and/or cooperative initiatives by national defense establishments and military practitioners for confidence building, trust creation, conflict prevention, and/or conflict resolution and Ireland, Israel, Italy, Japan, Luxembourg, Mexico, the Netherlands, New Zealand, Norway, Poland, Portugal, South Korea, Spain, Sweden, Switzerland, Turkey, the United Kingdom, and the United States. This sample is chosen due to the availability of data concerning country-specific immigration policies. (p. 567)

After the evaluation, Helbling and Meierrieks (2020) found: "a greater exposure to transnational terrorism is associated with stricter migration controls, but not stricter migration regulations regarding eligibility criteria and conditions" (p. 564). Helbling and Meierrieks (2020) also concluded:

> It points to the securitization of immigration, providing partial support for the notion that transnational terrorism incentivizes migration policy change towards greater restrictiveness. However, the policy response appears to be surgical (affecting only migration controls) rather than sweeping (and thus not influencing broader migration regulations) for the countries in our sample. (p. 564)

Omenma and Hendricks (2018) evaluated the impact of civilian interventions in counterterrorism in Africa. After their evaluation, Omenma and Hendricks (2018) concluded: "The main contributory factor was the shift in active and passive supports of the civilian population to the military, which increased the strategic and operational intelligence gathering, combat strength, and more proactive military in counterterrorism" (p. 764).

Murray and Blannin (2017) explained about the types of diplomacy of the war on terror, which are the following: (a) summit diplomacy, (b) defense diplomacy, (c) secret diplomacy, (d) public diplomacy, and (e) digital diplomacy. Based on previous studies, Murray and Blannin (2017) precised the definitions of the types of diplomacy as follows:

- Summit diplomacy, which consists of meetings among incumbent heads of government and/or state, or political leaders (p. 5).
- Defense diplomacy, which is the collective application of pacific and/or cooperative initiatives by national defense establishments and military practitioners for confidence building, trust creation, conflict prevention, and/or conflict resolution (p. 6).
- Secret diplomacy, which is the practice of intentionally concealing information from other governments, the media and/or the public and can also involve private, informal and clandestine backchannel meetings—particularly between states or state and non-state actors that share a publically adversarial relationship—as well as any number of activities associated with the murky world of intelligence gathering (p. 6).
- Public diplomacy, which is the process by which direct relations with people in a country are pursued to advance the interests and extend the values of those being represented (p. 7).
- Digital diplomacy, which is the use of social media for diplomatic purposes or the exploitation of the internet and information communications technology in order to carry out diplomatic objectives, or solve foreign policy problems (p. 8).

About the terrorist organizations (TO) and their acts, Murray and Blannin (2017) commented:

At first glance TOs seem anything but diplomatic. They intentionally target combatants and noncombatants and engage in shocking acts of violence. Their actions are criminal and unlawful, and they demonstrate complete indifference to international norms, treaties, conventions and laws. For many outside observers it is difficult to see beyond the barbarism of TOs. However, most of them, even the nihilistic ones, have political goals they seek to realise through many means – violence, alliances with criminal organisations, exploitation of new ICTs, and, the subject of this section, diplomacy. (p. 11)

ICTs means Information and Communication Technologies, NGO means Non Governmental Organizations, and CT means Counter Terrorism (Murray & Blannin, 2017). About the characteristic of the diplomacy of TO, Murray and Blannin (2017) precised the following:

- First, and in terms of representation, more than a few TOs have a political office or embassy, staffed by individuals who symbolise the group core interests. This is nothing new. As they mature, some Tos develop political capacities (p. 12).
- Second, TOs also are more than capable negotiators, particularly when their power begins to waver. Recognising this ability has been vital to the de-escalation of unconventional conflicts involving TOs the world over (p. 12).
- Third, all TOs communicate political and diplomatic messages via old and new media. Indeed, violence itself is a form of communication (p. 13).

Murray and Blannin (2017) concluded: "To win the War, more diplomacy is required, not less. Of course, there will always be disenfranchised individuals and groups that will resort to terrorism, however with good diplomatic theory and practice it is possible to discourage and diminish its impact" (p. 15). Some practical recommendations of the study of Murray and Blannin (2017) were the following: (a) "diplomacy should compete with the military (or, at least, complement) as the default responder in the WoT" (p. 14) and (b) "for states to establish, manage and sustain CT networks composed of NGOs and other non-state actors (NSAs)" (p. 15).

3 Construction of the Index

This section shows the data sources and the methodology for the construction of the index. Jointly with the data sources, some criteria for the inclusion of incidents into them were explained. Additionally, the weights of the indicators and the damage levels of the GTI were explained in the methodology into this section.

3.1 Data Sources of the Index

This section contains the details of the data sources of GTI: Global Terrorism Database and Study of Terrorism and Responses to Terrorism (Institute for Economics & Peace, 2020) and the criteria for the inclusion of terrorist incidents in those data sources. The data of the GTI was taken from the Global Terrorism Database (GTD) and other sources, and is collected and collated by the National Consortium for the Study of Terrorism and Responses to Terrorism (START) at the University of Maryland including over 170,000 terrorist incidents since 1970 until 2019 (Institute for Economics & Peace, 2020, p. 2). About the criteria for including an incident into the GTD and the START, the specialists of the Institute for Economics & Peace (2020) wrote:

> In order to be included as an incident in the GTD, the act has to be 'an intentional act of violence or threat of violence by a non-state actor.' This means an incident has to meet three criteria in order for it to be counted as a terrorist act:
>
> 1. The incident must be intentional—the result of a conscious calculation on the part of a perpetrator.
> 2. The incident must entail some level of violence or threat of violence - including property damage as well as violence against people.
> 3. The perpetrators of the incidents must be sub-national actors. This database does not include acts of state terrorism.
>
> In addition to this baseline definition, two of the following three criteria have to be met in order to be included in the START database from 1997:
>
> - The violent act was aimed at attaining a political, economic, religious or social goal.

- The violent act included evidence of an intention to coerce, intimidate or convey some other message to a larger audience other than to the immediate victims.
- The violent act was outside the precepts of international humanitarian law (p. 6).

3.2 Methodology

The indicators, the weights of the indicators, the weights of the levels of damage for the calculation of the GTI, and the details of the sample for the construction of the GTI are explained in this section. The specialists of the Institute for Economics & Peace (2020) explained that GTI ranks 163 countries with the following four indicators: (a) total number of terrorist incidents in a given year, (b) total number of fatalities caused by terrorists in a given year, (c) total number of injuries caused by terrorists in a given year, and (d) a measure of the total property damage from terrorist incidents in a given year, and that all the indicators were weighted average over five years (p. 96). Each one of the factors is weighted between zero and three with a weighted average of its value considering five years (Institute for Economics & Peace, 2020, p. 96).

The weights of the indicators were the following: (a) 1 for the total number of incidents, (b) 3 for the total number of fatalities, (c) 0.5 for the total number of injuries, and (d) between 0 and 3 depending on severity for the sum of property damages measure (Institute for Economics & Peace, 2020, p. 96). Additionally, the weights for damage levels in the GTI were the following: (a) 0 for unknown property damage, (b) 1 for minor property damage (likely minor than one million dollars), (c) 2 for major property damage (likely between one million and one billion of dollars), and (d) 3 for catastrophic property damage (likely major tan one billion of dollars) (Institute for Economics & Peace, 2020, p. 96). Finally, the key findings of the GTI study were grouped into the following themes: (a) results, (b) economic impact of terrorism, (c) trends in terrorism, (d) the shifting landscape, and (e) systems and terrorism (Institute for Economics & Peace, 2020, p. 96).

GTI was developed in consultation with the Global Peace Index Expert Panel and scored the countries with a scale from 0 (no impact from terrorism) to 10 (the highest measurable impact of terrorism), with a ranking in descending order (Institute for Economics & Peace, 2020, p. 6). The 10 worst scores of the GTI were for the following most impacted countries: (a) Afghanistan (9.592), (b) Iraq (8.682), (c) Nigeria (8.314), (d) Syria (7.778), (e) Somalia (7.645), (f) Yemen (7.581), (g) Pakistan (7.541), (h) India (7.353), (i) Democratic Republic of the Congo (7.178), and (j) Philippines (7.099), and 29 countries were scored with zero as the best score (Institute for Economics & Peace, 2020, p. 8).

4 Views and Applications

Diverse studies which include the use of the GTI at the international level (Avdan & Uzonyi, 2017; Azam & Feng, 2015; Bardwell & Iqbal, 2020; Dunne, 2003; Elkatawneh, 2015; Ghatak et al., 2017; Jidane-Mazigh et al., 2019; Sjödin, 2019; Tahir, 2018) and at the national level (Asaad & Marane, 2020; Das & Halder, 2018; Khan et al., 2018) were found in the literature review. Some of them are detailed in this section.

4.1 At the International Level

Estimations of the global economic impact of the terrorism (Bardwell & Iqbal, 2020), the influence of the terrorism on the public debt (Jidane-Mazigh et al., 2019), the relationships of the identity with the affects and thinking and the loss of reality-testing when the group is dominated by schizo-paranoid anxiety (Sjödin, 2019), the impact of the per capita income, the political instability, physical capital stocks, human capital stocks, corruption, military expenditures, inflation on the GTI (Tahir, 2018), the relationship among the mass violence perpetrated by state agents and the domestic terrorism (Avdan & Uzonyi, 2017), the relationships among the type of political regime and the level of domestic terrorism (Ghatak et al., 2017), and the impact of the Fragile State Indicator (FSI), social indicators, economic indicators, and political and military indicators on the level of GTI (Elkatawneh, 2015) were found in the literature review. The details of the mentioned studies are in this section.

Bardwell and Iqbal (2020) estimated the global economic impact of terrorism in the period 2000–2018 with the framework developed by the Institute for Economics and Peace's GTI and "a cost accounting methodology that costs the deaths and injuries from terrorism incidents using an adjusted unit cost provided by McCollister et al. (2010)" (p. 2). In their study, Bardwell and Iqbal (2020) estimated the cost of terrorism for 163 countries and territories with the following four indicators: (a) deaths from terrorism, (b) injuries from terrorism violence, (c) property damage from terrorism, and (d) indirect GDP losses from terrorism (p. 7). Bardwell and Iqbal (2020) calculated the economic impact of terrorism around US$ 33 billion in 2018, and the cost of terrorism for the world economy was US$ 855 billion since 2000 until 2018 (p. 23).

Jidane-Mazigh et al. (2019) studied the relationship among terrorism as independent variable (measured by Global Terrorism Index) and public debt as dependent variable (measured by Debt-to-GDP ratio), with control variables such as: inflation, GDP per capital, total reserves minus gold, and trade balance, for 19 developed and developing countries affected by terrorism attacks frequently (9 MENA countries and 10 Western countries) since 2002 until 2017. MENA means Middle East and North Africa. The nine MENA countries were: Bahrain, Egypt, Jordan, Kuwait, Lebanon, Morocco, Saudi Arabia, Tunisia, and Turkey, and the 10 Western countries were: France, Spain, Ireland, USA, United Kingdom, Sweden, Greece, Germany, Italy, and Norway. The conclusions of the study of Jidane-Mazigh et al. (2019) were the following:

> public debt is cointegrated with economic growth in three regions. A long-run equilibrium relationship between these two variables is identified in all countries. In addition, based on a recently developed panel Granger causality analysis that accounts for cross-section dependence and heterogeneity, our results show the existence of unidirectional causal relationships between terrorism and public debt as well for MENA countries and Western countries.
>
> Thanks to the AMG estimation, our econometric results suggest that terrorist activity can effectively damage public debt and this effect is more pronounced in MENA countries, which are more vulnerable to violent attacks than richer and diversified countries. For control variables, we find that GDP is the significant determinant of debt. This finding is consistent with existing literature, which considered GDP as the most important determinant of debt. (Azam & Feng, 2015; Dunne, 2003)
>
> For MENA countries, a close examination of the relationship between the Global Terrorism Index and public debt is worthwhile, not only due to the unexpected results (especially, for inflation and trade balance) obtained but also due to the specificity of the region.

The analysis in this research demonstrates that the political authorities need to take into account the impact of terrorism for budget planning and expenditure allocation purposes, mostly in less developed countries. These economies must be financially supported in their fight against terrorism as they are the most economically vulnerable to these attacks. Indeed, the challenge of countering terrorism is not only concern target countries but also it is a worldwide defiance. (p. 19)

Sjödin (2019) studied the relationship among the identity as "an individual's feeling of being unique, having a coherent self while at the same time being part of a large group" (p. 25) and the "affects and thinking and the loss of reality-testing when the group is dominated by schizo-paranoid anxiety" (p. 25). For this purpose, Sjödin (2019) analyzed the power of identity and the search for meaning in the globalization, the rise of a network society, and disenchantment with the world. Finally, Sjödin (2019) concluded:

We also have to consider our clinical experience, from which we learn that distinguishing between inner reality and outer reality, as well as between self and other, is a prerequisite for autonomy and psychic health. Today we have to add the capacity to identify motives rooted in a large group from motives rooted in the individual, in its turn a necessity for the development of concern for our fellow human beings and responsibility for our own hostile impulses.

Tahir (2018) studied the impact of the per capita income, the political instability, physical capital stocks, human capital stocks, corruption, military expenditures, inflation on the GTI with a simple of 94 countries which were affected by terrorism, considering Muslim and non-Muslim countries and data since 2005 until 2016. The results of the study of Tahir (2018) revealed the following: (a) low per capita income growth and political instability are the main driving forces behind prevailing terrorism in Muslim and non-Muslim countries and (b) the growth of both physical and human capital stocks are inversely related with terrorism in entire sample as well as for Muslim countries.

Avdan and Uzonyi (2017) studied the relationship among the mass violence perpetrated by state agents and the domestic terrorism with data from GTD since 1971 until 2011, considering the state features as control variable. Avdan and Uzonyi (2017) concluded:

This study argues that government violence should influence the count of terrorist attacks within the state through the way in which these policies affect both opportunity and grievance. While other types of government abuse such as human rights violations and economic discrimination may increase resentment among segments of the population, and thus their willingness to use violence in retaliation against the regime, mass killings do so by fueling violence for the sake of vengeance. The atrocities provide a focal point to mobilize and unite terrorist groups. They also provide further justification for violence by exacerbating societal polarization. In other words, mass killings play into the hands of terrorist organizations. (p. 954)

Ghatak et al. (2017) studied the relationships among the type of political regime and the level of domestic terrorism using a dataset since 1990 until 2012 from the GTD. Ghatak et al. (2017) found that different characteristics of the democracy associated to the regime relate to domestic terrorism differently (p. 1). Additionally, Ghatak et al. (2017) concluded:

Higher levels of the rule of law tend to decrease terrorism, whereas electoral democracies tend to experience more domestic terrorism. However, domestic terrorism increases in every form of democracy in the presence of political exclusion. As such, an effective counterterrorism policy must address underlying grievances as democratization by itself may actually drive domestic terrorism up. (p. 1)

Elkatawneh (2015) studied the impact of the Fragile State Indicator (FSI), social indicators, economic indicators, and political and military indicators on the level of GTI. The social indicators were the following: (a) demographic pressure on the population related to natural disasters, disease, environment, food scarcity, malnutrition, water scarcity, population growth, youth bulge, mortality, and pollution; (b) group grievance when tensión and violence exist between groups, the state's ability to provide security is undermined, and fear and further violence may ensue; (c) refugees and IPD (Internally Displaced People); and (d) human flight and brain drain (Elkatawneh, 2015, p. 12).

The economic indicators of the study of Elkatawneh (2015) were the following: (a) uneven economic development and (b) poverty and economic decline (p. 13). Also, the político and military indicators were the following: (a) state legitimacy, (b) human right and the rule of law, (c) fictionalized elites, (d) public services, (e) security apparatus, and (f) external intervention (Elkatawneh, 2015, p. 14). After the evaluation with the mentioned indicators in a sample of 160 recognized or on the verge of recognition countries of United Nations (p. 17), Elkatawneh (2015) concluded that social indicators and economic indicators are predictors of the GTI (p. 22).

4.2 At the National Level

In the literature review, the following studies with the use of GTI were found: (a) the effect of the corruption, terrorism, political stability, and oil Price on the Iraq stock Exchange (Asaad & Marane, 2020); (b) the relationships among terrorism, economic growth, and human development in Pakistan (Khan et al., 2018); and (c) the estimation of the global connectedness in India, which is influenced by various macro environmental elements including the GTI (Das & Halder, 2018). The mentioned studies are detailed in this section.

Asaad and Marane (2020) studied the effect of corruption, terrorism, political stability, and oil Price on the Iraq stock Exchange since 2005 until 2019, using corruption perception index for measuring corruption, global terrorism index for measuring terrorism, the index of political stability of the World Bank for measuring the political stability, the WTI crude oil price per barrel from US Energy Information Administration Database for measuring the oil price, and the logarithm of the general index of Iraq Stock Exchange for measuring the Iraq Stock Exchange. The findings of the study of Asaad and Marane (2020) revealed:

> the levels of corruption, terrorism activities and political stability are significant predictors of Iraq stock exchange, referring that when the business environment in Iraq is stated as being more corrupt and less transparent, facing terrorism activities with presence of more violence and public possibility of destabilization, have a negative effect on the Iraq stock exchange performance. Hence, findings confirmed the adverse effect of corruption, terrorism and political instability on Iraq stock Exchange performance. (p. 637)

Khan et al. (2018) studied the relationships among terrorism, economic growth (measured with Gross Domestic Product), and human development (measured with human development index), with data from

Global Terrorism Database (GTD), World Bank, and Human Development Report, respectively, since 1990 until 2016 in Pakistan (p. 34662). Electric Power Consumption and Urbanization were also considered as independent variables for the evaluation of the relationships. The conclusions of the study of Khan et al. (2018) were the following:

- The impact of both economic growth and electric power consumption is insignificant.
- Furthermore, the coefficient of terrorism shows a negative relationship with the human development process.
- Moreover, the verdicts of long-run dynamics revealed that urbanization endorses human development index. Additionally, bidirectional causality reported between human development and terrorism incidents (p. 34671).

Das and Halder (2018) studied the global connectedness in India (through the Global Connectedness Index), which is influenced by various macro environmental elements, such as: Human Development Index (HDI), Corruption Perception Index (CPI), Global Peace Index (GPI), Global Terrorism Index (GTI), Inflation Rate, Dependency Ratio, Education Rate etc., since 2006 until 2015. Das and Halder (2018) indicated: "Global connectedness of a country signifies the connectivity with various nations through different forms of trading" (p. 9). Finally, Das and Halder (2018) concluded:

> corruption perception index and dependency ratio have significant effect and the effect of global peace index is not statistically significant. On the other hand human development index, global terrorism index, inflation rate and education rate unable to satisfy the hypotheses but effect of these all elements are significant. Hence, in India dependency ratio has been played a vital role for the as influencer of global connectedness, after that corruption perception index also play important role for creation a burden on global connectedness. It can be concluded that global connectedness will increase by reduction of corruption perception index and dependency ratio. (p. 14)

5 Discussion

GTI does not include the indicators related to the networking of the terrorist people who attacked the countries with the terrorist groups of other countries or states, which could be financing them. Besides, GTI does not include the indicators related to the quantity of people related to the terrorist groups which are inside the country which received the attacks. Additionally, GTI must consider 10 years and not only 5 years for valuing the history of the occurrence of the terrorist attacks and weights for the scores of the states related to the condition of sponsor of the terrorist attacks into the territories of the state or in other states.

The mentioned indicators are important for sincering the GTI index and reflect not only the received attacks, but also the networking and the sponsorship of the terrorism groups in the level of gravity of the terrorism in a state or country. Besides, found literature review about the terrorism and the GTI was focused on the impact of diverse economic indicators on GTI; however, there is a lack of deep focus of the scientific research on detailed indicators about the solutions to this global problem and their components or phases, which are necessary for contributing to the human development of all the countries or states.

Future research must be related to the comprehension of the diverse variables, dimensions, and indicators, which have effects on the terrorism. Besides the indicators that were mentioned as related to GTI 2020 in the report of the Institute for Economics & Peace, other social and culture indicators could be considered, such as: (a) Gini index; (b) the Hofstede's dimensions of culture: power distance, individualism, masculinity, uncertainty avoidance, long term orientation, and indulgence (Hofstede Insights, 2021); (c) competitiveness indicators by countries at the national, regional, and local levels; (d) human development index adjusted by inequality (United Nations Development Programme, 2020); and (e) good practices of the diverse types of diplomacies for combatting the terrorism (Murray & Blannin, 2017).

Future research must also include the effect on terrorism of the following indicators: (a) indicators associated to the COVID-19 pandemic's damages, (b) global health indicators including mental health indicators (Elkatawneh, 2015), (c) type of political regime (Ghatak et al., 2017), and (d) sustainable land management indicators jointly (including indicators according to the global conventions for the protection of natural resources of the United Nations, such as: UNCCD, UNCBD, and

UNFCCC) with risk management indicators (Alfaro, 2019; Elkatawneh, 2015). UNCCD is the United Nations Convention to Combat Desertification, UNCBD is the United Nation Convention on Biological Diversity, and UNFCCC is the United Nations Framework Convention on Climate Change. Finally, diverse studies about the solutions for the terrorism problem at the local, regional, national, and global levels, and their formalizations with methodologies must be developed for improving the human development in the world.

References

Alfaro, E. A. (2019). Sustainable land management: The forgotten pillar of competitiveness. *ICPE Public Enterprise Half-Yearly Journal, 24*(1), 30–67.

Alguliyev, R. M., Aliguliyev, R. M., & Niftaliyeva, G. Y. (2018). Filtration of terrorism-related texts in the e-government environment. *International Journal of Cyber Warfare and Terrorism, 8*(4), 35–48.

Anshori, A. B., Napang, M., & Nurhasanah, S. (2020). The threat of economic recession and its impact on global terrorism. *Journal of Terrorism Studies, 11*(1), 1–19.

Asaad, Z. A., & Marane, B. M. R. (2020). Corruption, terrorism and the stock market: The evidence from Iraq. *Journal of Asian Finance, Economics, and Business, 7*(10), 629–639. https://doi.org/10.13106/jafeb.2020.vol7.no10.629

Avdan, N., & Uzonyi, G. (2017). V for vendetta: Government mass killing and domestic terrorism. *Studies in Conflict & Terrorism, 40*(11), 934–965.

Azam, M., & Feng, Y. (2015). Does military expenditure increase external debt? Evidence from Asia. *Defence and Peace Economics, 28*(5), 550–567.

Bardwell, H., & Iqbal, M. (2020). The economic impact of terrorism from 2000 to 2018. *Peace Economics, Peace Science and Public Policy,* 1–34. https://doi.org/10.1515/peps-2020-0031

Berrebi, C., & Ostwald, J. (2016). Terrorism and the labor force. *Journal of Conflict Resolution, 60*(1), 32–60.

Butnaru, G. I., Mironiuc, M., Huian, C., & Haller, A. P. (2018). Analysis of economic growth in tourism under the impact of terrorism and of the waves of refugees. *Amfiteatru Economic, 20*(12), 885–904.

Byman, D. (2020). Understanding, and misunderstanding, state sponsorship of terrorism. *Studies in Conflict & Terrorism.* https://doi.org/10.1080/1057610X.2020.1738682

Byman, D. (2005). *Deadly connections: States that sponsor terrorism.* Cambridge University Press.

Çetin, I., Keser, H. Y., & Ay, S. (2019). Intercontinental and regional evaluation of terrorism and its economic effects. In *The impact of global terrorism on economic and political development: Afro-Asian perspectives*. https://doi.org/10.1108/978-1-78769-919-920191010

Chandra, V. (2020). India's counter-terrorism diplomacy at the United Nations: Progress and problems. *India Quarterly, 76*(1), 40–57.

Das, S., & Halder, G. (2018). Global connectedness of India: An analysis with environmental elements. *IOSR Journal of Business and Management, 20*(9), 9–15.

Desai, S. (2017). Economic effects of terrorism: Local and city considerations, priorities for research and policy. *Geography Compass*. https://doi.org/10.1111/gec3.12332

Dunne, J. (2003). The making of arms in South Africa. *Economists Allied for Arms Reduction (ECAAR) Review*, 1.

Elkatawneh, H. (2015). *Fragile states and global terrorism, the impact of social, economic, political and military indicators on the level of the global terrorism index/statistical analysis*. https://ssrn.com/abstract=2691598. https://doi.org/10.2139/ssrn.2691598

Elster, Y., Zussman, A., & Zussman, N. (2017). Rockets: The housing market effects of a credible terrorist threat. *Journal of Urban Economics, 99*(1), 136–147.

Ghatak, S., Gold, A., & Prins, B. (2017). Domestic terrorism in democratic states: Understanding and addressing minority grievances. *Journal of Conflict Resolution*, 1–29. https://doi.org/10.1177/0022002717734285

Harrigan, J., & Martin, P. (2002, November). Terrorism and the resilience of cities. *Federal Reserve Bank of New York Economic Policy Review*, 97–116.

Helbling, M., & Meierrieks, D. (2020). Transnational terrorism and restrictive inmigration policies. *Journal of Peace Research, 57*(4), 564–580.

Hofstede Insights. (2021). *Compare countries*. https://www.hofstede-insights.com/product/compare-countries/

Ikenberry, J. (2005). Recent books on international relations: Political and legal. *Foreign Affairs, 84*(6), 135–136.

Institute for Economic & Peace. (2020). *Global terrorism index 2020: Measuring the impact of terrorism*. https://www.visionofhumanity.org/wp-content/uploads/2020/11/GTI-2020-web-1.pdf

Jidane-Mazigh, L., Khefacha, I., & Chamakh, A. (2019). An empirical analysis of terrorism impact on public debt: A dynamic heterogeneous panel approach. *New Trends and Issues Proceedings on Humanities and Social Sciences, 6*(8), 11–20.

Khan, Z. H., Aftab, S., Naqvi, B., Zahoor, S., & Imdad, I. (2020). Psychological reactions to terrorist attacks in Baluchistan youth. *Pakistan Journal of Psychology, 51*(1), 67–83.

Khan, N. H., Ju, Y., & Hassan, S. T. (2018). Modeling the impact of economic growth and terrorism on the human development index: Collecting evidence from Pakistan. *Environmental Science and Pollution Research, 25*(1), 34661–34673.

Kovalchuk, O., & Shynkaryk, M. (2020). *The macroeconomic model of modern global terrorism.* 10th International Conference on Advanced Computer Information Technologies (ACIT). https://ieeexplore.ieee.org/document/9208963

McCollister, K. E., French, M. T., & Fang, H. (2010). The cost of crime to society: New crimespecific estimates for policy and program evaluation. *Drug and Alcohol Dependence, 108*(1–2), 98–109.

Murray, S., & Blannin, P. (2017). Diplomacy and the war on terror. *Small Wars Journal.* http://smallwarsjournal.com/jrnl/art/diplomacy-and-the-war-on-terror

Neagu, F. S. (2017). *The impact of the terrorism on North African tourism* (pp. 1081–1087). https://doi.org/10.1515/picbe-2017-0111. ISSN 2558-9652. Proceedings of the 11th International Conference on Business Excellence.

Newman, E. (2007). Weak states, state failure, and terrorism. *Terrorism and Political Violence, 19*(1), 463–488.

Omenma, J. T., & Hendricks, C. M. (2018). Counterterrorism in Africa: An analysis of the civilian joint task force and military partnership in Nigeria. *Security Journal, 31*(1), 764–794. https://doi.org/10.1057/s41284-018-0131-8

Rose, A., Avetisyan, M., & Chatterjee, S. (2014). A framework for analyzing the economic tradeoffs between urban commerce and security against terrorism. *Risk Analysis, 34*(8), 1554–1579.

Sabattini, F. (2018). Pengaruh global terrorism index terhadap foreign direct investment dan makroekonomi [The influence of the global terrorism index on foreign direct investment and macroeconomics]. *Jurnal Administrasi Bisnis* [Journal of Business Administration], *57*(1), 198–207.

Savitch, H. V., & Ardashev, G. (2001). Does terror have an urban future. *Urban Studies, 38*(13), 2515–2533.

Sjödin, C. (2019). Terrorism from a Swedish perspective. *International Forum of Psychoanalysis, 28*(1), 25–30.

Stankova, M., Tsvetkov, T., & Ivanova, L. (2019). Tourist development between security and terrorism: Empirical evidence from Europe and the United States. *Oeconomia Copernicana, 10*(2), 219–237. https://doi.org/10.24136/oc.2019.011

Tahir, M. (2018). Terrorism and its determinants: Panel data evidence from 94 countries. *Applied Research in Quality of Life.* https://doi.org/10.1007/s11482-018-9660-x

United Nations Development Programme. (2020). *Human development report 2020.* http://hdr.undp.org/sites/default/files/hdr2020.pdf

Upadhyay, S. (2020). Covid-19 and its impact on terrorism. *Artha Journal of Social Sciences, 19*(4), 37–62.

Varaine, S. (2020). Revisiting the economics and terrorism nexus: Collective deprivation, ideology and domestic radicalization in the US (1948–2016). *Journal of Quantitative Criminology, 36*(1), 667–699.

Index

B
Big Mac Index (BMI), 193–204, 208–211

C
Composite indices, 2–5, 7, 9, 10, 12–14, 21, 28, 29, 77, 78, 89, 260
Corruption Perceptions Index (CPI), 233, 234, 236–241, 243–247, 256–266, 289
Country performance, 12, 95
Country risk, 213, 215–227, 230, 251

D
Decision-making, 4, 13, 75, 90, 107, 109, 134, 137, 140–142, 144, 147, 150, 187, 222, 243, 248, 254, 263, 266, 275
Development, 2, 3, 7–9, 11, 14, 24–26, 58, 64, 77–79, 86–89, 96, 98, 103, 112, 116, 117, 121–124, 132, 139, 140, 143, 145–149, 157, 159, 163, 167, 168, 173, 177, 179, 188, 196, 203, 204, 222, 234–237, 239, 242, 248, 252, 253, 255, 260–264, 279, 286–290

E
Economic growth, 7, 20, 25, 47, 56, 76, 124, 125, 127, 143, 157, 158, 173, 187, 214, 234, 235, 237, 238, 241, 274, 285, 288, 289
Economic risk, 25, 215, 219, 223–226, 228, 230
Energy diplomacy, 158, 160, 161, 166, 169, 172, 173
Energy security, 158–168, 170, 172–175, 177–179, 184–187
Energy security risk index, 164, 165, 172, 173, 175, 177, 179, 180, 183–187
Environmental sustainability, 3, 25, 173

© The Editor(s) (if applicable) and The Author(s), under exclusive license to Springer Nature Switzerland AG 2022
V. Charles and A. Emrouznejad (eds.), *Modern Indices for International Economic Diplomacy*, https://doi.org/10.1007/978-3-030-84535-3

G

Gender equality, 3, 8, 9, 85–88, 92, 94, 95, 98, 107, 109, 115–117, 121–125, 132–134, 136, 139, 142, 143, 145, 147, 148
Gini index, 56–59, 62–79, 290
Global security, 271, 274
Global Terrorism Index (GTI), 272, 273, 275, 277, 278, 282–290

H

Human rights, 9, 121, 122, 185, 236, 251, 275, 287

I

Income distribution, 25, 56, 58, 59, 62, 63, 68, 73, 76, 79
Inequality, 7, 25, 55–60, 63, 64, 66, 68, 70–79, 85–89, 92, 95, 115–117, 122–124, 126–128, 140–142, 145, 148, 149, 173, 213, 214, 260, 261, 271, 290
International economic diplomacy, 1, 12, 20, 22, 24, 76, 78, 87, 123, 148, 201, 207

O

OECD Better Life Index (BLI), 20, 22–24, 27, 33, 34, 49

P

Policymaking, 3, 4, 9, 12, 14, 57, 58, 76, 78, 79, 123, 131, 143, 148, 173, 185, 194, 202, 204, 207, 209, 210, 214

R

Regional progress, 11

S

Social development, 124, 133, 145, 147
Social innovation, 87, 96–98, 104, 116, 117
Socio-economic indicators, 272, 274

W

Wealth, 25, 35, 56, 57, 59, 64, 68, 74, 79, 139, 159, 208, 214
Well-being, 2, 7, 8, 11, 19–27, 33, 46, 47, 49, 56, 72, 76, 77, 89, 103, 157, 158, 162, 209, 276

CPSIA information can be obtained
at www.ICGtesting.com
Printed in the USA
LVHW080719070422
715582LV00005B/100